FCCT | Free Church, Catholic Tradition

Barry Harvey and Bryan C. Hollon, editors

FORTHCOMING VOLUMES:

Scott W. Bullard, *Re-membering the Body: The Lord's Supper and Ecclesial Unity in the Free Church Traditions*

Free Churches and the
Body of Christ

Authority, Unity, and Truthfulness

Jeffrey W. Cary

CASCADE *Books* • Eugene, Oregon

FREE CHURCHES AND THE BODY OF CHRIST
Authority, Unity, and Truthfulness

Free Church, Catholic Tradition 1

Cascade Books
An Imprint of Wipf and Stock Publishers
199 W. 8th Ave., Suite 3
Eugene, OR 97401

www.wipfandstock.com

ISBN 13: 978-1-61097-637-4

Cataloging-in-Publication data:

Cary, Jeffrey W.

    Free churches and the body of Christ : authority, unity, and truthfulness / Jeffrey W. Cary.

    p.; 23 cm—Includes bibliographical references.

    Free Church, Catholic Tradition 1

    ISBN 13: 978-1-61097-637-4

    1. Church—Catholicity. 2. Baptists—Doctrines. I. Title. II. Series.

BV601.3 .C35 2012

Manufactured in the USA.

To Amy and the kids

There is one body and one Spirit, just as you were called
to the one hope of your calling,
one Lord, one faith, one baptism, one God and Father of all,
who is above all and through all and in all.

EPHESIANS 4:4–6

Contents

Series Preface

Barry Harvey and Bryan C. Hollon, editors

WHY A BOOK SERIES entitled *Free Church, Catholic Tradition*? As he does on so many other occasions, Augustine eloquently articulates the benefits of engaging in the kinds of conversations that we hope it promotes. "Dear reader," he writes near the outset of *De Trinitate*, "whenever you are as certain about something as I am go forward with me; whenever you hesitate, seek with me; whenever you discover that you have gone wrong come back to me; or if I have gone wrong, call me back to you. In this way we will travel the street of love together as we make our way toward him of whom it is said, 'Seek his face always.'" Though Augustine's words here are addressed to individuals, the wisdom of what he says extends to the ecumenical spirit of our times. When set in this ecclesial context, his admonition provides both the content and the spirit that we hope will characterize this series.

The immediate context for this series is the growing number of scholars in Free Church communions who are interested in drawing upon the great tradition of the church catholic to deepen and enrich their own denominational heritage with its wisdom. We hope in particular that it will offer an effective means for getting the work of scholars from these church bodies into the wider theological conversation and that it will encourage others to join this conversation. The larger context is the modern ecumenical movement, which was given birth early in the twentieth century, developed in a variety of ways over the next several decades, and now in the twenty-first century has taken on new and diverse forms.

While ecumenism has many facets to it—ecclesiological, political, cultural—Jürgen Moltmann has helpfully identified its theological significance in his book, *The Church in the Power of the Spirit*. The ecumenical movement, writes Moltmann, has moved the churches away from the anathemas of the past, and ushered them down a path marked by dialogue and co-operation, culminating in toleration and the arguing out of differences within the one church. The ecumenical path, says Moltmann, leads theologically to living in council. He concedes that though the hope of an ecumenical all-Christian council, where Christianity would speak with one voice, is not at all likely in the foreseeable future, that hope nevertheless already sheds light on the present "wherever the divided churches are beginning to live in council with one another."

Living in council entails, on the one hand, consulting other churches and searching other traditions when asking questions affecting one's own communion. The days of returning always to the same dry wells to resolve internal problems and answer pressing questions are over. In particular, Free Churches that have entered into council with other churches are discovering new insights and fresh reservoirs of meaning. The *Free Church, Catholic Tradition* series has its first and most pressing *raison d'être* here, as more and more believers in these churches find ways of life and thought in the great tradition of the church that in their opinion are desperately needed in their own communions.

In addition, says Moltmann, living in council means intervening in the questions of other churches in an effort to cut through old provincial divisions. Though the idea of intervention may sound overly-intrusive (one thinks of reality television shows in which friends and family members perform "interventions" on loved ones who are addicted or otherwise caught up in ways of life that are not healthy), if it is in fact the case that the whole church is present in every individual church, what one body finds problematic or troublesome has important implications for the others: "it is then impossible to say that the controversy about papal infallibility is 'an internal problem for Catholics' or that the dispute about infant baptism is 'an internal problem for Protestants.'" Of course, if such interventions are not done prudently, carefully, humbly, and above all charitably, they will be of no avail.

The volumes in this series thus seek to cut across some of these well-established, though theologically problematic, divisions that have kept Free Church communions in particular from the riches of the Catholic intellectual, moral, and liturgical tradition, and to reconnect believers in these churches with the insights and wisdom of the church catholic. We also hope that Catholic theologians, together with Protestants from the magisterial traditions, would also find in the series a forum for shared inquiry with their "separated brethren," that together we might seek the face of God in the midst of our fragmented context.

Preface

THIS BOOK IS FUNDAMENTALLY about Christian unity, and I wrote it primarily for those within the free church tradition. Although I raise some pointed questions concerning this tradition, I want to state clearly that I honor this capacious tradition, not least because of my own home within the fellowship of churches known as the Churches of Christ. It is where I first learned about Jesus. Its people have consistently tutored me in the language of faith and worship. In its warm communion, I am regularly instructed in the love of God and neighbor. I have spent a number of years in its educational institutions, all of which I owe a debt of gratitude: Lubbock Christian University (where I now happily teach theology); Abilene Christian University; and Harding Graduate School of Religion. It is within the vibrant life of this heritage that I met my wife, Amy. It is within this loving context that we are nurturing our own children, their own lives already having been powerfully shaped by countless "parents and grandparents," Bible class teachers, ministers, and friends.

Churches of Christ represent one of the branches of a larger movement known as the Restoration (or Stone-Campbell) Movement, which arose as a unity movement in frontier America near the beginning of the nineteenth century. Recent historians of the movement have observed that its earliest hopes for broad Christian unity were ultimately overwhelmed by other concerns, particularly concern for uniformity of certain practices. Lamentably, this shift may have contributed to the very kinds of divisions, even within the movement, its initial leaders sought to overcome. In recent years, notable scholars and ministers within the Restoration Movement have given sustained historical and theological attention to the fractured state of Restoration churches in order to move the divided wings of this movement back toward their historical roots and thus back toward each other.

I gladly lay claim to these unitive roots as an heir within this tradition. This particular study, however, is not directed specifically at concerns within the Restoration Movement. My considerations here are directed more toward the free church ecclesial arrangement in general, especially as it relates to Christian unity. While my focus is broader than my own specific tradition, this broader engagement has introduced me to a host of conversation partners whose gifts I hope to bring to those within my own heritage, gifts I pray will bring further healing of divisions.

My initial academic considerations about unity grew out of questions about authority with which I was wrestling during seminary training. The Restoration heritage has expressed itself historically as a kind of "Bible only" tradition on matters of authority. Through both academic training and observing debates internal to my own heritage, I encountered what countless others have noticed—namely, that there is inevitably the pesky issue of *interpretation* that opens a host of further issues. I wondered how the Bible and its interpretation could be separated from historical contingency. The further I followed this trail, the more convinced I became of the necessity of a communally oriented engagement with Scripture; and the more I moved in that direction, the more I became aware of its implications for church unity.

As a result, when I entered my doctoral studies at Baylor University, the questions most alive to me were questions relating to authority. During my first semester there, I encountered the patristic tradition in a way that reframed for me certain questions concerning authority. During that same semester I had my first real encounter with John Henry Newman, the celebrated nineteenth-century theologian who migrated from Anglicanism to Roman Catholicism precisely over questions of authority. I recall going to Dr. Barry Harvey, who later became my dissertation advisor, and asking him, "What if Newman is right?" I suppose I expected him to rescue me from my disorientation over Newman because Dr. Harvey is, after all, a Baptist (at the time I had no idea what *kind* of Baptist I was dealing with). To my surprise, Dr. Harvey responded with something along the lines of, "Well, you should make that the question of your graduate studies, and don't be afraid to pursue it wherever it may lead."

This book is one of the fruits of that counsel; it is my doctoral dissertation with minor additions and revisions. I hope that it raises key questions and that it presses the conversation forward a bit. I do not pretend to provide much in the way of satisfactory answers to these questions, partly because it is a work in progress and partly because I do not think we can say prior to particular historical situations how any of this might find specific application.

I offer this work with the prayer that God may somehow use it to stir up within its readers a greater desire for what Jesus himself desires: that they may all be one.

Acknowledgments

IT TRULY TOOK A village for this project to reach its fruition, and I regret that I can mention only a few of the villagers here. There are some, however, whom I must name.

First, I must thank those who generously served on my dissertation committee: Barry Harvey, Ralph Wood, Scott Moore, Paul Martens, and Jonathan Tran. I extend special gratitude to Barry Harvey. He has been a wise and encouraging mentor along the way. I am very thankful for his commitment to this project and, more broadly, for his centrally formative role in my theological development. Special thanks go also to Ralph Wood and Dan Williams. Each, in his own way, has been crucially important in deepening my appreciation for the richness of the Christian tradition. I must also thank Chad Pecknold, whose acquaintance I did not make until after the defense of this project. Not only did he recommend it to the great people at Cascade Books, but he has also served as a very helpful conversation partner as I have prepared this work for publication.

Most of the daily encouragement I received during the course of this study came from friends in Lubbock, Texas. My colleagues in the Bible department at Lubbock Christian University made every accommodation to help me complete this project. Their encouragement and friendship have meant very much to me along the way. I am also grateful beyond words for the "Panthers" of the Broadway Church of Christ. Their undying commitment to praying for me and their support for my family during the dissertation phase regularly mediated the peace of Christ to me.

I am profoundly grateful to my parents, Wayne and Debbie Cary, for introducing me to Jesus and to his church. I am also thankful for their prayers on my behalf, which began long before this project and faithfully continued through it.

Further, I owe a huge debt of gratitude to my parents-in-law, Steve and Emily Lemley, to whom no parent-in-law joke has ever applied. Their support and encouragement have been unwavering, and their regular hospitality in California provided crucial time and space for completing this study.

I cannot imagine having undertaken or completed this project without the daily encouragement I received from my children: Anna, Tyler, and Olivia. Their laughter and vibrancy for life very often kept me from taking myself too seriously. Their nightly prayers included, "Help daddy to finish his dissertation." I am sure it is to their prayers above all that God graciously responded. While that prayer was a constant encouragement, I must confess that I will be glad never to hear it again.

There are simply no words to adequately express how much I owe my beautiful wife, Amy. I am certain that without her perennial patience, sacrifice, encouragement, prayer, and, yes, prodding, I would never have completed this project. She, more than any other person, helped me believe I could do it, often during those most ominous hours between night and day. I am blessed beyond measure to be married to the best person I know.

Finally, I thank my God (Father, Son, and Spirit), who enabled me to see this project to its end. I pray that whatever is of value in this work will bring him glory and will contribute to the health of his people. *Soli Deo Gloria.*

1

Introduction

THEOLOGIANS FROM FREE CHURCH[1] traditions have long struggled to articulate from within their ecclesial contexts the importance of the unity of Christ's body. This is not to suggest that free church traditions have been unconcerned about Christian unity. It is only to say that an ecclesiological outlook that is fundamentally "free" in character poses certain problems with respect to speaking coherently about ecclesial unity.

The state of the church in the wake of the Reformation has fixed ecclesial unity as a perennial topic of theological concern. The solution to the problem of apparent disunity has sometimes been sought in the notion of the "invisible church." For example, Luther, Calvin, and Zwingli followed Augustine in distinguishing between the visible and invisible church. This move allowed them to contest the Roman Catholic equation of the true church with the visible Roman institution centralized in the Roman pontiff. There followed, then, a tendency to associate the true church with the invisible church in the theology of the early Reformers, yet without downplaying

---

1. The term *free church* is notoriously difficult to define. Curtis Freeman offers five descriptive traits of the free church tradition that will serve as a working definition for the purposes of this study: 1. freedom of governance (nonhierarchical order/congregational polity); 2. freedom of worship (nonprescribed liturgy/spiritual worship); 3. freedom of faith (nonbinding confession/gathered community); 4. freedom of conscience (noncoercive authority/soul liberty); and 5. freedom of religion (nonestablished religion/ separation of church and state), "Where Two or Three Are Gathered," 259 n. 3. For a similar characterization (though under the name "Believers' Church"), see also Durnbaugh, *Believer's Church*, 4–8.

In using the singular "free church tradition," I do not intend to suggest that there is in reality one such tradition. Rather, there exist various free church traditions. The singular is simply a convenient way to consider together those traditions that in large measure share these common characteristics.

the importance of its visible marks such as the preaching of the Word and the proper administration of the sacraments. These visible marks created a crucial link between the visible and invisible church.[2]

Modern Protestant heirs have often made heavy use of the concept of the invisible church to address the obvious fact of ecclesial division. Paul Tillich criticized the way many Protestant theologians had tended to draw so freely upon the distinction between the visible and invisible church.[3] Nonetheless, this distinction remained central to his own ecclesiology. He argued that Protestants understand that unity, when predicated of the church, has a paradoxical character. The predicate of unity applies not to actual churches but to the "unity of their foundation, the New Being which is effective in them." Sociologically speaking, the church cannot avoid divisions. No matter how much ecumenical efforts may accomplish in reuniting actual churches, new divisions will always arise because of the "ambiguities of religion." Thus, the church's essential unity is not to be sought in the existence of actual churches. Rather:

> The predicate [of unity] is independent of these empirical realities and possibilities. It is identical with the dependence of any actual church on the Spiritual Community as its essence in power and structure. This is true of every particular local denomination and confessional church which is related to the event of the Christ as its foundation. The unity of the church is real in each of them in spite of the fact that all of them are separated from each other.[4]

Or to highlight more clearly Tillich's point about the paradoxical character of the church's unity, "It is the divided church which is the united church."[5]

2. See Schreiner, "Church," 324–26. See also Avis, "Church," 418–19; Grenz, *Renewing the Center*, 298, 310–11. Ola Tjørhom asserts that while the Lutheran Reformers spoke of the church as hidden with reference to its true members, they did not understand the church to be essentially invisible. Subsequent Lutheran theologians have misinterpreted Luther on this point and argued for the essential invisibility of the church, *Visible Church—Visible Unity*, 71, 77.

3. Tillich insists that these terms be used not to indicate two churches but two aspects of the one church. When these terms are used to indicate two distinct churches, "the result is either a devaluation of the empirical church here and now or an ignoring of the invisible church as an irrelevant ideal." He argues that the first misstep has characterized certain Spirit movements in Protestantism and the second misstep has characterized much of Protestant liberalism. For Tillich, the quality that makes churches churches is "their invisible, essential Spirituality," which he calls an "essentialistic interpretation of the Spiritual Community," *Systematic Theology*, 3:164–65.

4. Ibid., 3:168–69.

5. Ibid., 3:170.

Within this kind of essentialistic ecclesiology, there is no pressing theological need for visible unity, as desirable as it may be, because the visible is merely a sociological reality. It is the invisible, essential quality of unity that is real and that is given by God.

A heavy dependence upon the idea of the invisible church is not limited to mainline Protestants. Stan Grenz contends that the distinction between the visible and invisible church has been the "operative principle of evangelical ecclesiology."[6] For example, in his discussion of the nature of the church, Wayne Grudem, a self-described conservative evangelical, states, "In its true spiritual reality as the fellowship of all genuine believers, the church is invisible." He then proceeds to define the invisible church as "the church as God sees it." Grudem acknowledges the visibility of the church but only as an aspect of the true church, which is invisible. The visible church is "the church as Christians on earth see it" and that will always include unbelievers.[7] Similarly, Millard Erickson, a significant voice among Baptist and other free church theologians, maintains the distinction between the visible and invisible church, the latter of which is the "true church" and contains only true believers. He asserts that Scripture gives priority to the individual believer's spiritual condition and in doing so gives precedence to the invisible church over the visible.[8]

---

6. Grenz, *Renewing the Center*, 297. See also Timothy George, who says similarly, "At the heart of Baptist and evangelical ecclesiology is . . . the Augustinian distinction between the church visible and invisible," "Sacramentality of the Church," 24.

Not all groups typically considered within the broadest conception of evangelicalism would accept this assessment. Free church scholar James W. Thompson has distinguished the Church of Christ tradition (of which I am a member) from what he calls evangelicalism, specifically in the area of ecclesiology. He claims that a "high ecclesiology" is a dominant feature of the Church of Christ tradition, evidenced by the fact that it has never accepted the distinction between the visible and invisible church. In rejecting this distinction, its members are expected to adhere to a communal ethic of holiness. According to Thompson, this high ecclesiology separates the Church of Christ tradition from evangelicalism's emphasis on faith as a private and individual response to God, "What Is Church of Christ Scholarship?" 36–37. While this may be somewhat true historically, it seems to me that this is a decreasingly persuasive evaluation of the current situation among Churches of Christ, which are increasingly indistinguishable from the broad evangelical current in any number of ways. For a brief discussion of the early Restorationists' interest in highlighting the visible church through visible unity, see Childers, Foster, and Reese, *Crux of the Matter*, 96–98.

7. Grudem, *Systematic Theology*, 856.

8. Erickson, *Christian Theology*, 1046–47.

Visible Unity and Authority:
Emerging Free Church Voices

In recent years, especially in the light of twentieth-century ecumenical efforts focused on visible unity, a growing number of theologians from within
the free church tradition have become decreasingly satisfied with discussing
Christian unity primarily with reference to the invisible church. Yet, there
is a certain tension that presents itself for those theologians within the free
church tradition who are increasingly highlighting the importance of the
visible church. How is one to speak intelligibly about the visible unity of the
body of Christ from within a free church perspective?

The struggle over the visible unity of the church continues to revolve
largely around the vexed issue of authority. Those from within the free
church tradition have (in theory) typically located authority primarily, if not
solely, in Scripture. Whereas much of the Christian tradition has recognized
that authority is manifested through a constellation of distinct but not mutually exclusive loci (especially Scripture, tradition, and a teaching office), the
free church tradition has been notable for transforming the Protestant *sola
scriptura* principle into a radical biblical reductionism funded by rapidly
eroding modern modes of thought, modes of thought that were eventually
capable of buttressing visible ecclesial fragmentation.

In the wake these collapsing modes of thought, there is an emerging
cadre of scholars within the free church tradition, especially Baptists, who
are now pressing for a deeper engagement with the church's wider theological and liturgical tradition as an important source of authority in the life of
the church. Such calls for free church Christians to recognize tradition as
authoritative to one degree or another are often designed to unmask the
myth of the *sola scriptura* doctrine as it has come to be understood by many
within the free church tradition. These free church scholars are arguing in
various ways that Scripture must be read consciously within the context of
the church's tradition.

To argue that the church should read Scripture in the light of the
church's theological tradition opens the door for some serious questions for
those within the free church tradition, especially regarding their relationship
to the broader Christian tradition. These fresh voices from within the free
church tradition are now saying that they are participants in and inheritors
of the "one, holy, catholic and apostolic" church and that this catholic tradition belongs to all Christian traditions (including the free church tradition)
that make up the one living body of Christ that spans time and place. While

there is much here that is ecumenically promising, there also remain difficult questions to consider with regard to visible unity for these free church scholars who are heavily emphasizing the visible church while also turning to the resources of the catholic tradition. Most pressingly, how is unity with this one church to be visibly demonstrated within a free church context and its traditional construals of authority?

Why This Book?

The primary purpose of this study is to build on the recent turn to tradition among free church theologians primarily by pressing the question of visible ecclesial unity and its relationship to the issue of authority. In his foreword to Steven Harmon's book that urges Baptists to account more fully for their relationship to the larger Christian tradition, Paul Avis congratulates Harmon on his "Baptist Catholicity" but then offers this observation:

> The threefold ministry is a topic related to tradition that is not addressed in this book. I am aware that some earlier Baptist pastors were titled "bishop" and that local self-governing congregation [*sic*] can be seen as a diocese in miniature. But I do not think that those factors entirely answer to the concern for unity of particular churches one with another, for teaching authority, for the pastoring of pastors and for the thickly textured fabric of visible unity— in all of which the bishop has *traditionally* had a pivotal role.[9]

My aim is to naturally extend the recent discussion among these free church theologians partly by attending to Avis's concern. Namely, can the contemporary pursuit of tradition as an authority be undertaken coherently apart from a demonstrative pursuit of visible unity beyond the local congregation, especially in the form of an authoritative extra-congregational teaching office of some kind? I shall argue that the one leads naturally to the other and that a rejection of a simplistic *sola scriptura* doctrine along with the affirmation of visible unity of the church substantiates and recommends the classic recognition of the triple loci of authority: Scripture, tradition, and some form of episcopal teaching office. There are some indications that free church theologians are beginning to acknowledge the resulting complexities of engaging the church's tradition within the context of a free church setting, but not nearly enough attention has yet been given to these issues, especially issues of visible unity and authority.

9. Harmon, *Towards Baptist Catholicity*, xviii.

After a century of ecumenical debate, it is still not certain what a workable solution toward visible unity among differing Christian traditions would look like, if even possible. It is important, nonetheless, for those in the free church tradition to join ecumenical conversations even more deeply and consider further the implications of embracing the authority of the church's tradition. Are Scripture and tradition alone sufficient, or is there also a need for a personal ecclesial authority that, among other things, serves as a living sign of the unity among churches and, as such, witnesses to the one body of Christ? Stephen Harmon suggests that since free churches have not typically given attention to the role of tradition in the theological enterprise, they need to listen to those who have already been engaged in discussions about the nature of tradition.[10] Likewise, those within the free church tradition can benefit from guides outside their own tradition to help facilitate reflection concerning the proper relationships between distinct yet related loci of authority and how the nature of these relationships must find expression in a postmodern context.

To help facilitate precisely this kind of reflection, I will take as my primary interlocutors for this study Robert W. Jenson and Rowan Williams, both of whom are located outside the free church tradition. Robert Jenson is a Lutheran theologian who has been at the center of Christian ecumenical dialogue during the latter half of the twentieth century.[11] Rowan Williams is currently serving as the archbishop of Canterbury within the Anglican Communion. Williams too has been a significant contemporary voice in the pursuit of visible Christian unity. I will be particularly interested to examine how each develops and draws upon the classical triumvirate of authority (Scripture, tradition, and episcopal authority) and then show how their conceptions of authority shape their particular conceptions of visible unity. For all the challenges their theologies put to those within the free church tradition, I believe they can be heard by those within the free church tradition because of their fundamental commitments, especially their commitments to the centrality of Scripture and the importance of the local church.

10. Ibid., 46.

11. Jenson attempted to write his *Systematic Theology* as an explicitly ecumenical theology. See *Systematic Theology,* 1:vii–x (hereafter *ST* I).

Method

Robert Jenson asserts that prolegomena of an "epistemologically pretentious sort are a distinctively modern phenomenon."[12] Thus, Jenson claims at the outset of his two-volume *Systematic Theology* a much more chastened role for theological methodology: "The most prolegomena to theology can appropriately do is provide readers an advance description of the enterprise."[13] Also reflecting this now widely accepted suspicion of an overly ambitious hope for what methodology can actually deliver, Dan Stiver suggests that methodology serves best in a clarifying role rather than a foundational role. It sketches the basic framework for doing theology.[14] Following this lead, what I offer here is a brief and modest description of the *style* of theology within which this study will operate, a style I will broadly categorize as tradition-based inquiry.

As the epigraph to his influential book *Arius: Heresy and Tradition*, Rowan Williams reproduces the following statement by the moral philosopher Alasdair MacIntyre: "Traditions, when vital, embody continuities of conflict."[15] MacIntyre has been an important voice advancing what he calls "tradition-constituted and tradition-constitutive enquiry."[16] MacIntyre argues that rational inquiry is essentially historical and communal in nature. His thesis is in direct contrast to Enlightenment accounts of rationality which sought to find liberation from authority and tradition so that truth could be pursued on the sure foundation of indubitable rational principles accessible to rational beings whatever their context. MacIntyre demonstrates that no such sure foundation has ever been found.[17]

In contrast to Enlightenment foundationalism, MacIntyre argues for the inherently traditioned character of rational inquiry. In one instance, he defines a tradition as

> an argument extended through time in which certain fundamental agreements are defined and redefined in terms of two kinds of conflict: those with critics and enemies external to the tradition who reject all or at least parts of those fundamental agreements, and those internal, interpretive debates through which the

12. Jenson, *ST* I, 6.
13. Ibid., 3.
14. Stiver, "Theological Method," 175.
15. MacIntyre, *After Virtue*, 222.
16. MacIntyre, *Whose Justice?*, 9.
17. See especially ibid., ch. 18.

meaning and rationale of the fundamental agreements come to be expressed and by whose progress a tradition is constituted.[18]

So to begin thinking is already to find oneself in the midst of an ongoing and traditioned argument, the future of which is not determined. Thus, the character of a tradition's future inescapably derives from its past.[19]

A tradition-oriented approach to rational inquiry has received several forms of theological expression in the twentieth century.[20] Two notable examples are the twentieth-century Catholic *ressourcement* movement and what has come to be known generally as postliberal theology. The first, led by such distinguished scholars as Henri de Lubac, Yves Congar, and Jean Daniélou, advocated that the most promising way into the future was the way back to the Christian sources (*ad fontes*). These scholars revitalized interest in patristic and medieval voices within the Christian tradition. The second, postliberal theology, is usually associated with a theological style that emerged from Yale University under the leadership of theologians such as George Lindbeck and Hans Frei. Lindbeck coined the term "postliberal theology" as an alternative to what he called "cognitive-propositionalist" and "experiential-expressive" approaches to theological discourse. He argued for a "cultural-linguistic" approach according to which "meaning is constituted by the uses of a specific language rather than being distinguishable from it."[21] According to Lindbeck, religion functions much like a culture which "shapes the subjectivities of individuals rather than being primarily a manifestation of those subjectivities."[22] In other words, the logic of Christian faith is inseparable from its character as a developing tradition. I will intentionally be operating within this basic methodological framework. Indeed, it is a methodological commitment to the necessity of tradition-based inquiry that raises some of my primary questions concerning the ultimate coherence of the free church tradition, which has historically given relatively little attention to the importance of tradition.

My methodological commitment to tradition-based rationality has played an important role in the selection of my primary interlocutors. Both

18. Ibid., 12.

19. MacIntyre, *After Virtue*, 223.

20. Harmon provides a helpful sketch of several different theological paradigms for a postmodern retrieval of tradition, *Towards Baptist Catholicity*, 46–63.

21. Lindbeck, *Nature of Doctrine*, 114.

22. Ibid., 33. Similarly, Milbank states, "The human mind does not 'correspond' to reality, but arises within a process which gives rise to 'effects of meaning,'" "Postmodern Critical Augustinianism,'" 234.

Jenson and Williams are fundamentally committed to tradition-based theological approaches that are richly textured and wide ranging. In a statement that strongly echoes Lindbeck's thesis, Williams states, "I assume that the theologian *is* always beginning in the middle of things. There is a practice of common life and language already there, a practice that defines a specific shared way of interpreting human life as lived in relation to God. The meanings of the word 'God' are to be discovered by watching what this community does . . ."[23]

I begin this study "in the middle" of the free church tradition and specifically *for* those within the free church tradition. Methodologically, this means that I must begin by arguing for a way of proceeding that allows the role of tradition more prominence in theological inquiry than it has normally received among free church theologians. Only then can we begin to examine what follows from granting a greater degree of authority to tradition.

Chapter Outline

An overview of the course of the book and its overall argument will perhaps be helpful. In the second chapter I will fill out what I have presented here in brief sketch with regard to the free church tradition. I will highlight some of the basic commitments that have characterized free church ecclesiology, especially with respect to issues of authority and ecclesial unity, and that have underwritten seemingly unending fragmentation. I will then demonstrate the recent and growing emphasis among free church theologians upon the visible church, an emphasis that is occurring concurrently with a developing recognition among certain free church scholars of the need to substantially appropriate the church's larger tradition as a hermeneutical authority within their own ecclesial contexts. While strongly affirming this recent shift toward tradition among free church theologians, I will argue that these recent scholars have, in general, not yet given sufficient attention to the issue of visible unity and *how* the larger tradition is to be appropriated as an authority apart from accountability to some form of extra-congregational structures, structures that were a critically important facet of the church's developing tradition over time.

In chapters 3 and 4, I will turn to the work of two non-free church theologians, Robert Jenson and Rowan Williams respectively. I will seek to

---

23. Williams, *On Christian Theology* (hereafter *OCT*), xii. For a very similar statement by Lindbeck, see *Nature of Doctrine*, 114.

demonstrate why each theologian believes it is necessary to attend to the constellation of Scripture, tradition, and an episcopal office *as authoritative*. Further, I will seek to uncover *how* they appeal to these loci as related authorities as well as what vision of ecclesial unity results from each one's construction. Though there is much in common between them, their visions for visible unity are somewhat different. For his part, Jenson ultimately argues that the church needs a universal pastor and concludes that the Roman pontiff is the most logical choice. Williams, on the other hand, argues for an ecclesial arrangement without such a focused centralization in which visible unity takes the form of a web of supranational church structures rather than a centralized institutional hierarchy, a generally conciliarist approach.

In chapter 5, I will engage the work of the Baptist theologian James Mc-Clendon, an influential free church theologian with ecumenical sensitivities and an expressed concern for visible ecclesial unity. In his work, McClendon consciously attempts to make room for the inevitable processes of tradition as well as the legitimacy of extra-congregational structures, yet in such a way that, in my view, fails to consider them as authoritative in any substantial way. As a result, he fails to account fully enough for the visible unity of the one body of Christ. Against the backdrop of Jenson and Williams, I will demonstrate why McClendon's congregationally rooted polity, represented by the image of a Ferris wheel, is ultimately insufficient. Specifically, I shall argue that his ecclesiological insufficiencies result, in part, from an unintended ahistorical strain in his theology as well as an insufficient soteriology that does not give enough attention to the notion of union with God. In these and other areas, Jenson and Williams will provide needed supplement and correction to McClendon's valuable contributions.

In the conclusion, I will inquire how those from within the free church tradition can enter the space opened up by the consideration of Jenson and Williams taken together both in their similarities and differences. I will argue that many recent free church theologians have begun advancing in the areas in which James McClendon appears to be deficient, and precisely because of those advances, the case for a free church polity as a desirable goal becomes even more problematic. I will suggest that these free church theologians need to wrestle more overtly with whether their continued defense of the free church tradition is a *truthful* result of their recent moves toward the wider Christian tradition.

2

Recent Developments within
the Free Church Tradition

IN THE INTRODUCTION, WE briefly observed that those within the free church tradition have often tended to account for ecclesial unity by appealing to the notion of the invisible church. In this chapter I will first demonstrate a recent move among certain free church theologians to reject such a move and instead focus more attention upon the visible church as the proper agent of discussions regarding ecclesial unity. Since issues of visible unity are so closely bound up with issues of authority, I will then highlight typical perspectives on authority within the free church tradition and how recent accounts of authority by certain free church theologians present a challenge to the typical perspectives on authority within their own tradition. Specifically, I will demonstrate how these new theological voices within the free church tradition are challenging an account of authority that is rooted in an overly simplistic embrace of *sola scriptura*. Instead, they are advocating a conscious embrace of ecclesial tradition as a necessary authority within the life of free churches. Finally, after affirming these recent turns toward attending to the visible church and embracing tradition as a locus of authority, I will raise questions that arise from making such moves. Specifically, I will ask whether those within the free church tradition can make these moves coherently without also embracing the need for a third locus of authority, an extra-congregational teaching office.

A Free Church Turn to Visibility

In 1977, a group of American evangelical theologians, some of whom were from the free church tradition, drafted a document titled "The Chicago Call:

An Appeal to Evangelicals." In it, the signatories decry "the scandalous isolation and separation of Christians from one another," and assert that "such division is contrary to Christ's explicit desire for unity among his people and impedes the witness of the church in the world." They reject "church union-at-any-cost" but also reject "mere spiritualized concepts of church unity." Further, they state forthrightly that "unity in Christ requires visible and concrete expressions," and then they call upon evangelicals to "cultivate increased discussion and cooperation, both within and without their respective traditions, earnestly seeking common areas of agreement and understanding."[1]

Stan Grenz observes the generally cautious response among neo-evangelicals to the kind of ecumenical challenge represented by "The Chicago Call." On the one hand, because modern evangelicalism was born out of an ecumenical impulse, these evangelicals do not openly oppose movements toward unity among separated confessional traditions. However, the typical evangelical impulse, which would certainly include most within the free church tradition, is skeptical toward attempts at unity that center on organizational union. As Grenz argues, this skepticism is partly rooted in the evangelical commitment to convertive piety with its primary attention on individual believers.[2] The result is what Grenz calls a "believer ecumenism" among evangelicals, as opposed to a "church ecumenism." The former is focused on unity among individuals rather than confessional groups, and the focal point for the unity among these believers is usually cooperative involvement in projects that they have in common.[3]

Millard Erickson and Wayne Grudem are illustrative of the kind of response outlined by Grenz. In his summary comments on Christian unity, Erickson affirms that the one church of Jesus Christ is his spiritual body, and that the spiritual unity shared by believers who are in this body should "come to expression in goodwill, fellowship, and love for one another. We should employ every legitimate way of affirming that we are one with Christians who are organically separated from us."[4] Note that Erickson does not indicate that organic separation is inimical to Christian unity. Rather, in the midst of organic separation, Christians should find ways to express their spiritual unity. True unity is spiritual (i.e., invisible). Erickson then reveals what he has in mind by saying that spiritual unity should come to

1. "The Chicago Call," 16.
2. Grenz, *Renewing the Center*, 305–6.
3. Ibid., 308.
4. Erickson, *Christian Theology*, 1146.

expression. He states, "Christians of all types should work together whenever possible. . . . Cooperation among Christians gives a common witness to the world and is faithful stewardship of the resources entrusted to us."[5] In other words, the visible expression of spiritual unity takes the form primarily of voluntary association and is oriented toward the accomplishment of certain joint interests and tasks of mission. For Erickson, visible unity is functional and ad hoc rather than necessary.

Wayne Grudem reflects a similar perspective. He admits the New Testament teaches that Christians should work toward not only the purity of the visible church but also the unity of the visible church. But this visible unity does not require one worldwide ecclesial governing structure over all Christians. Rather, the spiritual unity of believers (which is already actual) is supposed to be demonstrated visibly and "is often demonstrated quite effectively through voluntary cooperation and affiliation among Christian groups." These distinct and organically separated Christian groups are not necessarily a contradiction to the unity of the body of Christ.[6] Again, we see here the conviction that visible unity of Christians has more to do with voluntary association of particular Christian groups to accomplish certain tasks than with structural unity of all Christians, a structural unity that would be organically related to the actual unity of Christ's body.

In spite of this skeptical reaction among some free church theologians, the turn toward the visible church, and thus to visible unity, has gained momentum among other free church theologians. The Mennonite theologian John Howard Yoder was a pioneering figure in this regard. Yoder was intensely interested in and highly involved with the ecumenical efforts of his day. For Yoder, the imperative of visible Christian unity is fundamentally a theological imperative. He eschews any effort to ground visible unity in "good manners" or any simply utilitarian rationale that seeks greater efficiency through visible cooperation among Christian groups. Rather, for Yoder, the imperative for visible unity is rooted in the church's identity as a witnessing community. And this ecclesial identity is in turn rooted in a christological reality.

To underscore this christologically centered ecclesial identity, Yoder appeals to two biblical texts that have been central to ecumenical discussions in recent years: John 17:20ff. and Ephesians 2–3. In the Johannine text, Jesus prays that future believers would be one just as the Father and the Son are one. The unity of the Father and Son provide the model for Christian unity.

5. Ibid.
6. Grudem, *Systematic Theology*, 876–77.

Further, this unity among believers has a functional element, and it is here that we clearly see the church's identity as a witnessing community. As Yoder states it, "The function of the unity of the future believers is, therefore, to make credible the fundamental Christian claim ('that the world might believe,' said twice) and to reflect the nature of the unity between the Son and the Father, to render that credible witness substantial." In the Ephesians text, the focus is on God's cosmic purpose to make one humanity out of heretofore divided Jews and Gentiles. Once again, the church is called to witness to the reality of this new humanity before the observing world. And thus, "Where Christians are not united, the gospel is not true in that place." Yoder explicitly rejects conceptions of unity that require only occasional manifestations of visible unity and otherwise settle for invisible unity, what sometimes passes under the label "spiritual" unity. [7] The church is a sociological reality independent of the sociological structures of surrounding culture. As such, Yoder advocates that a more useful distinction than that between the visible and invisible church (or any other distinction between "realms of reality") is the more biblical distinction between those who confess Jesus as Lord and those who do not.[8]

James McClendon has also been an influential free church theologian who has given increased attention to the visible unity of the church. At the beginning of an extended treatment of ecclesiology, McClendon clarifies his own ecclesiological starting point as a "baptist"[9] theologian. He states, "My own orientation is toward a 'gathering church' or 'local' style ecclesiology. The doctrine of Christian community begins with (though does not end with) the actually meeting, flesh-and-blood disciples assembly." Whatever he says about the universal dimension of Christian community depends upon "the character of the church as tangible, as local, as gathering."[10] Therefore, to speak of Christian unity is to speak primarily about tangible, visible unity. On this account, doctrinal division among Christians is problematic. The community Jesus prays for in John 17 is not represented well by such

7. Yoder, "Imperative of Christian Unity," in *The Royal Priesthood*, 289–99, esp. 291.

8. Yoder, "Let the Church Be the Church," in *The Royal Priesthood*, 168–80, esp. 170–71.

9. McClendon regularly uses the term *baptist* (distinguishable from *Baptist*) to indicate a broad but discernible theological vision shared by a variety of groups with roots in the Radical Reformation. This theological vision certainly includes Baptists but also encompasses many other groups such as Disciples of Christ, Churches of Christ, Mennonites, and Assemblies of God. For his full discussion of the "baptist" vision, see *Ethics*, 17–35.

10. McClendon, *Doctrine*, 327–28.

divisions. McClendon acknowledges that theology has often contributed to such divisions and must now seek to be part of the solution, working toward visible unity.[11] He demonstrates the importance of visible unity by stating, "The fellowship of the Spirit is not even imaginably ours until it *takes shape as a fellowship of peace and love* open to the neighbor—even the enemy neighbor—as to the Lord."[12]

Similarly, Baptist theologian Stan Grenz has been a noteworthy free church voice advocating attentiveness to the visible unity of the church. He approvingly cites David Watson, an evangelical Anglican, who writes, "The time has come when we can no longer excuse our disunity by appealing to the invisible unity of all true Christians."[13] Grenz argues that distinguishing sharply between the visible and invisible church leads to an elevation of the latter above the former, in which situation the former becomes soteriologically irrelevant.[14] He partly grounds his call for attentiveness to the visible church in the apologetic role of the religious community that has come to the fore within a postmodern context:

> In such a situation, the ecclesiological question can no longer be answered merely by appeal to the true church as an invisible, spiritual reality, together with the denominationalist compromise. Rather, the postmodern, pluralist context calls for an apologetic evangelical theology that reaffirms the place of the church as a people and, in a certain sense, as a soteriologically relevant reality.[15]

That is, the church is now expected to be the visible demonstration of the social reality it proclaims. The church's unity is its witness.

11. Ibid., 332.

12. Ibid., 330, emphasis added. In a coauthored essay, McClendon and Yoder argue that the unity that is crucial to the church is not merely the acknowledgment of one Lord but also of one faith and one baptism. They state clearly, "That is, the Spirit gives unity, not only of commitment but also of doctrine and of practice. . . . We believe Christians have a fundamental duty to realize this unity," "Christian Identity in Ecumenical Perspective," 561.

13. Watson, *I Believe in the Church*, 351, cited in Grenz, *Renewing the Center*, 305. See also the free church theologian Miroslav Volf on this point. He maintains that one must distinguish theologically between the *ecclesia visibilis* and the *ecclesia invisibilis*, but that they may not be separated, because in separating them, one risks abusing the notion of the invisible church to justify separation from visible churches, *After Our Likeness*, 173.

14. Grenz, *Renewing the Center*, 299.

15. Ibid., 308.

Visible Unity and Authority

There is a tension that emerges for those theologians within the free church tradition who are increasingly highlighting the importance of the visible church. When the notion of the invisible church is not available to carry the weight it has often carried within this tradition, how is one to speak intelligibly about the unity of the body of Christ from within a free church perspective? How are those within free church settings to account seriously for Jesus' high priestly prayer for unity in John 17, along with all the other New Testament injunctions toward ecclesial unity? How is this particular church to be united with that particular church? How are these particular churches to be united with those particular churches of differing times, places, and traditions?

The issue of visible unity has been one of the most pressing theological concerns of the last century.[16] While much good has come from these processes, large-scale movements toward visible unity have not yet resulted. The struggle over the visible unity of the church continues to revolve largely around the vexed issue of authority. The move toward greater visible unity will depend, in large part, on whether greater consensus can be reached regarding what counts as legitimate authority in the church and how that authority is to function. If this is true, then it is imperative that each Christian tradition spend significant energy honestly reviewing and analyzing its own understanding of authority, both in theory and in practice.

Those from within the free church tradition have, in theory, typically located authority primarily, if not solely, in Scripture. Though the original Reformers did not conceive of *sola scriptura* as abrogating the authority of the church's larger (especially early) tradition,[17] subsequent forms of Protestantism have tended to reduce the scope of authority to Scripture alone and, only secondarily, to forms of congregational governance that could be justified clearly within the New Testament. This is especially true for most within the free church tradition.[18] For free churches, the church's tradition

16. Though, as Yoder has noticed, free church representation has been largely absent from these discussions, "Nature of the Unity We Seek," in *The Royal Priesthood*, 221–30, esp. 225.

17. See D. H. Williams, *Retrieving the Tradition*, ch. 6.

18. My own location is within the Restoration heritage, particularly the most conservative wing known as Churches of Christ. Over time we developed what Restoration scholars typically label a "pattern hermeneutic," which viewed Scripture (particularly the New Testament) as primarily providing a pattern or blueprint to which subsequent congregations must rigorously adhere. Scripture is *the* authority in matters of church

has historically received very little play, and rarely does it function *overtly* as a locus of authority. This is most evident in the rejection of all creeds within the worship of most free churches. Further, for most free churches, there is no adherence to any official teaching office or authority outside the local congregation. Whereas much of the Christian tradition has recognized that authority resides in a constellation of three distinct but not mutually exclusive loci (especially Scripture, tradition, and a teaching office), the free church tradition has been notable for transforming the *sola scriptura* principle into a radical biblical reductionism.

The consequences of this biblical reductionism are manifold, two of which are of direct importance for this study. First, the move away from submission to tradition and an official and authoritative teaching office in the church occurred alongside and from within the epistemological foundationalism that developed during the Enlightenment. This epistemological shift resulted in both a liberal Protestant attack upon the veracity of Scripture and the counterreaction of conservative theologians whose primary burden was to defend Scripture from within the same reigning epistemological foundationalism. These defenses, still common among conservative evangelicals, have come under heavy attack by so-called postmodern ways of thinking which resist foundationalism and insist upon the contextual and traditioned character of all knowledge.[19]

A second significant result of Protestant biblical reductionism has been the proliferation of individualism, and its concomitant disunity. When tradition and any extra-congregational teaching authority are severely reduced in significance, or eliminated altogether, what usually remains is Scripture as it is interpreted by each individual, and the result has been unending fragmentation. Even an ardent supporter of congregationalism such as John Yoder can observe that while the Reformers did not intend for division and individualism to result from their convictions about the perspicuity of Scripture and the priesthood of all believers, nevertheless, "that openness to unaccountable individuality was potentially present in their logic."[20] This "openness" unfortunately has become a tragic reality.

---

practice and doctrine. To ensure proper adherence to biblical mandates as well as to deal with other issues that may arise, each congregation is autonomously governed by a plurality of elders and deacons. This arrangement was supposedly the clear pattern for ecclesial organization read directly off the pages of the New Testament.

19. For an account of this history, see Murphy, *Beyond Liberalism and Fundamentalism*.

20. Yoder, "Hermeneutics of Peoplehood," in *The Priestly Kingdom*, 15–45, esp. 24.

A Free Church (Re)Turn to Tradition

Partly in response to postmodern criticisms of foundationalism, partly in response to the individualism rampant within free church settings, and partly out of ecumenical concerns for a greater demonstration of visible unity, there is a recent and swelling movement among free church theologians to recover the wider Christian tradition in significant ways beneficial for their own tradition. In recent years a spate of books and articles has appeared by these revolutionary scholars challenging the biblical reductionism and individualism of their own tradition and encouraging attentiveness to the larger Christian tradition, increasingly in ways that overtly conceive of this tradition as authoritative to one degree or another.[21]

Among free church theologians, the pioneering work of scholars such as the aforementioned Mennonite John Howard Yoder and the Baptist James McClendon has been influential in turning other free church scholars toward the resources of Christianity's long history. For both Yoder and McClendon, one of the motivations for engaging the breadth of the Christian tradition is the concern for visible Christian unity. We will briefly consider each of these theologians in turn, as well as the Baptist Stanley Grenz.

---

21. Alongside the more academic discussion of retrieving the church's larger tradition, there is a corresponding popular movement among many free churches and other evangelicals toward embracing tradition as well. A 2008 issue of *Christianity Today* has as its cover story a Wheaton Theology Conference whose theme was "The Ancient Faith for the Church's Future." Its author cites the influence of men such as Robert Webber, Peter Gillquist, and Tom Oden as being significant in leading evangelicals back to the resources of the Christian tradition. Some younger evangelicals are apparently driven by an impulse toward greater rootedness in a fragmented world and by a desire for worship renewal that leads to greater authenticity. While there is much to applaud in this general instinct toward the past, one also gets the sense that such "retrievals" are often further instances of the worship consumerism often found within these traditions. As Chris Armstrong puts it in this article, this youth movement says, "Embrace symbols and sacraments. . . . And break out the candles and incense. Pray using *lectio divina*. Tap all the riches of Christian tradition you can find," "Future Lies in the Past," 26.

The more difficult discussions are happening at the level of scholarship as a new wave of free church scholars are discussing not only retrieving the tradition, but the importance of being answerable to it somehow, approaching it not so much as consumers but as learners and inheritors. Resources by noteworthy scholars aimed at thoughtful nonspecialist audiences will be of immense value in the coming years to provide guidance for what is currently a more popular engagement with the tradition. One such resource is the expanding series of books titled Evangelical *Ressourcement* edited by D. H. Williams. Williams has authored the first two books in the series, *Evangelicals and Tradition* and *Tradition, Scripture, and Interpretation*. The subsequent two volumes are Craig Allert's *A High View of Scripture* and Ronald Heine's *Reading the Old Testament with the Church*.

John Howard Yoder

Across the breadth of his career, Yoder was intensely interested in ecumenical dialogue, which for Yoder never amounted to cheap ecumenism or unity that merely pursued a least common denominator.[22] This commitment to dialogue, of course, forced Yoder to deal with the role and weight of tradition within Christian theological discourse. As one consistently arguing for the important contributions of the free church tradition, Yoder was keen to repeatedly bring Scripture to the center of ecumenical discussion, sometimes seemingly to the point of naïveté. For example, in one of his earlier ecumenically oriented essays published in 1957, Yoder asserts the following:

> If the locus of our given unity is Jesus Christ, it would seem that the only feasible solution to the problem of authority would be to declare inadmissible the attribution of authoritative character to any particular historical development and to recognize, as the only legitimate judge, *Christ himself* as he is made known through Scripture to the congregation of those who seek to know him and his will.

He then states that this would not necessarily condemn all post-scriptural doctrinal development, nor would it necessarily lead to a simplistic literalism in the use of Scripture. But it *would* preclude "recourse to any particular evolution as a canon of interpretation. Neither what the modern mind can accept, nor what the medieval mind could accept, nor what one of the Councils of Constantinople could accept, would have the right to stand above, or beside, or even authoritatively under Christ and Scripture."[23]

In a later essay (1984) titled "The Authority of Tradition," Yoder reflects more positively on the importance of tradition.[24] Here Yoder responds to Roman Catholic critics who charge evangelicals with biblicism (in the pejorative sense of what Yoder elsewhere calls "infantile literalism"[25]) and who assert that evangelicals, too, interpret Scripture within a context, make

22. E.g., see Yoder, "Nature of the Unity We Seek," in *The Royal Priesthood*, 229–30. For focused attention to Yoder's ecumenical agenda, see Nugent, *Radical Ecumenicity*.

23. Yoder, "Nature of the Unity We Seek," in *The Royal Priesthood*, 225.

24. In comparing these two articles, I do not necessarily intend to demonstrate an evolution in Yoder's thought in this area. Much of Yoder's writing is for specific contexts that would call for differing emphases at different points. My primary aim is to show that while Yoder can sometimes make statements that *appear* quite biblicist (in a pejorative sense) in nature, these must be balanced by his more generous appraisals of the role of tradition in the theological enterprise.

25. Yoder, "Nature of the Unity We Seek," in *The Royal Priesthood*, 225.

assumptions, etc. Yoder recognizes this truth but limits the wide, sweeping force of the attack by countering that it adequately applies only to a naïveté among certain precritical evangelicals. It does not, however, apply to the evangelical theological tradition "which in its original age (that of Wyclif and Hus or of Luther and Calvin) was by no means naïve nor disrespectful of tradition as a hermeneutical matrix." Yoder proceeds to affirm the need for a "hermeneutical matrix" when reading Scripture, but will not allow this matrix to usurp or even stand on equal footing with Scripture itself as an authority. Analogously, one must have recourse to a microscope in order to observe microorganisms, but the microscope remains distinct from the microbe, the latter of which retains its priority as an object of knowledge.[26]

What about doctrinal development as enshrined in Christian tradition? For Yoder, it is appropriate to speak of legitimate change as long as one is equally willing to acknowledge the real possibility of error. The real tension is not between Scripture and tradition; rather, it is between faithful tradition and unfaithful tradition. In saying this, Yoder locates Scripture within the broader category of tradition. Scripture "comes on the scene not as a receptacle of all possible inspired truths, but rather as a witness to the historical baseline of the communities' origins and thereby as link to the historicity of their Lord's past presence."[27] Scripture has priority within the tradition because it brings us within the hearing distance of the "original traditions." In an obvious counter to John Henry Newman's organic metaphor for doctrinal development,[28] Yoder states that the wholesome growth of tradition is less like the growth of a tree and more like that of a vine. It is a story in which organic growth is constantly interrupted by pruning. Pruning is the church's appeal to its original traditions, especially represented in Scripture. It is not idealistic primitivism, but rather a "'looping back,' a glance over the shoulder to enable a midcourse correction. . . ." Pruning is designed to "provoke new growth out of the old wood *nearer to the ground*, to decrease the loss of food and time along the sap's path from roots to fruit. . . ."[29]

It is clear that Yoder is greatly concerned about origins, wanting to reduce the gap between *then* and *now* as much as possible, as partly indicated by his vinedresser's metaphor. This movement toward reaching for origins is itself found within the original traditions enshrined in Scripture. Thus, the

26. Yoder, "Authority of Tradition," in *The Priestly Kingdom*, 63–79, esp. 66.

27. Ibid., 69.

28. For its classic statement, see Newman, *Essay on the Development of Christian Doctrine*.

29. Yoder, "Authority of Tradition," in *The Priestly Kingdom*, 69, emphasis added.

center of the Christian tradition is not propositions, scriptural or otherwise, which are authoritative by virtue of some inspired status free from historical contingencies which move them beyond the reach of hermeneutical debate. Rather, the center of the Christian tradition is itself an impulse toward the earliest memories of the foundational event itself.[30] Yoder does not hesitate at all to affirm continuing revelation. In fact, he points to Jesus' promise that there would be continuing revelation (e.g., John 14:12–26; 16:7–15). Yoder only insists that all new revelation and development be measured at the bar of Scripture, which most notably enshrines the original traditions.[31]

Yoder acknowledges and even embraces the process of tradition. He is willing to acknowledge that the logic of the Christian faith evolves in particular directions in response to particular historical contingencies. Many of these changes are natural outgrowths of the "original event." Others are aberrations or dead ends that need to be trimmed back and recognized as unfaithful departures, or unfruitful at best. What Yoder is not clear about in these texts is how post-biblical tradition functions *authoritatively*, and how the church locates those areas of the tradition that are most centrally germane to function as the miscroscope that we need in order to observe Scripture rightly. Nonetheless, Yoder is a free church voice acknowledging that we must somehow attend to genuine change within the Christian tradition.

James W. McClendon Jr.

James McClendon is another significant free church voice demonstrating greater sensitivity to the role of tradition than is normally found within the free church tradition. Veli-Matti Kärkkäinen labels McClendon the premier theologian of the free church tradition and describes his theology as "rooted in the rich classical tradition in both the East and West, at the same time contemporary and often creative in its constructive proposals."[32] We will attend to McClendon more fully in the fifth chapter. For now I simply want to register that the church's tradition is important to McClendon's theological enterprise, both methodologically and as a theological resource.

With regard to methodology, McClendon has strong affinity for the work of philosopher Alasdair MacIntyre, who argued that moral inquiry can only take place within a community over time, a living tradition of receiving

---

30. Ibid., 70.

31. Ibid., 72.

32. Kärkkäinen, *Introduction to Ecclesiology*, 142.

and handing on formative skills and practices. McClendon came to some of these insights independently of MacIntyre's work, but he found great affinity between his work and MacIntyre's and subsequently drew upon it. McClendon argued that a traditioned community is a necessary condition for a believer's knowledge of God because it forms the community's life and informs its teaching through shared practices extending over time and space.[33]

McClendon also draws upon the Christian tradition as a theological resource. As with most "baptists," for McClendon Scripture rests at the very heart of the theological enterprise. Nonetheless, Kärkkäinen is correct in saying that McClendon is "rooted" in the classical theological tradition. One may well question what the term *rooted* means here, but at the very least it means that McClendon widely and freely engages the broad Christian tradition, especially in his volume on Christian doctrine. At times, he engages the tradition in a posture of forthright critique and challenge. At other times, he draws upon insights from the tradition and honors these insights as belonging to all Christians, including free churches.[34]

Like Yoder, ecclesial unity is one of McClendon's motivations for engaging the broad Christian tradition in such constructive ways. Since, as we noticed earlier, McClendon locates the nature of the church primarily in its

33. McClendon, *Doctrine*, 316. For more on this, see McClendon and Smith, *Convictions*. This is one of the reasons McClendon began his *Systematic Theology* with a volume titled *Ethics*. For one instance of his defense of the uncommon method of beginning a systematic theology with ethics, see McClendon, *Ethics*, 41ff.

34. As an example of the latter, in his discussion of the atonement, McClendon speaks appreciatively of the major theories of atonement present within the Christian tradition. After addressing the ways in which these theories do and do not belong to contemporary believers, he suggests that each is worthy of a place within contemporary theology, but only to illuminate Scripture (as a form of Chrsitian midrashim), not to replace it, *Doctrine*, 232.

While helpful for certain general purposes, McClendon's categorization of these theories of atonement is too tidy. As only one example, he relies on Gustav Aulén's now classic work and assigns the *Christus-victor* model of atonement to "this 'first thousand years' of atonement teaching," *Doctrine*, 203. While Aulén certainly was helpful in bringing this emphasis of early Greek thought to the fore, later studies demonstrated that his conclusions were a bit oversimplified and that early atonement teaching was more nuanced and varied than Aulén's account would lead one to believe. See, for instance, Turner, *The Patristic Doctrine of Redemption*.

In the final chapter, we will consider other ways in which McClendon's treatment of tradition is less than satisfactory. My immediate goal is to notice the fact that he takes the tradition more seriously than have most free church theologians. But as we will see, there is a new generation of free church scholars who are engaging the tradition with far greater attention and precision than McClendon himself, something he would no doubt celebrate and affirm.

local "gatheredness," he believes Christian unity must work toward visible unity. Together with Yoder, he says that "the Spirit gives unity, not only of commitment but also of doctrine and practice. . . . We affirm here our commitment to that unity for which Jesus prayed and which the Spirit, speaking in the Apostle [i.e., Eph 4:6], commands. . . . We believe Christians have a fundamental duty to realize this unity."[35] Having said that, McClendon is not optimistic about any fully realized visible unity short of the eschaton. Consistent with his eschatologically oriented theology, McClendon believes that the different "types"[36] of Christian expression are all provisional expressions on the way to eschatological unity. Nonetheless, Christians should work to realize what unity they can in the present.[37]

Thus, McClendon's ecumenicity can be seen as a mutual sharing and contributing among the different types of Christian expression. This is not to say that each type is equal in McClendon's eyes. Presumably one participates in any given type out of the conviction that it is superior to the others. Nonetheless, each is a partial expression of a greater whole. We can then understand McClendon's engagement with non-baptist strands of the Christian tradition as an honest attempt at listening to the fuller voice of God as it is expressed through the Christian "other."

While McClendon has led free church theologians into greater contact with the tradition, and partly out of ecumenical intent, he does not provide much in the way of explicit reflection on the value of engaging tradition or how tradition functions authoritatively. What he does say is remarkably brief. For instance, for McClendon Scripture plays a central role of authority in the Christian community. But in his discussion of authority, McClendon says surprisingly little about the role of tradition in the formation of Scripture, a point Catholic theologians have been stressing now for centuries. He acknowledges that tradition preceded Scripture but not as a rival to it. He also acknowledges that there is some agreement now between Catholics and other Christians that Scripture and tradition are not two sources of authority but one and that early Christians saw creeds as hermeneutical guides to reading Scripture. He then asks the pressing question, what authority do these creeds have? His conclusion is that they are "monuments of tradition"

---

35. McClendon and Yoder, "Christian Identity in Ecumenical Perspective," 561.

36. McClendon follows Lesslie Newbigin's typology (found in *The Household of God*) of Western Christian groups into Catholic, Protestant, and Pentecostal, the latter of which McClendon terms *baptist*. For this discussion, see *Doctrine*, 334ff.

37. McClendon, *Doctrine*, 336–37, 344. Cf. McClendon's similar discussion using the models of a tree and river in *Witness*, 333–34.

showing us how people at other times have read Scripture and inviting us "to read it that way if we can." He finally states that they are "simply hermeneutical aids and like every reading strategy must remain subordinate to the scriptural texts we hope to read (partly) by their help."[38]

It is not at all clear in McClendon's brief discussion what kind of authority attaches to tradition, especially the creeds he mentions. We are simply encouraged to use them as hermeneutical lenses "if we can." There is much ambiguity in this latter phrase, and again, in the fifth chapter we will return to this and other ambiguities in his treatment of authority. At this point, however, we see McClendon urging Christians to try to read Scripture by the light of these ancient creeds, even if his rationale for doing so is not readily apparent. This is at least a step in the direction of taking tradition more seriously than have many within the free church tradition.

We must notice one final point with regard to McClendon's view of tradition as an authority. On the surface, it is a bit surprising that when he locates centers of Christian authority (namely experience, Scripture, and community), he does not give sustained attention to tradition as a center of authority (or as a major theological category). He provides a brief rationale for such a decision. In the avalanche of material dealing with the role of tradition, it has taken on different meanings and included more and more things (e.g., the complex of doctrines, practices, patterns of life, etc.). As a result, McClendon says that Christian tradition is not an authority on or in Christianity but simply *is* Christianity. As the term includes more and more, there is less need to contrast it with other authorities.[39] There is, of course, a certain truth in this observation, but there is also the potential for using it as a quick way out of some very complex and thorny issues, issues that do not get much press in McClendon's work.

Stanley J. Grenz

One other exemplary free church theologian I wish to single out is the Baptist theologian Stanley Grenz, who has been a formative influence for many recent students within the free church tradition. Mark Medley surveys a list of several influential Baptist theologians ranging from the mid-nineteenth century to the present and concludes that among them, James McClendon

---

38. McClendon, *Doctrine*, 470–71. See also his brief discussion (one paragraph) a bit further on in which he suggests the use of the longer Catholic canon (though he doesn't mention the even longer Orthodox canon as an option), 476–77.

39. Ibid., 470.

and Stanley Grenz produce the most constructive discussion of tradition.[40] We have already seen that McClendon's explicit treatment of tradition is not extensive. Grenz offers a bit more.

In his systematic theology, Grenz lists tradition as the second of three norms or sources (i.e., Scripture, tradition, and culture) for doing theology and gives roughly one page to its treatment. Nowhere else in this lengthy volume does he engage in any kind of extended discussion of tradition as a theological category. However, he does heavily engage the church's tradition throughout the work. The terms he uses when he explicitly discusses tradition as a theological source are instructive. He says that past theological discussions and conclusions are "significant" and "important" for today's theologians, especially as they are "instructive in our quest for relevant theology." Certain historical formulations have withstood the test of time (i.e., creeds) and carry "special significance" and "special relevance for every age." Because we want to participate in the one body of Christ, we must "take seriously" the doctrine of the church across the ages. Because the theology of these formulations is embedded in the great theological literature of the ages, we can read it "with profit." Finally, he adds the cautionary word that these formulations are "not binding in and of themselves. They must be tested by the Scriptures and by their applicability to our cultural situation." Further we must understand them within their own historical and philosophical contexts.[41]

Several years later Grenz coauthored a book attempting to give shape to a specifically postmodern theological methodology that moved beyond foundationalism. Here again, he offers tradition as the second of the same three theological sources he provides in his systematic theology. Here, however, he devotes an entire chapter to tradition. Much of the same language appears again. The tradition is an "important reference point,"[42] and classical formulations such as widely accepted creeds have "special ongoing significance."[43] There is, however, a new tone that makes its way into this discussion. First, the question of canon formation emerges in a way that it does not in his systematic theology, so that now Grenz can say, "Apart from the *authority* of the Christian community, there would be no canon of authorized texts."[44] Second, Grenz takes on the problems surrounding the

40. Medley, "Catholics, Baptists, and the Normativity of Tradition," 119–20, n. 2.

41. Grenz, *Theology for the Community of God,* 18–19.

42. Grenz and Franke, *Beyond Foundationalism,* 118.

43. Ibid., 123.

44. Ibid., 115, emphasis added.

Protestant *sola scriptura* slogan. He argues that Scripture and tradition are "inseparably bound together." Then, appealing to Robert Jenson, he states, "For this reason, to suggest that the Protestant slogan *sola scriptura* implies an authority apart from the tradition of the church—its creeds, teachings, and liturgy—is to transform the formula into an oxymoron."[45] Third, with respect to widely accepted creedal statements, he now calls them a "vital" resource for theology. As he did in his systematic theology, he roots this assessment in unity of the church, except it receives stronger statement now:

> So also, in confessing the one faith of the church in the present we become the contemporary embodiment of the legacy of faith that spans the ages and encompasses all the host of faithful believers. . . . Hence, although our expression of faith is to be contemporary, in keeping with our task of speaking the biblical message to the age in which we live, it *must also* place us in continuity with the faith of the one people of God, including both our forbears who have made this confession in ages past and our successors who will do so in the future . . . . Because we are members of this continuous historical community, the theological tradition of the church must be a *crucial component* in the construction of our contemporary theological statements, so that we might maintain our theological or confessional unity with the one church of Jesus Christ.[46]

Finally, flowing from all of this, and drawing upon Alasdair MacIntyre's work on the nature of tradition, Grenz concludes that although Scripture functions as the norming norm, "the tradition of the community provides a *crucial and indispensable* hermeneutical context and trajectory in the construction of faithfully Christian theology."[47]

Whether Grenz intended it nor not, there is a marked development in his language from the first book to the second which we have briefly surveyed here. What he initially described merely as important and of special significance has now become vital, crucial, indispensable. It has become *authority* in explicitly stated terms. My goal here is not to delve into *how* it functions authoritatively in Grenz's work. I simply want to point to the intensification of language that this high profile, free church theologian is using with respect to tradition. It is an intensification that is increasingly shared by others in this tradition as we shall shortly see. I also want to highlight how

45. Ibid., 117.
46. Ibid., 123–24, emphases added.
47. Ibid., 129, emphasis added.

Grenz's emphasis on tradition is expressly rooted in (among other things) a fundamental conviction concerning the unity of the church.

A Swelling Free Church (Re)turn to Tradition

There is an emerging cadre of scholars from the free church tradition, especially Baptists, who are now pressing for an even more thickly textured engagement with the church's tradition than that advocated by Yoder, McClendon, and Grenz. In his recent book, *Towards Baptist Catholicity*, Baptist patristics scholar Steven Harmon highlights and summarizes this "emerging trend" among Baptist theologians and points toward its important ecumenical implications. He states that Baptist theologians "are increasingly invoking tradition as a source of religious authority, reflecting on tradition as a theological category, offering constructive proposals for a Baptist or Free Church retrieval of tradition, and utilizing tradition as a resource for constructive theology."[48] Curtis Freeman has coined the term "catholic baptists" (following McClendon's lowercase spelling of *baptist*) to describe those from this tradition who are seeking to locate themselves more fully within the broader Christian tradition.[49]

As Harmon observes, these catholic Baptists (using the uppercase spelling since he is dealing specifically with those from the Baptist tradition)

48. Harmon, *Towards Baptist Catholicity*, 2.

49. Freeman, "Confession for Catholic Baptists." Some of those who have come to be known by this label are represented in a collective flagship statement in which its authors make "a beginning" at moving Baptists in a new theological direction that includes, among other things, a commitment to "look to the church catholic as it appears throughout the world and throughout history for other examples of faithful communities." This manifesto and a list of its authors can be found in Harmon, *Towards Baptist Catholicity*, 215–23. For a recent doctoral dissertation studying this loosely affiliated group of scholars, see Jorgenson, "Bapto-Catholicism."

Although Baptists are leading the way among free church theologians with respect to engaging the church's tradition, they are not alone. For example, from my own tradition a recent book by Ron Highfield makes some surprisingly strong claims for the role and status of tradition, though his account carries with it some of the deficiencies I will soon argue are present in some of these Baptist theologians as well, *Great Is the Lord*, esp. 28ff. Further, Leonard Allen, also an influential theologian within this tradition, has begun advocating a connection with "the Great Tradition." See "The Future of the Restoration Movement." It is a start, but there are many questions that remain, and those within my own tradition are just beginning to wrestle with these issues. Another recent free church ecclesiology authored by non-Bapist theologians is refreshing in its positive and broad engagement with the church's larger tradition. See Harper and Metzger, *Exploring Ecclesiology*.

explicitly recognize tradition as a source of authority.[50] Philip Thompson has called upon Baptists to seriously consider "the normativity of tradition."[51] Mark Medley affirms Thompson's call and suggests that it should involve engaging in ecumenical conversation with those who have reflected on tradition, which he models in this article by providing an in-depth review of Terrence Tilley's (a Roman Catholic) *Inventing Catholic Tradition*.[52] D. H. Williams argues for the particular normativity of the patristic period and claims that contemporary evangelicalism, including free church traditions, cannot remain doctrinally orthodox or faithful to Scripture apart from integrating the tradition forged during this pivotal period.[53]

These calls for free church Christians to recognize tradition as authoritative usually directly challenges the myth of the *sola scriptura* doctrine as it has come to be understood by many within the free church tradition. Common to some within the free church tradition is the slogan "no creed but the Bible,"[54] whether it is overtly stated or held only implicitly. What has long been argued by Catholics, and what is now being affirmed by this new wave

50. Harmon, *Towards Baptist Catholicity*, 7. This is the first of seven marks of Baptist catholicity Harmon provides in this chapter.

51. Thompson, "Re-envisioning Baptist Identity," 302.

52. Medley, "Catholics, Baptists, and the Normativity of Tradition," 121. Medley has reproduced some of these same ideas in "Stewards, Interrogators , and Inventors." See also Steven Harmon, who says that since Baptists (and this would be true of other free church groups as well) "lack a tradition of traditions," they need to be in dialogue with other proposals for engaging the early Christian tradition in a postmodern context, *Towards Baptist Catholicity*, 46.

53. D. H. Williams, *Retrieving the Tradition*, 13. Williams contends that without serious recourse to this ancient tradition, free churches 1) will increasingly perpetuate an ahistorical and subjectivist sectarian approach to Christian faith, and 2) will silently compromise the uniqueness of the Christian identity by accommodating it to a pseudo-Christian culture, 14. For an attempt to put this retrieval of the church's classic tradition into practice, see this collection of essays by free church theologians: D. H. Williams, *The Free Church and the Early Church*.

54. This slogan emerged initially within the Stone-Campbell Restoration movement. The Restoration movement began as a unity movement that held out the promise of unity based on a "back to the Bible" approach governed by a hermeneutical outlook influenced partly by Scottish Common Sense philosophy. The leaders of this movement believed unity could be achieved if only the centuries of dogmatic separations represented by competing creeds could be eliminated in favor of returning to the true source of unity, the clear teachings of the Bible. See Boring, *Disciples and the Bible*, 16–30. William Tabernee has rightly noticed, however, that Alexander Campbell himself had a more positive view of the resources of the patristic period, including ancient creeds, than is sometimes realized by caricaturing his position with slogans like "no creed but Christ" or "no book but the Bible," "Alexander Campbell and the Apostolic Tradition."

of free church "catholics," is that Scripture has never been the sole means of authority that mediates the Christian faith. In fact, *sola scriptura* for the early Reformers did not mean discarding all tradition in favor of "simply reading the Bible." It meant delivering the Bible as it was interpreted by the early Christian tradition from the abuses and hegemony of certain medieval Roman traditions which had suffocated the proper interpretation of Scripture. The magisterial Reformers made strong appeal to the interpretations of the church fathers and to the catholic creeds that emerged during those formative centuries. They believed themselves to be making rightful claim to those sources.[55]

Later Protestants have not been so wise in practice, especially those in the free church tradition. They have not realized the need to acknowledge other sources of authority that are inevitably at work in the process of interpreting Scripture. An outsider to the free church tradition has unmasked this tendency well with specific reference to trinitarian theology. George Lindbeck has insightfully recognized that "most biblicist Protestants" affirm, in practice, postbiblical Trinitarianism. They accept Nicene theology while overtly ignoring the creed itself and act as if this theology emerges clearly and effortlessly from the pages of Scripture.[56] Fresh free church voices are calling for a climate in which ancient creeds and confessions, among other expressions of the tradition, would play some kind of authoritative role in theological formation. They realize what many in the Christian tradition have known for a long time, but what many contemporary Christians have lost sight of—namely, that everyone must have a hermeneutical lens for reading Scripture. These classic creedal lenses, understood rightly, are not a competitive authority over against Scripture. Rather, they were understood by their framers as a summary of the purport of Scripture, the key to reading the whole correctly. This consensual creedal tradition (undergirded by earlier local baptismal formulas) and Scripture function in a symbiotic fashion.[57]

55. D. H. Williams, *Retrieving the Tradition*, ch. 6; D. H. Williams, "Scripture, Tradition, and the Church." See also Harmon, *Towards Baptist Catholicity*, 32; Holmes, *Listening to the Past*, 14–17.

56. Lindbeck, *Nature of Doctrine*, 74. For the same point made by free church theologians, see among others Harmon, *Towards Baptist Catholicity*, 71–87; D. H. Williams, *Evangelicals and Tradition*, 51; *Retrieving the Tradition*, 29.

57. See D. H. Williams, *Retrieving the Tradition*, chs. 3 and 5. See also Harvey, "Doctrinally Speaking," 56–57; "Where, Then, Do We Stand?" 371–79; Newman, "Priesthood of All Believers," 56. See also a formal and collective statement to this effect by Curtis Freeman, Steven Harmon, Elizabeth Newman, and Philip Thompson, in which these

This symbiotic relationship between Scripture and tradition surfaces some important issues with respect to canon formation. Free church theologians are increasingly inclined to highlight the fact that a vibrant process of traditioning was a prerequisite for the formation of the biblical canon. D. H. Williams points to the fact that prior to the biblical canon, there was a canon of faith at work, what the church believed and professed, best represented perhaps in the pre-creedal "rule (or canon) of faith."[58] This has implications for *how* Christians appeal to the Bible as an authority. Barry Harvey poignantly expresses the importance of keeping the church's tradition wedded to the reading of Scripture:

> Once we exit the ecclesial house of tradition like prodigal children, then, we leave behind the Bible as a unified set of texts that functions as the norming norm of their common life and language. Appeals to the authority of Scripture made apart from this ecclesial process . . . eventually undermine that authority and deepen the authorial void that looms beneath our feet.[59]

The very shape of the Bible rests on the theological outlook preserved and enshrined in the tradition as it is reflected in baptismal formulas, creedal formulas, liturgies, catechetical instruction, etc. Free church scholar Craig Allert has recently given book-length treatment to canon formation, a book aimed specifically at evangelicals. His thesis is that a "high view" of Scripture must be just as concerned with how Scripture came to be as in what it says. Thus, he concludes:

> Appeal to the Bible as authority is essential, but not without a similar appeal to the proper lens of interpretation. That proper lens of interpretation has been the ecclesial canons of the church in which the Bible grew. . . . If we are to do justice to and cherish God's word to us, we must be aware of the means God used to deliver it to us, and in that, the church has been central.[60]

---

authors jointly call upon Baptists churches to include a weekly recitation of either the Nicene Creed or the Apostles' Creed, "Confessing the Faith," in Harmon, *Towards Baptist Catholicity*, 225–26. The Disciples of Christ (Restoration heritage) scholar Boring has also advocated the use of creeds as a way of demonstrating connection with the wider Christian tradition, *Disciples and the Bible*, 429–30.

58. *Evangelicals and Tradition*, 55; *Retrieving the Tradition*, 45. See Norris, "Canon of Scripture in the Church," 3–25.

59. Harvey, "Where, Then, Do We Stand?" 374.

60. Allert, *High View of Scripture?*, 175.

To reject naïve expressions of *sola scriptura* and to acknowledge that the church together with her tradition supplies the proper hermeneutical context for reading Scripture is simultaneously to press some very difficult questions for the free church tradition, specifically with regard to its relationship to this broad and ancient Christian tradition. Rather than continuing to say that theirs is the only true form of church, or that the true church is the (invisible) sum total of all who belong to God, some from the free church tradition are now saying that they are participants in and inheritors of the "one, holy, catholic and apostolic" church of the Nicaeno-Constantinopolitan Creed, and that this catholic Christian tradition belongs not just to the Roman Catholic or Orthodox traditions, but it belongs to all Christian traditions (including the free church tradition) that make up the one living body of Christ that spans across time and place.[61] While there is much here that is ecumenically promising, there also remain difficult questions to consider with regard to visible unity for these free church scholars who are heavily emphasizing the visible church while also turning to the traditional resources of the "one, holy, catholic and apostolic church." Perhaps the most pressing question is, how is unity with this one church to be demonstrated, visibly?

Questions Going Forward

As stated in the introduction, the primary purpose of this study is to build on the recent turn to tradition among free church theologians primarily by pressing the question of visible ecclesial unity and its relationship to the issue of authority. We can now begin to uncover some of the tensions that arise for free church theologians as they attempt to embrace the authority of tradition. In the midst of these new and provocative moves among these theologians, there resides an oddity. They often speak about retrieving the catholic tradition "for the free church tradition" or "as Baptists" or "as evangelicals." Notice, for example, the opening sentence of Steven Harmon's preface to his outstanding book *Towards Baptist Catholicity*. Here he states that his book "contends that the reconstruction of the Baptist vision in the wake of modernity's dissolution requires a retrieval of the ancient ecumenical tradition that forms Christian identity through liturgical rehearsal, catechetical instruction, and ecclesial practice."[62] This initial statement announces that

61. E.g., see Harmon, *Towards Baptist Catholicity*, 3, 82, 149; Holmes, *Listening to the Past*, 18–36; D. H. Williams, *Retrieving the Tradition*, 205ff.

62. Harmon, *Towards Baptist Catholicity*, xix.

reconstruction of the Baptist vision is the primary aim of the book, and that retrieval of the ancient catholic tradition serves this more foundational purpose of Baptist self-reconstruction. Elsewhere, he states that Baptists must give greater attention to the relationship of the catholic tradition and the church which formed it and "for which it has *some* normative function. A Baptist hermeneutic of tradition will maintain a place for the ecclesial distinctiveness of Baptist communities while becoming more open to the traditional resources of the larger Christian community."[63] Again, the explicit aim does not seem to be that Baptists should seek to enter full communion with other Christians. Rather what is sought is a specifically "Baptist hermeneutic of tradition" that will not eclipse Baptist distinctiveness in the end.[64] Further, there are "ways in which Baptists may affirm their connection to the larger Christian community to which they belong, and thus to its tradition, without yielding the distinctiveness or *authority of their own communities*."[65]

On the other hand, in his answer to the question of why he is still a Baptist in light of his developing views about traditional catholicity, Harmon acknowledges that those who abandon their Protestant traditions to join the Roman or Orthodox Church are taking steps toward full visible unity. He then explains his own decision to remain a Baptist:

> Nevertheless, I am of the considered opinion that before the separated churches can move towards visible unity, they must first go deep within their own traditions in order to recover elements of catholicity that once characterized their own churches but have subsequently been neglected and in order to identify the sources of the present barriers to a mutually realized catholicity.[66]

Similarly, in the last sentence of his book, he expresses his hope that his Baptist readers "will love Christ's church deeply enough to regard our cherished constructions of Baptist identity as temporary way stations en route to the realization of the visible unity of the Body of Christ in one Eucharistic

63. Ibid., 63, emphasis added.

64. This kind of language is also common among scholars of my own Church of Christ tradition. One commonly hears calls to unity, but these calls often come with admonitions to "preserve our Restoration distinctives." The list of so-called "Church of Christ distinctives" has rapidly decreased over the last several years as other free church groups have taken up a "higher" view of baptism and weekly observance of the Lord's Supper, both of which have been central in the Church of Christ tradition. Congregational autonomy is one characteristic many in this heritage still treasure and seek to maintain.

65. Harmon, *Towards Baptist Catholicity*, 64, emphasis added.

66. Ibid., 203.

fellowship."[67] For Harmon, eucharistic fellowship is the primary visible expression of catholicity, the latter term referring primarily to a *"qualitative fullness of faith."*[68] Thus, for Harmon, it seems that recovering the catholic tradition *as Baptists* and for Baptist reconstruction is a temporary agenda on the way toward full unity, which of course would not then be "Baptist" in character.

Consider also the way in which D. H. Williams discusses these matters. He believes that retrieving the ancient tradition is crucial for free churches, and while he sees ecumenical potential in such an undertaking,[69] he makes the interesting claim that "one ought not to have to leave the Free Church in order to embrace the norms of the ancient Christian Tradition."[70] Indeed, according to Williams, "Appropriating such roots is essential if free church and evangelical Protestantism is going to *preserve its identity* in light of its present tendencies toward internal fragmentation and accommodation to Western culture."[71] One wonders what the "ecumenical potential" of engaging the larger tradition might mean if "preserving the identity" of one's particular tradition is a noble aim that one should not have to abandon.

Elsewhere, Williams worries that the free church traditionless and noncreedal approach "lacks the centripedal force necessary to keep its tendency toward fragmentation and detachment at bay."[72] Again, he says he is not trying to undermine the free church spirit, but that a rigorous understanding of local congregational autonomy "provides a false security for maintaining Christian truth." Free churches need the "external check" of the church's theological history and doctrinal standards to prevent the current slide toward fragmenting sectarianism found among much of the evangelical world, including the free church tradition.[73]

Herein lies the oddity in how both Harmon and Williams speak of free churches engaging the church's catholic tradition as a touch point of authority. The free church tradition is marked, at least in part, by its commitment to local congregational autonomy. Does not an appeal to an authority (other than Scripture) coming from outside the congregation begin to call the entire free church polity into question? As we have just seen, Williams seems to

67. Ibid., 212–13.

68. Ibid., 204.

69. D.H. Williams, *Retrieving the Tradition*, 8.

70. Ibid., 31.

71. D. H. Williams, *Free Church and the Early Church*, x, emphasis added.

72. D. H. Williams, *Retrieving the Tradition*, 208.

73. Ibid., 204.

acknowledge this difficulty and challenges overly rigorous understandings of congregational autonomy. But his "external check" is simply the ancient tradition, which raises other problems. Which parts of the tradition are to receive central attention? Who says? What are the mechanisms for receiving and handing on this tradition? Who interprets the tradition and determines how it should be understood and applied in the present? How can we speak of the ecumenical potential of a retrieval of tradition if what we are left with is individual congregations taking up the tradition without accountability to each other with regard to how they are reading the tradition? Would this not simply become a form of congregational individualism?[74]

These questions raise further and important questions. Namely, if some free churches continue to give increased attention to the visibility of the church, and if these same churches become increasingly serious about submitting to the authority of the catholic tradition, is it possible for them to pursue unity through this tradition without global, extra-congregational structures of authority that serve to facilitate and demonstrate the visible unity among congregations? If the answer to this question is no, at what point do they cease to be free churches and become something else? And what is it that they become?

In a letter to Eberhard Bethge in 1940, Dietrich Bonhoeffer made the following observation:

> [I]t became quite clear to me again that the struggle regarding the church government [Kirchenregiment] is actually the question necessarily emerging from church history regarding the possibility of a Protestant church for us. It is the question, whether following the separation from papal and worldly authority in the church, an ecclesial authority can be erected that is grounded in word and confession alone. If such an authority is not possible, then the final possibility of a Protestant church is gone; then there truly remains only a return to Rome or a state church or the way into isolation, into the "protest" of true Protestantism against false authorities.[75]

It seems that some of the free church theologians advocating a return to tradition believe that authority can be located solely in Scripture and confession, especially if by "confession" we mean the normativity of what we might loosely label "Nicene theology" as it is reflected in ancient creeds, liturgy,

---

74. After this chapter was written, these almost identical questions were put to Williams in a review of another of his books that contains similar arguments. See Martin, "*Evangelicals and Tradition.*"

75. Bonhoeffer, *Conspiracy and Imprisonment*, 78.

etc. It is not obvious, however, that a specifically congregational adoption of these classical expressions of faith is enough to maintain their theological integrity over time. If it is not, could we rephrase Bonhoeffer and ask whether the last possibility of a free church ecclesiology is dead? Given the challenges that come with embracing the authority of tradition, is it ultimately coherent for free churches to continue speaking in terms of a *"Baptist* engagement with the tradition" or an *"evangelical* recovery of the tradition"?

Michael Hollerich speaks to these concerns in a remarkable article that traces the contours and implications of a lively correspondence between Adolph von Harnack and Erik Peterson in 1928. While critiquing the kind of undogmatic Protestant liberalism represented by Harnack, Peterson found himself needing to justify dogma and eventually could not do so without actually becoming a Roman Catholic, which he did in 1930. Peterson realized that with the collapse of the church's legal-political expression of *Öffentlichkeit* (i.e., public character) under the Weimar Republic, the church's public character now had to be grounded in dogma. But having to ground the German Protestant church's public character in dogma "meant facing up to the absence of an authority which sanctioned dogma." The church no longer had the state to function as a quasi-dogmatic office in regulating the church's doctrine, which in Peterson's thinking created a dogmatic vaccum. Peterson believed that if the church sought a public identity, then some kind of magisterium was imperative for the formation and preservation of dogma, a point obviously precluded by Protestant presuppositions.[76]

Hence, Peterson spoke of a "dogmatic deficit." This deficit was unrecognizable for a while since the Protestant church still had recourse to various confessional documents, but the binding authority of these confessions rested on the state, not the church. Hollerich observes, "The state's abdication of its religious character now left the confessions dangerously exposed. And Peterson was not as sanguine as Harnack that historical inertia would suffice for a considerable time to keep the tradition together. Far from possessing an indelible character, it might be liable to rapid erosion."[77] Traditional Protestantism had long been connected to its Catholic roots in a "complex dialectical relationship which confessional politics could never obscure" (e.g., liturgical resemblances, a common dogmatic basis reflected in the ancient creeds, etc.). Peterson argued that the consciousness of these

---

76. Hollerich, "Retrieving a Neglected Critique," 325.
77. Ibid., 326. Cf. Lindbeck, *Nature of Doctrine,* 77ff.

historical connections with Catholicism faded in time because of shifts that occurred within modern Protestantism that changed its ontological basis.[78]

We can observe some parallels between this exchange and contemporary free church issues. As we have noticed, several free church theologians have highlighted the fact that free churches have been dependent on traditional catholic theological developments (e.g., the doctrine of the Trinity), even if they have explicitly rejected the ancient enshrinements of those developments (e.g., classical creeds). Free churches have, often unknowingly, been in a "complex dialectical relationship" with the catholic tradition. But do we have any reason to believe this will continue? Can we simply assume that those within the free church will continue to "play close to home" in a postmodern context, especially in the absence of formal points of connection such as recourse to creeds, ancient liturgies, etc.? And would the simple embrace of ancient instantiations of the tradition be sufficient?

Peterson claimed that for the church to have a public character grounded in dogma, it needed a public authority to sanction the dogma. If tradition is not static, and if tradition is as much about process as content, then we must have trustworthy mechanisms by which we continually receive and learn to enact the tradition. This was equally true for the period in which Scripture itself and the classical creeds emerged. As Barry Harvey asserts, "Apart from the institutions and deliberations that were indelibly inscribed within the process, the Bible's normative status can never be anything more than an arbitrary imposition on the competency of an individual's soul by a particular church."[79] One of these institutions was the episcopacy which served as a focal point for retrieving and passing on the tradition within the church in a way that highlighted the unity among churches with respect to this tradition. Free church scholar Frederick Norris says more bluntly, "Bishops shaped the canon."[80] Norris is not arguing that monepiscopacy is essential to the church. Rather, he is arguing that an extra-congregational office of authority played a central role in the formation of the biblical canon. Instead of asking whether any such structure is found in Scripture and is

---

78. Hollerich, "Retrieving a Neglected Critique," 326. Peterson argued that modern Protestantism developed three ways to compensate for the loss of "public character" that had resulted from legal disestablishment: the substitution of "universal truths of reason" for pure doctrine; inward piety (mysticism); and church activism. He believed that if these were pursued apart from awareness of Protestantism's dialectical relationship with Catholicism, then they inhibited the restoration of Christianity's public character, which he was convinced could only happen through dialogue with Catholicism, 327.

79. Harvey, "Where, Then, Do We Stand?" 374.

80. Norris, "Canon of Scripture in the Church," 16.

essential, we should be asking whether it leads to well-being. Although mon-episcopacy is and was capable of grave abuses, it also proved healthful in the early centuries for gathering Scripture and clarifying the church's faith.[81]

Could it be that in an ecclesial context of increasing fragmentation and postmodern challenge, those within the free church tradition need to give more serious attention not only to recognizing the authority of the catholic tradition, but also to the need for authoritative structures that would facilitate a healthy reception and interpretation of the tradition? Could it be that these structures might make possible a more visible demonstration of unity between churches gathering around this tradition such that the church understood as the one body of Christ would gain more coherence among believers and be a more compelling visible witness to an observing world?

There are some indications that free church theologians are beginning now to deal with these questions which arise naturally out of a deeper engagement with the church's tradition. Baptist scholar Paul Fiddes has emphasized the importance of visible unity beyond the local congregation and what kinds of supra-congregational structures might be necessary for more fully realizing such unity. In addressing the question of episcopacy, he says, "It seems that there will be no real hope of visible unity in the church of Christ without some agreement on this personal sign of being apostolic."[82] Similarly, Barry Harvey has stated that Baptist (and this would apply to other free church traditions as well) polity must prove that in the current post-Christian context, it can navigate the difficult terrain between the church's central practices and the institutions that cultivate those practices. After observing James McClendon's model of a Ferris wheel in which these different facets of authority within congregational life are connected with no top chair, Harvey states in a footnote, "It is becoming increasingly clear that Baptists and other Free-church traditions need to revisit the question of apostolic succession, and in particular the validity of the dichotomy between episcopal and so-called 'spiritual' secession [sic]."[83]

Aside from such brief observations by free church scholars, the question of some kind of living and extra-congregational teaching authority that facilitates visible unity along with a faithful transmission of the church's tradition has not received nearly enough attention among free church theologians who are more fully engaging the church's tradition. More work is needed on the implications of embracing the authority of the catholic

81. Ibid., 17–18.
82. Fiddes, *Tracks and Traces*, 225.
83. Harvey, "Where, Then, Do We Stand?" 379, n. 81.

tradition. Is Scripture and tradition sufficient, or do we also need a personal authority that serves as a sign of the unity among churches and witnesses to the one body of Christ?

To provide guidance in forming a response to this and the other pressing questions I have raised in this chapter, I will now turn to the work of Robert Jenson and Rowan Williams. I will demonstrate that for each theologian, the church's unity is best facilitated by the mutually dependent and interactive authority of Scripture, tradition, and some form of a global teaching office.

3

Robert W. Jenson on Unity and Authority

Introduction

ROBERT JENSON'S THEOLOGICAL JOURNEY has taken him from deep Lutheran roots and commitments in an increasingly ecumenical direction, marked by an all-encompassing concern for visible ecclesial unity.[1] To observe the centrality of ecclesial unity in Jenson's work, one may simply read the preface to his *Systematic Theology*. These four pages are governed by a singular goal: to frame the entire work as an ecumenical contribution, doing theology for the one church. Jenson resists the tendency toward particularistic theologies such as Lutheran theology, Reformed theology, Catholic theology, etc. Such monikers might be used innocuously as historical descriptions, but when they mark the course for theology, the result either limits the scope of "church" or debilitates the task of theology.[2] Theology, defined as "the church's enterprise of thought," is done for the church, and "the only church conceivably in question is the unique and unitary church of the creeds."[3] The latter claim is, of course, contestable, especially among many within the free church tradition (at least in the terms expressed here), but it expresses

1. Together with his longtime friend Carl Braaten, Jenson founded the Center for Catholic and Evangelical Theology and launched the theological journal *Pro Ecclesia*, both of which have been important ecumenical forums. In his personal memoir of Jenson, Braaten selects Ephesians 4:4–6 ("There is one body and one Spirit . . . ") as an epigraph that expresses the central pulse of their shared theological vision, "Robert William Jenson—A Personal Memoir," 9. From 1998–2005, Jenson served as the Senior Scholar for Research at Princeton University. He describes himself during this final period of his academic career as a "catholicizing, Lutheran/Epis-copalian," "Theological Autobiography, to Date," 53.

2. Jenson, *ST* I, vii.

3. Ibid., ix, vii.

Jenson's firm commitment to let the ecumenical agenda take precedence over specific traditions or those agendas that tend toward balkanization and that subsequently have increased difficulty accounting for *the* church, the one body of Christ.

In the face of ecclesial division, Jenson registers one of his central convictions—that is, that the present church exists in a state of eschatological anticipation. The church is awaiting her fullness, and she must view this time of waiting as "the most creative of activities." Theology need not wait for an undivided church to do theology for that church, because theology "is itself a form of the waiting we must practice."[4] His is a theology that is marked by just that sort of waiting.

While there are parts of Jenson's theology that are controversial regardless of where one is on the theological spectrum, I believe that his is a voice that those from the free church tradition can appreciate. First and foremost, he is a profoundly biblical theologian who takes great care with scriptural exegesis.[5] Further, Jenson is especially effective in demonstrating why a typical free church account of *sola scriptura* is not a truthful way forward and why the church's Bible is inevitably bound up with the church's tradition. While some theologians in the free church are coming to similar conclusions about tradition, Jenson demonstrates why there is the further need for an authoritative teaching office. Yet even on that point, perhaps Jenson can at least be heard by those in the free church because he does not make overly ambitious claims about what a teaching office actually provides, and he shows himself ready to critique episcopal systems as they have often been practiced. Finally, even though he argues for an extra-congregational teaching office, Jenson also places a very high priority on the local church gathering and the Spirit's work in such gatherings, something free churches can obviously appreciate. In the end, he displays a portrait of visible ecclesial unity that relies upon a healthy and fruitful exchange among the three classic loci of authority.

In order to appreciate how Jenson develops and relates these loci of authority, we must begin with the overall shape of his ecclesiology. First, we will outline the basic structure of the *communio* ecclesiology he espouses.

---

4. Ibid., viii.

5. This feature of Jenson's theology is usually acknowledged, even by his critics. For example, David Hart registers his profound disagreement with almost every part of Jenson's theological program, but he praises him for his attention to the breadth and depth of Scripture, "Lively God of Robert Jenson," 33–34. See also Robert Wilken who praises Jenson's theology for being surprisingly biblical as well as being deeply Trinitarian and immersed in the church fathers, "Is Pentecost a Peer of Easter?" 176.

We will then briefly explore Jenson's understanding of the church as the body of Christ and how that understanding in turn shapes his commitment to visible unity. Finally, we will examine how Jenson develops and relates each of the three loci of authority under discussion toward the goal of visible ecclesial unity.

Communio Ecclesiology

Jenson's ecclesiology is rooted in what he takes to be the proper *telos* of humanity, namely, the classic notion of participation in the divine life, or *theosis* (i.e., deification or divinization), which is especially prominent in Eastern theology. Jenson pointedly asserts, "The patristic concept of *theosis* is the most precise and compendious possible evocation of the end for which God creates us."[6] The central role of *theosis* in Jenson's theology finds expression in Rowan Williams's theology as well. The implications of this doctrine are wide ranging, and I will eventually argue in chapter 5 that the relative absence of *theosis* in McClendon's theology is, in part, what allows him to defend a congregational polity. By contrast, Jenson's apology for institutional visible unity is deeply rooted in his commitment to *theosis*.

His commitment to a soteriology oriented toward *theosis* leads Jenson to fully embrace *communio* ecclesiology, which has become a "major achievement of ecumenical consensus."[7] In brief summary, *communio* ecclesiology asserts that the foundation, model, and goal of the church's communion (*koinonia*) is the *koinonia* of the triune life. Since participation in the Trinitarian life is at the root of *communio* ecclesiology, it is important to make some brief observations about Jenson's Trinitarian theology, the facet of his theology for which he is probably best known and which will probably rub against the grain of most free church sensitivities.[8]

Perhaps the most consistent and driving impulse of Jenson's theology is his unflinching commitment to the notion that God is not identified *by*

6. Jenson, "Church as *Communio*," 3. Paul Cumin refers to the doctrine of *theosis* as the climax of Jenson's theology, "Robert Jenson and the Spirit of It All," 178. It would be difficult to consider this an overstatement.

7. Jenson, "Church as *Communio*," 1; Jenson, *Systematic Theology: The Works of God*, 221 (hereafter *ST* II). The Orthodox tradition has been especially influential in developing this ecumenical ecclesiology. Two notable promulgators of this teaching are the Orthodox theologian John D. Zizioulas (*Being as Communion*) and the Catholic theologian J.-M.-R. Tillard (*Church of Churches*).

8. Now in retirement, Jenson himself refers to the doctrine of the Trinity as "ever more decisively the key in all my thinking," "Theological Autobiography, to Date," 54.

the events recorded in Scripture but *with* them. For example, the Son is always only the Son by virtue of his incarnation and resurrection; thus, these historical events become constitutive of the identity of God.[9] Jenson is so committed to identifying God *with* the events of the biblical narrative that he is willing to follow his logic to its conclusion: an overt challenge to the traditional teaching that God's "being" is "timeless," a view he ascribes to a corrosive Hellenistic influence upon Christian thought.[10] In Jenson's view, God becomes himself through time, which has certainly been the most controversial of Jenson's propositions, since it seems to compromise God's freedom and sovereignty.[11] Jenson attempts to answer such objections by appealing to (his reading of) Barth's doctrine of election, according to which God is not "bound" by history, sin, and death, because the incarnation was his eternal free choice.[12]

9. This basic conviction gets worked out in numerous places in Jenson's corpus, largely because it is so foundational to his theology. Among many places, see e.g., *A Religion Against Itself*; *Christian Dogmatics*, vol. 1, chs. 1–6; *ST* I, esp. 42–60; *Story and Promise*, 103–28; *The Triune Identity*; "The Triunity of Truth," in *Essays in Theology of Culture*, 84–94; "Does God Have Time?" in *Essays in Theology of Culture*, 190–201.

10. The rejection of timelessness in God has been one of the constant themes of Jenson's theological career. For Jenson's early critique of "religion" as an attempt to escape time, and the influence this has had on Christian theology, see *A Religion Against Itself*. See also his early adamant rejection of the notion of a timeless God in *Alpha and Omega*.

11. David Hart offers one of the more clear critiques of this aspect of Jenson's theology. While Hart himself affirms Rahner's famous maxim that the economic Trinity is the immanent Trinity and the immanent Trinity is the economic Trinity, he argues that Jenson goes wrong by collapsing the necessary analogical interval between the economic Trinity and the immanent Trinity, "Lively God of Robert Jenson," 30–31. For further critique of Jenson on this controversial point, see Di Noia, "Robert Jenson's 'Systematic Theology': Three Responses," 103; Farrow, "Robert Jenson's 'Systematic Theology': Three Responses," 91; Forde, "Robert Jenson's Soteriology," 136ff.; Gunton, "Creation and Mediation in the Theology of Robert W. Jenson"; Hunsinger, "Robert Jenson's *Systematic Theology*," 176–79; Ive, "Robert Jenson's Theology of History," 155–57; Mattes, "Analysis and Assessment of Robert Jenson's *Systematic Theology*," 484; Molnar, "Robert W. Jenson's *Systematic Theology*," 130; Sholl, "On Robert Jenson's Trinitarian Thought," 31–32; Wainwright, "*Vera Visibilia*," 297; Fackre, "Lutheran *Capax* Lives," 98. Peter Ochs, a Jewish scholar, sees all these concerns about Jenson's "immanentism" as unproblematic if Jenson is read as a corrective to excesses in modern theology rather than as a time-independent system, "Jewish Reading of *Trinity, Time and the Church*." Ochs' easy dismissal of these concerns, however, does not take seriously enough the potency of Jenson's ontological assertions.

12. Jenson wrote his doctoral dissertation on Barth's doctrine of election. See *Alpha and Omega*, 47ff., 60–63. Paul Molnar challenges Jenson's appeals to Barth's idea of the eternal decision of God as a way of protecting God's freedom. Molnar contends that Barth does so in such a way that the Godhead still remains transcendent to Christ's humanity (he refers explicitly to *Church Dogmatics* IV.2, 63), "Robert Jenson's *Systematic Theology*," 120–21.

Having freely chosen to become himself through the course of contingent historical events, God's self-identity is "constituted in *dramatic coherence*" of his "eventful actuality." Since dramatic coherence is determined by a drama's resolution, God is what he is by *anticipation* rather than by persistence of some immutable essence.[13] According to this logic, the life of God is "constituted in a structure of relations, whose own referents are narrative." These narrative referents as poles of time relate to the triune identities in the following way for Jenson: "The Father is the 'whence' of God's life; the Spirit is the 'whither' of God's life (i.e., 'God coming to us from the last future'); and we may even say that the Son is that life's specious present."[14] This point will become significant in our discussion of authority when Jenson directs our attention to the Spirit of the future in order to assess the necessity of a teaching office. Jenson supports his temporal-relational understanding of God through appeal to Thomas Aquinas's teaching of the triune identities as "subsisting relations" and through heavy appeal to the Cappadocian insights of God's "being" as *perichoresis*. God's "being" is not *a* something but an *event*.[15] It is truly an eternal *conversation* of personal and loving discourse between the Father, Son, and Spirit.[16]

Putting this perichoretic understanding of the Trinity together with Jenson's narrative-constituted Trinity, we can better understand why Jenson believes *theosis* is the appropriate soteriological end not just for individual humans but for the church. For Jenson, the identity of the second person of the Trinity is *eternally* the God-man Jesus Christ.[17] This means God has

13. Jenson, *ST* I, 64–66. Jenson follows Aristotle's account of dramatic coherence "in which events 'occur unexpectedly but on account of each other,' so that before each decisive event we cannot predict it, but afterwards see it was just what had to happen."

14. Ibid., 218–19. For a critique of Jenson's assignment of the triune members to the three poles of time, see Watson, "'America's Theologian,'" 219–23; Crisp, "Robert Jenson on the Pre-Existence of Christ," 34–37.

15. Jenson, *ST* I, 212–15. See also Jenson, *Story and Promise*, 118ff. We should note that neither Thomas nor the Cappadocians connected these "subsistent relations" with poles of time. For the problem of reading narrative events back into the life of God, see Milbank, "Second Difference," in *The World Made Strange*, 171–93, esp. 178–80.

16. Jenson, *ST* I, 223; *Story and Promise*, 122ff. For Jenson, "conversation" is not a metaphor for God's being: "God is ontologically specifiable as a *conversation*." See *Knowledge of Things Hoped For*, 179.

17. See Jenson, *ST* I, 138ff. That the identity of the second person of the Trinity is *eternally* the God-man leads Jenson to reject the class notion of the *logos asarkos*. Jenson suggests that what ontologically precedes the Son's birth to Mary is not an unincarnate *state* of the Son, but a "narrative pattern of *being going to be* born to Mary," a pattern of movement within the pattern of the triune God's life, 141. It is not clear to me how a pattern of movement ("being going to be born") has ontological status. But Jenson is

freely and eternally determined to work himself out in relation to others. Thus, Jenson determines that "the sole object of eternal election is Jesus with his people, the *totus Christus*."[18] For Jenson, not only the man Jesus but the *totus Christus* is definitive of the divine life. Francis Watson goes to the heart of these implications in his construal of Jenson's claims: "If God is not God without Jesus, it is for that very reason that God is not God without the church."[19] Since, according to the principle of dramatic coherence, the church receives its character from what it can expect from the future, and because the triune conversation has been opened to God's creatures who are destined to be united in Christ, the church anticipates its *theosis*, being fully incorporated into that perichoretic life.[20] *Communio* ecclesiology emphasizes that the one church is a communion of communions, where finally the local church is a communion of persons who find their *koinonia* in joint participation in God's triune *koinonia*. Central to this ecclesiology of communion is the Eucharist, where the communion between God and his people is most centrally enacted. For that reason, we must briefly consider Jenson's treatment of the church as the body of Christ.

The Church as the Body of Christ

Modern ecumenical theology has developed its discussion of the church largely around three headings taken from the New Testament: the people of God, the temple of the Holy Spirit, and the body of Christ. The latter has proven especially significant, and it is central to Jenson's own ecclesial vision, so we will briefly observe his provocative development of this theme, since it is so closely tied to his vision for visible ecclesial unity.

---

willing to endure this conceptual strain in order to follow Barth's notion of the Father's eternal election of Christ. The confusion over Jenson's rejection of the *logos asarkos* is also expressed by Pannenberg, "Eternity, Time and the Trinitarian God," 68 n. 8. See also Crisp, "Robert Jenson on the Pre-Existence of Christ."

18. Jenson, *ST* II, 175. Jenson takes the phrase *totus Christus* from patristic literature. E.g., see Augustine, *In Johannem*, 11.8; *Contra Faustum*, 1.12.

19. Watson, "'America's Theologian,'" 211. James Buckley refers to this mutual determination of God and the church in Jenson's work as the "central shock to a frequently shocking theology," "Intimacy," 13.

Again, Jenson will always assert God's freedom of choice against such criticisms, but never in such a way as to skirt the fact that God does not become himself without us. Notice this particularly compact and striking formulation: "The God of the gospel narrative freely determines himself to need us," "Male and Female He Created Them," 188.

20. Jenson, "Church as *Communio*," 2.

Jenson states that too much of twentieth-century theology has treated "people," "temple," and "body" as tropes that need to be balanced or variously emphasized. While "temple" may be used as a simile for the church, "people" is clearly not a metaphor or a simile. For Jenson, once Paul is interpreted correctly, it also becomes obvious that Paul did not intend "body of Christ" as a metaphor for the church.[21] Surely, Jenson is not the first to argue this position, but he does present it in a fairly unusual way.

The scriptural foundation for Jenson's position arises from exegetical attention to certain passages in Paul's first letter to the Corinthians. Paul says to the Corinthians, "You are the body of Christ" (12:27). For Jenson, "body of Christ" functions as a proposition rather than a trope, although it may enable similes such as that of a body and its members which Paul elsewhere draws upon:

> Precisely to enable the similes of body and members, the proposition, "the church is the body of Christ" must itself be an *ontic identification*, like the regularly paired, "You are the community of the Spirit." We are the body of Christ, according to Paul, in that we have been "baptized into" it (12:13). And what we have been baptized into is simply "Christ" (12:12). Again, we are "one body" in that we do something that can equivalently be described as "sharing in the body of Christ" and partaking "of the one bread" (10:16–17). In the complex of these passages, there is no way to construe "body" as a simile or other trope that does not make mush of Paul's arguments.[22]

The reason that this must be a proposition, according to Jenson, is because of the *bodily* resurrection of Jesus that the church confesses. Since Jesus is raised as the God-man, his humanity must persist beyond resurrection, in which case he must now exist somehow in bodily form.[23] Thus, Paul's expression leads us to the conclusion that "the church is ontologically the risen Christ's human body . . ." This body, of course, is not a biological human body. Paul was able to think in terms of a spiritual body (*sōma pneumatikon*) that succeeds the biological body (*sōma psychikon*) after the resurrection but that still serves as a real and necessary personal embodiment (15:42–44).

---

21. Jenson, *ST* II, 189–90.

22. Jenson, *ST* I, 204–5, emphasis added. See also Jenson, "Church and the Sacraments," 209–10.

23. *ST* I, 201. Appealing to Luther, Jenson states, "Were Christ's presence in the assembly disembodied, it would be his presence as God but *not* his presence as a human, for as a human he is a risen body," *ST* II, 214.

For Paul, embodiment means primarily *availability* to other persons. So the church is the availability of Christ in the world, and as such, his ontological embodiment.[24]

The reason it is important to notice Jenson's emphasis on personal embodiment is that Jenson concludes from it that the church is the *visible* gathering of God's people in the world. This runs counter to much of the history of Christian thought, influenced largely by Augustine, according to which the true church is considered an invisible entity, a view that we have noticed has a history in the free church tradition as well. Jenson curtly remarks:

> The concept of the invisible church has occasioned little but trouble through theological history, and no use will be made of it in this work. The church is not an invisible entity; she is the, if anything, all too visible gathering of sinners around the loaf and the cup. What is invisible is that this visible entity is in fact what she claims to be, the people of God.[25]

Although Jenson clearly argues for a (startling!) ontological identification of Christ with the visible church, he attempts to qualify this identification by incorporating Paul's teaching on the Eucharist. In 1 Corinthians 10:16–17, Paul refers to the eucharistic bread as the body of Christ. Jenson states that the church is the risen body of Christ "because the bread and the cup in the congregation's midst is the very same body of Christ." Returning to the notion of *availability*, Christ's risen body is whatever object serves to make Christ available to us as subjects. Therefore, since Christ promised his presence in the objects of the bread and the cup, we must be able to locate and respond to him precisely there.[26] The church assembly is the body (availability) *of* (identification) Christ to the world, and the Eucharist is the body (availability) of Christ *to* (distinction) the church.[27] Both have ontological force for Jenson.

24. *ST* II, 212–3; *ST* I, 204–5. Catholic scholar Richard Neuhaus uses the term "radical realism" to describe Jenson's articulation of Christ's embodiment in the church, "Jenson in the Public Square," 246.

25. *ST* II, 174. David Yeago provides an interesting essay on Jenson's repudiation of the notion of the "invisible church." He sets Jenson in contrast with much of his Lutheran background in which the invisible church was seen as the "true church" and the visible church as a necessary but secular institution, largely as a result of Pietism, "Church as Polity?"

26. *ST* I, 205–6. Jenson argues that the Protestant hesitation to fully affirm the presence of Christ in the substances of bread and cup is a result of its "spiritualizing conception of personhood," *Unbaptized God*, 32.

27. *ST* II, 213, 168; *ST* I, 205. Paul Molnar challenges Jenson's view that Jesus rose

That Jenson wants to advocate distinction as well as identification is plainly seen in this statement: "We may not so identify the risen Christ with the church as to be unable to refer distinctly to the one and then to the other."[28] In order to explain this complex relationship of identification and distinction, Jenson appeals to the subject-object distinction found within German idealism, a distinction he initially applies to the inner triune relations.[29] The idea, located in Hegel's *Phenomenology of the Spirit*, is that the two parties of a relationship must be both a subject and an object if there is to be a free relationship; there must be *reciprocal availability*.[30] This is why, for Jenson, a real embodiment of Christ is necessary. If Christ is only present in thought and feeling as believed by most Protestants (certainly most free churches) and many Catholics, then this disembodied personal presence can only mean bondage since there is no subject-object reciprocity.[31] Here, then, is how Jenson explains the identification and distinction: the body of Christ is the church (subject) gathered around the Eucharist (object).

It is obvious at this point that the Eucharist is central to Jenson's vision of the church's identity as the body of Christ, something free church

---

"into the church and its sacraments," which thereby constitute his resurrected body. According to Molnar, Jenson compromises the distinction between Christ and the church. It is Jesus himself who rose from the dead, and it is the God-man (not the church and the sacraments) who appeared to his disciples. Further, Molnar concludes that Jenson's view implies that Christ needs the church as the church needs Christ, "Robert W. Jenson's *Systematic Theology*," 126–27. We have already seen earlier how Jenson might attempt to blunt the latter criticism. He would likely say that Christ only "needs" the church because the Father has freely decided that the second person of the Trinity finds its complete identity as the *totus Christus*. Thus, for Jenson, it is a freely chosen "need."

28. *ST* II, 213.

29. See, e.g., *Triune Identity*, 146. For an insightful critique of Jenson's application of this idea to the inner triune life, see Burgess, *Ascension in Karl Barth*, 176–78. David Demson suggests that in spite of Jenson's attempts to distinguish Christ and his church as subject and object, his particular conception of the *totus Christus* suggests reciprocity in such a way that just as Jesus constitutes his community, the community also constitutes him, "Robert Jenson's *Systematic Theology*: Three Responses," 97. See also Schwöbel, "Once Again, Christ and Culture," 124.

30. *ST* II, 214; *ST* I, 155–56. The notion that embodiment means primarily reciprocal availability has long been important in Jenson's understanding of the body of Christ. E.g., see his *Visible Words*, 18–25. See also "Church and the Sacraments," 211.

31. *ST* II, 214. See also "Autobiographical Reflections," in *Essays in Theology of Culture*, 220. Though surprisingly he does not appeal to it at this point in his *Systematic Theology*, Jenson earlier described the Suffering Servant of Isaiah as the servant *and* the community to be served by the servant. The same sort of idea was expressed by the church fathers who spoke of the *totus Christus*, which referred to the risen Christ including and included in his community, *ST* I, 81.

traditions have not typically espoused. Based on 1 Corinthians 10:16–17, Jenson states that as the church shares in the eucharistic body of Christ, they are united in communion (*koinonia*) not only with him but with each other. There Paul states, "The bread that we break, is it not a sharing [*koinonia*] in the body of Christ? Because there is one bread, we who are many are one body for we all partake of the one bread." Therefore, in receiving the sacramental body of Christ, the church becomes the ontological body of Christ making the churchly and eucharistic communion inseparable.[32] But again, Jenson moves beyond simply saying that the Eucharist is Christ's embodiment *for* us. He posits an ontological identification between Christ's body and the church gathered around the Eucharist. He states, "Christ, as the second identity of God, is at the right hand of the Father, and just so can find his Ego in a community of earthly creatures and have that community as his body."[33] As we have seen, Jenson's theology results in Jesus' knowing himself rightly only as he encounters himself as object, his body, the church.

Like others previously mentioned, Susan Wood expresses concerns about Jenson's formulation of the relationship between Christ and the church. As a Catholic, she appreciates his attempt to make a strong connection between Christ and the church, but she believes he makes the identification too directly and relies too heavily on German idealism, according to which the church becomes Christ's objective self. She proposes that a better way to conceive of the relationship between Christ and the church is through the category of sacrament, where the church *itself* is a sacrament with the resurrected Christ as the referent. According to Wood, the category of sacrament allows for precisely the identification and distinction Jenson attempts (but perhaps fails) to achieve, because a sacrament contains a reality that is still beyond itself.[34]

---

32. Jenson, *ST* II, 211–12.

33. Ibid., 254. Boldly he states, "Where does the risen Christ turn to find himself? To the sacramental gathering of believers," "Church and the Sacraments," 211.

34. Wood, "Robert Jenson's Ecclesiology," 180–84. In another research context I have fruitfully followed Wood's suggestions and explored the thought of Henri de Lubac along these lines. By focusing on the church itself as a sacrament, de Lubac is able to develop an understanding of the body of Christ in which there is a strong and organic relationship between Christ and the church, centered around the Eucharist, and which is necessarily visible, but also mystical, preserving a proper distinction between Christ and the church. See especially these works by de Lubac: *Catholicism*; *The Splendour of the Church*; *The Church*. See also Susan Woods' helpful exposition of de Lubac's thought, *Spiritual Exegesis and the Church in the Theology of Henri de Lubac*.

Jenson apparently believes himself to be following such a line as suggested by Wood. He speaks affirmatively of ecumenical discussion growing out of the Second Vatican Council according to which the church is declared to be "a sacrament, as it were."[35] Although Jenson does repeatedly attempt to distinguish between Christ and the church,[36] it is difficult to reconcile these attempts with his other statements which, growing out of his particular narrative reading of the Trinity, seem to imply Jesus' dependence on visible embodiment, not only for his church but for his self-identification. It is not clear how the church can be the body of Christ in any way other than the way in which it receives the body of Christ, which Jenson acknowledges is a sacramental reception.

While there are some potentially problematic aspects of Jenson's Christology and eucharistic theology, his striking claims are perhaps effective at getting those from within the free church to think more about the ontological implications of the Eucharist and the church's relation to the risen Christ. We can see that Jenson's driving concern is that since *theosis* is the ultimate outcome for the church, and that since this comes about by participating in Christ, it is very important for Jenson that Christ be *really* present so that communion can *really* occur. Christ has told us where to find him (the eucharistic meal) and that by participating in this meal, Christians commune with Christ and with each other, making one body. As Jenson says it, "The communion of the church is then actual as the Eucharist; the Eucharist does not merely enable or manifest the communion we call church. It *is* that communion."[37]

The visibility of the eucharistic act cannot be underestimated in Jenson's thought. Jenson often describes sacraments in Augustinian language: they are "visible words." The gospel is spoken not only in audible but visible words, and visible words (embodiment) are important for true community to occur. Visible words are objective availability and objective address.[38] These visible words announce the gospel by making a promise. They promise,

35. "*Uti sacramentum,*" *Lumen Gentium,* 1.1. Jenson, "Church and the Sacraments," 207–8.

36. For another particularly strong example, "The church now possesses her Lord sacramentally only, that is, actually and truly but still in faith and not by 'sight.' Indeed, the eschatological separation is constituted in the sacramental relations themselves: the church, community of disciples, is now the presence of Christ *only in that* within her that same Christ is present as an other than she, and there only as a sign signified by other signs," *ST* II, 334, emphasis added.

37. Jenson, "Church and the Sacraments," 215.

38. For this general discussion, see Jenson, *Visible Words,* 3–25.

"*There* is my body in the world, and you here eating and drinking commune in it. It promises: *there* is the actual historical church and you are she. That the risen Christ is not present merely 'spiritually' is itself a vital promise of the gospel, and the one made specifically by the bread and cup."[39] It is through the eucharistic *act* that communion occurs. As Jenson says, when the action is not carried out, there is nothing for the promise to be about.[40]

Since there can properly be only one great communion as *the* body of Christ, each local and visible eucharistic gathering can only know itself as the one great communion by its openness to other communions (at whatever level), an openness that expresses itself in eucharistic fellowship, mutual reception at the eucharistic table. Since the Eucharist is the central act by which the church is communion, then Jenson can say, "If an assembly of persons claims to be church, and if that assembly recognizes another assembly as church, and yet these two assemblies cannot celebrate together, both claims are—at the very least—in extreme jeopardy."[41] So for Jenson, visible unity, expressed chiefly in demonstrable and mutual eucharistic reception, is an imperative because the eschatologically achieved communion with the triune life (which is the church's ultimate end) is truly participated in now through participation in the visible words of the promise that the Eucharist announces. If unity occurs centrally in the Eucharist in the way that Jenson has outlined, then recourse to the notion of invisible unity is simply not an option. One need not adopt every aspect of Jenson's theology to appreciate the cogency of his understanding of visible unity facilitated primarily through eucharistic communion. Free churches have not historically been known for eucharistic theology that makes strong claims concerning ontological participation with Christ and his church. At the very least, Jenson's thought-provoking exegesis of the relevant passages in 1 Corinthians, together with his commitment to *theosis* as the proper end of humanity, challenge free churches to revisit their own views on such matters.

Authority within the Body of Christ

With Jenson's theological rationale for visible ecclesial unity in view, we may now proceed to observe how he accounts for the authorities by which the integrity of this unity should be maintained. How one conceives of these

39. Jenson, *ST* II, 220.
40. Ibid., 216.
41. Jenson, "Church and the Sacraments," 218.

authorities depends, at least in part, upon what one perceives to be the central task of the church. Jenson's consistent answer is that the church's mission is to maintain and see to the speaking of the gospel (to the world as proclamation and to God as appeal and adoration), where the gospel is specifically, "The God of Israel has raised his servant Jesus from the dead," and where this resurrection is understood as establishing Jesus as Lord of all.[42] The church is the gathering that occurs around the telling of the gospel, whether using audible or visible words (sacraments). As such it is a *visible* entity, not an "invisible fellowship of kindred spirits."[43]

Since speaking the gospel is the church's *raison d'être*, the unity with which the church must be concerned is above all unity tied directly to the mission of speaking this gospel which constitutes the church's identity. Therefore, it is crucial that the church be able to distinguish between what is and what is not the gospel. The gospel is news; more specifically, it is apostolic news with discernible content. One of the most pressing questions faced in the years after the death of the apostles was how the church and her mission would be preserved without the apostles. The beginnings of this struggle are already evident in the Pastoral Epistles, and the struggle eventually produced the mutually interdependent trio of scriptural canon, creed, and office as "an interim surrogate for living apostles."[44] Apostolic continuity is crucially important when the gospel is understood fundamentally as an announcement founded in and inseparable from specific historical content "back there,"[45] as opposed to accounts of the gospel that might pursue some "meaning" (e.g., existential or moral) behind historical events precisely by abstracting from them. Jenson uncovers the implications of such a historically rooted understanding of the gospel for the church's self-understanding:

> When the church accepted that her Lord had deposited her in history, that the time between Resurrection and fulfillment would not be a historical instant but had occupied and therefore might yet occupy a succession of generations, she might have confessed her hope refuted. . . . If she was nevertheless to carry on, her self-identity as the church of the apostles would now be an identity

42. E.g., see Jenson, *ST* I, 4, 11, 23.

43. Jenson, *Story and Promise*, 2.

44. Jenson, *ST* I, 23. Jaroslav Pelikan provides a helpful overview of the process by which the authority of canon, creed, and office outlined by Irenaeus emerged among "orthodox" Christians. This development occurred partly (but only partly) in response to early doctrinal challenges such as those posed by Marcion, various Gnostic groups and Montanism, *Christian Tradition*, 1:107–20.

45. On the gospel as historical specificity, see Jenson, *Story and Promise*, 4–6.

mediated through an acknowledged interval of past time, and she would have to live it in the way of such historical self-identity, that is, in the continuity of a recognized *tradition*. And she would have to make arrangements for carrying the self-identity so constituted into a future of her own for *perpetuating* the apostolic tradition; that is, she would have deliberate *institutions* that would be constitutive of her life.[46]

It is the fact that the church must be the church of the apostles that drives the church to understand her identity as being historically mediated and requiring instruments aimed at historical continuity with the apostles.

There are two pitfalls to avoid at this point, according to Jenson. On the one hand, Catholic theology is tempted to take as unproblematic the development of these institutions of historical continuity. On the other hand, Protestant theology tends to take these same developments as illegitimate. Most within the free church tradition surely fall within the latter group. According to Jenson, both paths are equally erroneous. Contra the Catholic perspective represented here, there *are* problems with the "early catholic" developments, especially when compared with the apostolic period. Contra the Protestant position, Protestants who appeal to the normativity of the first generation in such a way that illegitimatizes subsequent "early catholic" developments, deny by this very move the authenticity of the gospel as it was proclaimed in subsequent generations "and so deny, among other things, that they are in a position to make any such critique."[47]

The purpose of the church's tradition is not merely to sustain the existence of the community. Rather, the church's tradition seeks to preserve the community around specific content. But the process of tradition is notoriously a threat to such content. It is because of this realization about the threatening nature of tradition that Jenson makes one of his most important and undergirding observations. It is worth quoting at length:

> No structures of historical continuity merely as such can assure the integrity of witness to reality that is other than the transmitting group, at least if that witness is such as to require hermeneutical reflection. Thus neither Scripture nor creed nor liturgy nor teaching office, nor yet their ensemble, can as historical structures guarantee the fidelity of our proclamation and prayer to the apostolic witness. Affirmation that the church is still the church pledges the certainty of a historical continuity that no structures of

46. Jenson, *ST* I, 23–24.
47. Ibid., 24.

historical continuity can make certain. This affirmation therefore reaches beyond its immediate object to be faith that *God* uses the church's communal structures to preserve the gospel's temporal self-identity and so also the temporal self-identity of the gospel's community. . . . Faith that the church is still the church is faith in the Spirit's presence and rule in and by the structures of the church's historical continuity.[48]

We see here that certainty is not Jenson's aim. He does not attempt to construct a foundationalist apologetic for these instruments and structures, including Scripture. Rather, he forthrightly admits that these instruments cannot guarantee anything. We can only affirm their reliability *by faith*, and it is primarily faith in their *usefulness*, that is, that God has used and still may use them to preserve the integrity of the church's witness to the gospel. And we can only affirm their reliability because of an antecedent belief that the church is still the church. Those within the free church tradition may find in Jenson a friend to help them think about the normative function of Scripture as foundationalist arguments continue to erode. Further, his chastened claims for what tradition and a teaching office actually provide may help free church theologians hear him with less initial defensiveness.

The structural norms (i.e., authorities) that Jenson names within the church's tradition are: 1) the canon of Scripture (Old and New Testaments); 2) the continuity of instituted liturgical action; 3) the dogmatic tradition; and 4) succession in ministerial office.[49] We will follow Jenson's lead here in separating these areas only for purposes of analysis, but because the tradition is one reality, it is impossible to keep them separate. As we address one, we will by necessity be touching on the others. The distinctions, however, will allow us to bring each into specific focus. Instead of four norms of tradition, we will operate with three, lumping together the liturgical and dogmatic tradition (as well as other instantiations of the tradition such as theological treatises, catechetical material, etc.) under the more general heading of "tradition."[50] We will consider these three in the following order: Scripture, tradition, and the teaching office of the church.

48. Ibid., 25.

49. Ibid., 26.

50. This is in harmony with Jenson's own recognition of the ancient trio of Scripture, tradition, and ecclesial teaching office, *ST* I, 23. For a clear ancient reference to this trio, see Irenaeus, *Against Heresies*, 3.3.

The Authority of Scripture

The decision to begin with Scripture follows Jenson's own rationale. It does not indicate a foundational order of authorities, since tradition (oral and otherwise) and teaching office facilitated the collection of these writings. Rather, it follows the ecumenical consensus that, although prior authorities facilitated the formation of Scripture, once Scripture arises, it has a privileged position of authority. In Reformation terminology, Scripture is the *norma normans non normata*, even though it may need other authorities for its proper functioning.[51]

The Nature of Scriptural Authority

Contrary to many conservative Protestant (including free church) accounts of Scripture, Jenson does not seek to establish the authority of Scripture on some prior doctrine of inspiration. *That* the Bible is authoritative for the church is not something one must argue. It is an observable fact in the church's life. What one must argue is that this authoritative status is necessary if the existence of the church is willed by God.[52]

The most elemental doctrine of Scripture is not proposition *about* Scripture. It is simply that it should be read, and that it should be read in the church (the only place it *could* be read). In fact, the churches that are in

51. Jenson, *ST* I, 26. Elsewhere, Jenson relates this to an argument he advances with regard to the offices of ministry; namely, that because of the reality of the Spirit, something can appear historically in the church that can yet belong to the *foundation* of the church, "Response to Watson and Hunsinger," 226–27.

52. Jenson, "Second Thought about Inspiration," 393. Jenson states here that in his career, he has intentionally not relied on the phrase "Scripture is inspired," since it has often been used as an attempt to establish Scripture's authority, even for those outside the church. Jenson does not use a doctrine of inspiration for establishing Scripture's authority either for those inside the church (since it is already an observable fact) or for those outside the church (since Scripture has no authority or even any existence there). Outside the church, Scripture as a unified canon falls apart into a disparate collection of ancient documents elucidating ancient Near Eastern and Mediterranean religion. Its unity (and thus its existence *as Scripture*) arises from churchly convictions outsiders do not hold. In this article, a late article in Jenson's career, he returns to reclaim the doctrine of inspiration, not to ground the authority of Scripture but to ground a specifically Christian reading of the Old Testament. In other words, it seems that, for Jenson, a useful doctrine of inspiration does not so much say *whether* or *why* one should read this book; rather, it instructs those with a prior faith commitment concerning *how* to read this book (especially the Old Testament). We will return to this below. For an even more recent and similar statement, see Jenson, "On the Authorities of Scripture."

actuality most faithful to Scripture are those that regularly and thoughtfully read and listen to Scripture, not those that enumerate propositions attempting to secure Scripture's position of authority. Jenson states the most basic teaching concerning Scripture thus: "*Privilege* this book within the church's living discourse." Scripture's fundamental authority is that its living voice is present in the church to shape all aspects of the contemporary lives of believers.[53]

The question then becomes *why* Scripture should have a privileged voice. For Jenson, the answer is tautologous. The gospel is a narrative and the Bible is the rehearsal of that narrative to which all other Christian rehearsals appeal.[54] Since the church's task is to speak the gospel as narrative, this book then becomes normative for the church's own speaking. It is the norm of proclamation. Speaking the gospel can go wrong since it is a historical activity, so we must have ways of determining whether what we are saying is *the* gospel. We look, then, to others who have spoken the gospel. Of course, any of these may be themselves questioned, only until we come to the apostles, for "if they did not speak the gospel, no one did." It is impossible to get behind the apostles since they only spoke and did not hear the gospel, so they are the final appeal.[55]

Beyond privileging Scripture because it is the foundational telling of the gospel that we are to be speaking, the church should privilege this book because the reading of the Bible is living speech, since what the gospel does is make promises, which can never be a static word of the past. As living speech, it is primarily the Word of God (i.e., the living Christ) who addresses its hearers in promise. There is a sacramental relation between Christ's living address and the public reading of Scripture. Yet this living voice of Scripture is not immediately that *of* a living person. It comes to the present listener with all the weight of historical conditioning involved in language, writing, editing, transmitting, etc. How can such a collection of historically conditioned documents be the living voice of Christ? Because the Spirit freely makes it so.[56] For Jenson, then, Scripture's privileged voice in the church is

53. Jenson, *ST* II, 273.

54. Ibid., 274.

55. Jenson, "On the Problem(s) of Scriptural Authority," 238.

56. Jenson, *ST* II, 275–76. Jenson develops this account of Scripture as the sacramental living Word of Christ in partial contrast to earlier Protestant accounts of inspiration which made inspiration a predicate of the processes by which these writings came to be written down. Inspiration of the writing of *these words* was supposed to guarantee the truth contained in the documents. The problem is that such an account made unnecessary, even impossible, a sacramental relation between God's Word and the actual

rooted in a pneumatology according to which the Spirit who is present to the church liberates these historically conditioned texts to be the living Word of God (i.e., the risen Christ) in the actual practice of their reading.[57]

When Scripture functions in liturgical usage, its authority is immediate because it is (sacramentally) the authority of God's own presence to create and nurture faith through the word. Jenson distinguishes between the authority of the living Word of God (Scripture's liturgical authority) and its authority as a norm in the church's theological enterprise of reflecting upon and learning to speak the gospel. This recognition allows Jenson to address the age-old chicken and egg dilemma concerning Scripture's relationship to the church. In its liturgical function, Scripture, as the living Word of God, is prior to the church. In its canonical and theological mode, it is subsequent to the church.[58] Those from the free church tradition should be able to appreciate Jenson's strong emphasis on the importance of reading Scripture in worship gatherings. In fact, Jenson's account of the sacramental presence of Christ's living voice through Scripture takes the local gathering even more seriously than do many free churches, since many in the free church tradition would tend to locate the authority of Scripture in some account of its inspired words rather than in Christ's presence through the reading of the words in the Spirit-inspired community. Jenson provides a way for free churches to continue to embrace the priority of Scripture to the

---

reading of these texts. So instead of appealing to a theory of inspiration to authenticate these words independent from all subsequent history, Jenson appeals to the active Spirit of God in the church who freely works within the reflection, writing, collection, editing, transmission, and contemporary reading of these texts to make them, in the midst of all historical conditioning, the living Word of God to the Church.

57. Given this exposition, it is perplexing to read Francis Watson's criticism that Jenson lacks an account of Scripture as the living "word of God" and advocates instead the sheer factual presence of this list of books and the demand that it be read, "'America's Theologian.'" Jenson shares this perplexity in his response and clarifies that he wholeheartedly agrees with Watson's proposition that "texts do not merely report the divine speaking, they enact it," and that enacting is a central notion in his theology, "Response to Watson and Hunsinger," 226.

58. Jenson, *ST* I, 28–29. Jenson notices this distinction among certain Lutheran scholastics, especially Johannes Musaus, *Introductio in theologiam* (1679), ii.iii. He argues, however, that this healthy distinction was dropped by later theologians to provide resistance to the Catholic argument that the church was the authority behind the canon. The distinction maintained by those such as Musaus collapsed into a third and complex sense in which Scripture was simultaneously seen as word of God and written record and taken as such for theological purposes. Jenson argues that under the pressure of the Enlightenment, this conflation became the only sense in which Scripture was understood, and modern biblicism was the result.

church while dealing truthfully with the ways in which the church is prior to Scripture. Free churches have not yet given enough attention to this latter issue, and Jenson's nuanced assessment of the different modes of Scripture is helpful toward that end.

The real problem is *how* Scripture functions authoritatively for the church, not whether it does. When it comes to the problem of describing how Scripture functions authoritatively in the church, Jenson argues that there is not one problem but several, some more significant than others, since some are either blunders or pseudoproblems from the beginning. One such pseudoproblem is that in attempting to articulate *the* authority of Scripture, we suppose that this authority is one particular relation between what Scripture says and what we now say. Rather, there are a variety ways in which Scripture "*in fact,* and in the *complexity* of all fact" functions authoritatively, even when people despair of now being able to locate *the* authority of Scripture.[59]

When we seek to discover how Scripture in fact functions authoritatively, we must look to operations. Jenson locates three specific authoritative operations of Scripture which correspond to the three parts of the statement: Jesus is risen. That Jenson would begin with this statement is not surprising since the mission of the church is to speak the gospel, the speaking of which is a particular kind of event. The gospel is "any act of human communication in which two specific givens meet and interpret each other." The first is the claim that Jesus is risen. The second is the always changing structures of hopes and fears of those who come to articulate this claim. The second pole here is a matter of hermeneutics, to which we will attend shortly. Regarding the first pole, Jenson argues that we can see the actual authoritative functions of Scripture by mapping them onto the three parts of the claim: Jesus is risen.[60]

The name *Jesus* functions grammatically in this statement to identify the one who has risen. But when a name alone does not sufficiently identify a person, we are in need of identifying descriptors in the form of "the one who . . . and who . . ." until the listener can say, "Oh, that one." The Bible provides just such an ensemble of identifying descriptions. As Jenson states, "A Gospel is simply a long 'The one who. . . , and who. . . ,' with an abruptly

59. Jenson, "On the Problem(s) of Scriptural Authority," 240. For the same general discussion that follows here concerning the variety of Scripture's authoritative modes, see also Jenson, *ST* I, 29–33.

60. Jenson, "On the Problem(s) of Scriptural Authority," 240–41. For a brief account of these three functions of Scripture, see Jenson, "On the Renewing of the Mind," in *Essays of Theology in Culture,* 168–70.

stated 'is risen' at the end." But beyond the Gospels themselves, there is the tradition of Israel mediated through her Scriptures which further enables the identification of Jesus. The first authoritative function of Scripture, then, is to identify *who* is risen, which occurs in the church as *scholarship*. Identifying Jesus can only occur through the study of texts, and this pressure has always been felt by the church whatever theories about Scripture have come and gone or whatever changes have occurred in scholarship through modern historical sensitivities. From the writers of the Gospels forward, these texts have provided the only material by which the church has sought to ascertain the identity of Jesus; thus, they simply are authority.[61] This is true, of course, only if the church believes its primary task is to proclaim "Jesus is risen." Where a church loses sight of this central missional conviction and makes any other agenda its central motivation disconnected or only marginally connected to the proclamation "Jesus is risen" (whether social justice, or meaningful worship experience, or any other of a number of properly derivative candidates vying for supremacy which seek to distract the church from her central identity), Scripture simply will not function authoritatively in this way of identifying Jesus.

With the word *risen*, we can ascertain a second authoritative function of Scripture. Jenson observes that such loaded terms only work within a specific semantic and syntactic structure. For example, at Mars Hill when Paul spoke of Jesus' resurrection, his listeners thought he was introducing a new deity. In the statement "Jesus is risen," the term *risen* takes on its specific meaning only within Israel's language tradition. Therefore, the church's missionary proclamation of the gospel cannot merely be a simple saying of the proposition "Jesus is risen." It must also be an immersion into the language tradition that gave rise to such a proclamation. Thus, a second authoritative function of Scripture is "to maintain the liveliness and authenticity of the language in which 'Jesus is risen' can be said, to continually reestablish the church as a community whose common bond is the language-tradition of Israel." This second function of biblical authority occurs in a *liturgical* mode. It occurs in that Scripture is carefully read and listened to, that its images and stories come to fund our own expressions of prayer and adoration. Scripture functions authoritatively in this way because "we read and hear Scripture in order to learn to talk rightly."[62]

In a slightly more ambiguous way, Jenson relates a third authoritative function of Scripture to the "is" portion of "Jesus is risen." Whereas the first

61. Jenson, "On the Problem(s) of Scriptural Authority," 241–42.
62. Ibid., 242.

was related to scholarship and the second to liturgy, this third function is the domain of *theology* proper. As Jenson repeatedly states, theology is "thinking about what to say to be saying the gospel." In conversation with the always shifting hopes and fears of history, theologians ask questions such as, "What is to be said because it is *Jesus* who is risen?" or "What is to be said because he is *risen*?" Scripture functions authoritatively in two key ways for the task of theology. First, since the gospel is whatever the apostles said, their thinking is *de facto* acceptable. Jenson states that "samples of apostolic theologizing are guaranteed samples of authentic theologizing, though not necessarily the best theologizing."[63] Their authority is an authority of paradigms. We are not to merely repeat what they said. This would not be the gospel, since the gospel is a lively exchange between the proclamation of Jesus and any particular set of hopes and fears. Rather, the apostolic scriptural authority with respect to theology is methodological. We learn how to do what they did by watching how they did it, and then we "gradually mix in." There are many others to watch throughout Christian history, but the apostles "are those who, although they may not be the smartest or most powerful, are for certain actually doing what we want to do."[64] For example, the fundamental way in which the apostles went about their gospel-speaking was in their reading and exegesis of Israel's Scripture in light of what happened with Jesus. So in our attempt to speak the gospel that the apostles spoke, we must submit ourselves to the same texts they did. Apostolic use establishes the authority of the Old Testament for the church.[65] Jenson's account of New Testament

63. Ibid., 243. Jenson mentions the epistles as the most notable examples of apostolic theologizing, but also includes redaction criticism of the Gospels as instances of authoritative theologizing.

64. Ibid., 243. For Jenson, that the Bible's authority with regard to theology is methodological relieves the potential embarrassment about the theological pluralism discovered in the New Testament through modern biblical studies (see, for example, the classic article by Helmut Köster, in which he highlights the theological variety among canonical and noncanonical documents to challenge the idea of an early defined orthodoxy, "GNOMAI DIAPHOROI"). Against this kind of argument, Jenson's focus on theological methodology argues that the New Testament initiates us into the activity of interpreting human concern in light of the resurrection of Jesus rather than into the activity of reproducing the material theology of the New Testament, as if there were just one.

65. Jenson, "On the Problem(s) of Scriptural Authority," 239. Jenson claims that the primary documentary control of our attempt to say what the apostles said is that we pursue the same interpretive act they performed, and apart from which they could not have preached the gospel. That is, we, like they, must "interpret what happened with Jesus by Israel's Bible and Israel's Bible by what happened with Jesus." He argues that we should not even speak in terms of the apostles "appropriating" or "adopting" Israel's canonical Scriptures since the origin of the church depended on these Scriptures. The church has

texts as authoritative in a methodological sense is not likely one that would be familiar to many within the free church tradition, but when one accepts his understanding of what it means to speak the gospel, his account is persuasive. Further, his account opens the door for the importance of tradition and a teaching office, a point to which we shall return later in the chapter.

The second way that Scripture functions authoritatively in its theological operation is that, for the reason given above (i.e., Scripture is the foundational point of reference for speaking the gospel narrative), all theological propositions must be tested against Scripture. This testing does *not* occur merely by asking, "Is this what Scripture says?" which in most cases would be answered "yes and no." Rather, the test of any theologoumenon (or theological system) occurs at the first-level discourse of the church's life. Does it, as a hermeneutical principle, result in successful exegesis with respect to the church's liturgical uses of Scripture?[66] In constantly running up against the texts of Scripture, a theology is tested by whether it helps the theologian "deal with actual texts without pressing them." As Jenson says, "'Theology' that leaves daily exegesis unaffected is no theology; it is ideology. Theology that regularly fights texts is in process of refutation."[67]

Again, Jenson wants to speak of Scripture's authority as an ensemble of the different ways in which Scripture *in fact* functions in the life of the church, which together are its authority. This is yet another reason he is typically dismissive of theories of inspiration, inerrancy, etc. According to him, all such theories are in search of *the* authority of Scripture. Since there is no such thing, these attempts are wrongheaded. In general, whether or not we adopt any of these theories of inspiration, we would keep reading Scripture in the ways outlined above. We do not need theories about Scripture (whether "high" or "low"); rather, we need to be attentive to what Scripture actually does in the church, its operations.[68] Free churches have tended to locate the authority of Scripture in the text itself or its character as a divine product and have not tended to think about the authority of Scripture in terms of its actual operations within the church's life.

---

just as much claim to these Scriptures as does modern Judaism, since both appeared simultaneously within Israel's history, *ST* I, 30, including n. 23.

66. Jenson, *ST* I, 33. To illustrate, Jenson imagines that in preparing a sermon from a text in Galatians, one could say, "The Spirit 'proceeds from the Father through the Son,'" and then conclude, "*That* is why Paul could say to the Galatians that no experience could verify a variant gospel." With regard to theological systems, they are tested by their success as a hermeneutical principle for Scripture taken as a whole.

67. Jenson, "On the Problem(s) of Scriptural Authority," 244.

68. Ibid., 245.

Hermeneutics

As we noticed earlier, for Jenson, the gospel is the mutual interpretation of the proclamation "Jesus is risen" and the antecedent hopes and fears that this proclamation confronts at any given time and place. The pressing question then becomes how to go about interpreting the gospel as it is attested in Scripture so as to address contemporary and historically specific hopes and fears.

Once again, Jenson insists on a churchly reading of Scripture. That is, the primary hermeneutical principle for the church's reading of Scripture is the church's own life reflected in its liturgy, devotion, catechesis, and homiletics (where all of these are properly directed to speaking and enacting the gospel). Jenson makes this point against the interpretation of Scripture being primarily located among academic specialists with no commitment to the gospel, but the point is equally valid against free church interpretation strategies that are not necessarily rooted in the church's communal worship and that easily become individualistic in orientation. The Bible only exists *as canon* for those with a shared commitment to speaking the gospel (i.e., the church). Where a shared commitment to the gospel is absent, the Bible disintegrates into discrete parts, and it is no longer "the Bible" that they are interpreting. Jenson derides the "drastically misnamed Society for Biblical Literature" for treating biblical texts as essentially no different from other ancient religious texts, texts that were "luckily preserved for scholarly ex-Christians from which to make a living."[69]

Of course, there are points in the church's life where its liturgy, devotion, and catechesis are not the direct hermeneutical principle. In these areas the church *thinks* about how to understand Scripture, how to struggle to say what the Bible says. Jenson takes Irenaeus as his guide at this point, largely because Irenaeus's situation was comparable to our own in that he was combating the pretentious and scholarly interpretation of his gnostic opponents, which he found at odds with the church's purposes. The two major errors of this gnostic exegesis were: a) regarding Scripture as a collection of discrete sayings, stories, laws, etc., which can be mined for whatever over-riding purpose for which they wanted to use them; b) the notion that the theological meaning of a text is something above or behind what it actually says. In response, Irenaeus provided a short list of hermeneutical rules for a necessarily churchly reading of Scripture, which Jenson displays and fully endorses. Briefly stated they are:

69. Jenson, "Hermeneutics and the Life of the Church," 90.

1. Scripture is a whole.

2. Scripture *is* a whole because and only because it is one long *narrative*.

3. To be able to *follow* the single story and grasp Scripture whole, we need to know the story's general plot and *dramatis personae*.

4. It is the *church* that knows the plot and *dramatis personae* of the scriptural narrative, since the church is one continuous community with the story's actors and narrators, as with its tradents, authors, and assemblers.

5. The church's antecedent knowledge of Scripture's plot and *dramatis personae*, without which she could not read the Bible as a whole, is contained in what Irenaeus calls the "rule of faith."[70]

With the first two rules, we are brought back around to something we have already registered as being central to Jenson's theology; namely, that Scripture presents us with a narrative. He states that it is axiomatic in much of twentieth-century theology that "narrative is Scripture's encompassing genre."[71] And as we observed earlier, the narrative of Scripture serves primarily to identify its particular God and the relation of all else to him in a dramatic and coherent fashion. The Bible tells the true story of the world. As such, it must not be fitted into some larger story; it tells *the* true story in which all other true stories find their place. Scripture is read authoritatively by the church when it is read in such a way as to let the entire narrative of Scripture shape its own life.[72] How the church is to read the Bible as a whole relates to the last three of Irenaeus's five rules mentioned above, and treatment of that matter must wait until we attend to the authority of tradition.

70. Ibid., 95–98. These same rules, along with others, can be found in one form or another among the "Nine Theses on the Interpretation of Scripture" compiled and agreed upon by the Scripture Project of which Robert Jenson was a part. The collected essays of this project appear in *The Art of Reading Scripture*.

71. Jenson, *ST* I, 57. He is following Hans Frei's widely influential terminology in *The Eclipse of Biblical Narrative*.

72. Jenson, "Scripture's Authority in the Church," 32–34. In a wonderfully insightful essay, Jenson challenges the church to deepen its engagement with and liturgical performance of the grand narrative of Scripture in the face of a postmodern world that is increasingly relinquishing the supposition that life ought to make some sort of dramatic sense, "How the World Lost Its Story."

Historical-Critical Exegesis

To focus on Scripture as a whole raises some questions concerning historical-critical exegesis, which has exercised a functional methodological hegemony with regard to biblical interpretation in the modern world, especially since historical-critical methods as they have been employed have tended to act corrosively precisely on the unity of Scripture. Jenson claims that a churchly reading of Scripture is not one that follows some particular methodology. Rather, it is an interpretive process that occurs in the activities specific to the church, and there is no way to say in advance how Scripture will function in these activities in the course of historical changes.[73] According to Hans Frei, with whom Jenson is largely in agreement regarding scriptural hermeneutics, "It is doubtful that any scheme for reading texts, and narrative texts in particular, and biblical narrative texts even more specifically, can serve globally or foundationally."[74] Yet, the historical-critical method is still taught as the "one fully legitimate way to read the Bible" in most schools of theology, in spite of the more recent acknowledgments of its deleterious effects on the church.[75]

Earlier, we noticed that Jenson rejects the idea that the problem of scriptural authority is singular. Rather there are several problems, and some are only apparent problems. At this point, there is a real theological problem. Modern historical consciousness seriously challenges the idea that ancient texts can make any kind of meaningful or authoritative claim upon us. The modern historical consciousness that underlies historical-critical reading maintains a critical awareness of *historical difference* and seeks to keep this historical distance open. In fact, what is eventually troubling to the theological enterprise are not historical-critical techniques but this foundational policy calculated to maintain awareness of historical distance.[76]

The problem deepens. If Scripture is to function authoritatively, we must guard this distance so as to protect its independence from us. If Scripture is to be authoritative, we must assume that it might have something to say other than what we thought it said or expected it to say. These texts are ancient texts, emerging out of ancient language traditions and symbols. If

73. Jenson, *ST* II, 277.

74. Frei, "'Literal Reading' of Biblical Narrative in the Christian Tradition," 70.

75. Jenson, *ST* II, 277. The seminaries in my own tradition, similar to most Baptist and other free church seminaries, teach biblical studies primarily from a historical-critical perspective, increasingly making use of other more recent critical methodologies such as literary criticism, rhetorical criticism, sociological criticism, etc.

76. Jenson, "Hermeneutics and the Life of the Church," 103.

they are going to be free to address us, we must preserve this distance, which means Scripture can be an authority for us now only if we intentionally read it historically-critically.[77]

Once the historical distance is necessarily recognized as genuine difference, the "hermeneutical gap" seems to widen continually. The first object of historical critique was the Bible with the intended consequence of silencing the Bible to allow other voices to be heard. Other critics then attempted to salvage the faith by silencing the apostles so that the historical Jesus could be heard, a process that once in motion must silence Jesus as well. Once Jesus' teachings are interpreted in their own contexts, it is increasingly difficult to see what any of it has to say to contemporary readers. And now we arrive at the crux of the problem. "If Scripture—or any body of tradition—is to be authoritative," says Jenson, "we must read it historically-critically. If we do, methodically rather than by undeliberated necessity, it falls existentially silent. There is the problem."[78] Preachers and teachers become crushed under the strain of the historical difference and cannot seem to address contemporary listeners with these texts with any degree of conviction or confidence. The result for many conservative preachers, including many in the free church tradition, who want to affirm the authority of Scripture is that they end up turning a blind eye to its historical differences, or they increasingly rely on moralizing or spiritualizing reading strategies that allow them to "apply" these ancient texts that have fallen silent through historical-critical reading practices.

Beyond (But Not without) Historical-Critical Exegesis

The deleterious effects of historical-critical readings of Scripture upon the life of the church in many instances have led some contemporary theologians to react against historical-critical methodologies to one degree or another.[79] Jenson's solution to this genuine problem is *not* to abandon

77. According to Jenson, guarding this historical distance was not a requirement for pre-Enlightenment scholars since they operated with a metaphysics of timelessness. In this view, the stretch of time between what was ancient and what was contemporary was seen as continuity. This changed in the eighteenth century with the advent of the intellectual policy of "critique of appearances" which caused the stretch of time to be experienced as separation (e.g., "I know that's what Caesar's text *says* happened in Belgium; but did it *really*?"), "On the Problem(s) of Scriptural Authority," 245; *ST* II, 277–78.

78. Jenson, "On the Problem(s) of Scriptural Authority," 246.

79. E.g., see the well-known article by Steinmetz, "The Superiority of Pre-Critical Exegesis."

historical-critical reading, since if we are to read Scripture authoritatively, we must read it in this way. We cannot return to a precritical age. Rather, he rejects historical-critical exegesis as the *sole* methodological reading strategy as it is usually practiced in the academy.[80] Further, he has an interesting way of addressing the problem of the widening hermeneutical gap that results from historical-critical reading, and his solution is rooted in his ecclesiology, particularly his understanding of the church as an ongoing process of traditioning.

Jenson argues that the main reason that the historical-critical reading of Scripture has created such a problem for the church and for faith is because of a simple but profound mistake concerning the nature of the historical difference in view. In the modern world, we have too often supposed that the historical distance that is opened up is that between the world of Scripture and our own, between the communities of Israel and the early church, on the one hand, and our own community, on the other. Jenson emphatically rejects this supposition. Whatever hermeneutical gaps we must deal with in reading Scripture, it must be clear that "there is *no* historical distance between the community in which the Bible appeared and the church that now seeks to understand the Bible, because these are the same community."[81]

The error of most modern biblical interpretation is the assumption that the church for which the biblical writers wrote is historically distant from the church that reads what they wrote. It is an assumption that "there is no one diachronically identical universal church: nearly all modern biblical exegesis in fact presumes a sectarian ecclesiology."[82] Jenson states, "But when the church reads Scripture in course of her own worship and catechetics and preaching, her interpreters cannot give up so easily, because they are themselves at stake." It is in the struggle to keep saying what Scripture says, believing that it does say *something* to contemporary readers, that those within the church recognize and maintain its authority, especially those who are ministers and scholars.[83] Thus, it is Jenson's ecclesiology, with its emphasis on the diachronically unified body of Christ, which initially allows him to challenge this defect in the usual practice of historical-critical read-

---

80. His rejection is increasingly shared by some within the free church tradition. We will notice in the fifth chapter, for instance, that James McClendon similarly rejects the hegemony of historical-critical exegesis, though he does not provide as much as Jenson regarding its importance for contemporary reading.

81. Jenson, *ST* II, 279; "Hermeneutics and the Life of the Church," 103–4.

82. Jenson, *ST* II, 279.

83. Ibid., 280.

ing. The church from which and for which Paul wrote is the same church that reads and interprets his writings in any subsequent age. The notion of a diachronically unified body of Christ has not figured prominently in most free church theology. Free churches have often tried to make immediate connection with Scripture, which increased engagement with historical-critical reading strategies have made difficult.

We have just seen that Jenson's denial of a radical chasm between present readers and ancient text stems first and foremost from a theological argument rooted in his ecclesiology. He provides further support, however, through recourse to Gadamer's thought, what he calls "the most percipient of twentieth-century hermeneutical theory." In fact, he says Gadamer's explication of hermeneutics must hold true in the church if nowhere else. He summarizes it in this way: "Our present effort to understand a handed-down text cannot be hopeless, since it is merely the further appropriation of a continuing communal tradition within which we antecedently live." Past and present cannot be irredeemably bifurcated since the past is already mediated to the present through the continuity of the community's language.[84]

Thus, Jenson advocates the necessity of keeping open historical distance (something especially conservative free church theologians need to hear), but not between *the* ancient community and our own. Rather, historical-critical reading properly helps us maintain the differences between the various voices of Scripture and between any of those voices and ourselves. In his view, it is important to see the historical distances within Scripture itself—between Moses and later prophets, between Jesus and Paul, between Paul and ourselves—but never between the biblical story as a whole and our own, or between "the biblical community" and the contemporary church. The differences within Scripture itself form the "historical *compass*" of the one community from Israel to the present church, the one community to whom this book belongs and by whom it is to be interpreted.[85]

There *are* differences in theological perspective among the various biblical voices. Historical-critical reading rightly helps us highlight those differences clearly. But this is only an initial step. It helps us see the individual

84. Ibid.

85. Jenson, "Hermeneutics and the Life of the Church," 104; *ST* II, 281. In the article just referenced, Jenson concludes a discussion on the problem of hermeneutics (including historical-critical exegesis) with the following statement: "Readers will have noticed that at nearly every step, the positions I advocated demand reckoning with the *church*. That is no accident. In my judgment, reclaiming the Bible for the church is in very large part accomplished by remembering that there *is* the church for which to claim the Bible," "Hermeneutics and the Life of the Church," 105.

moments within a larger story. Thus, churchly interpretation must proceed to locate these individual instances coherently within the larger story of God and his people. Jenson relates this latter move to what the church has traditionally called "spiritual exegesis." In explicating the character of spiritual exegesis, Jenson generally follows the work of Henri de Lubac, the mid-twentieth-century Catholic theologian, who is largely responsible for recovering spiritual exegesis from its ghetto, a position it had acquired both through irresponsible practice and by confused polemic against "allegory."[86]

Spiritual exegesis was primarily Christian exegesis of the Old Testament, working from the conviction that the events of the Old Testament find their fulfillment in the events of the New Testament. In this view, events of the Old Testament can be read as "figures"[87] of later events. This reading practice is not to be confused with "spiritualizing" Old Testament texts, which has sometimes occurred within free churches in their attempts to recognize the authority of the Old Testament. Rather, spiritual exegesis relies on the "literal" meaning of these texts and then places them in an overarching eschatological plot. The process is (or should be) controlled by the New Testament accounts of Christ (and his anticipated kingdom, and the moral life resulting from participation in Christ).[88] It is an attempt to read Christ at the center of all history, which of course depicts history as having a discernible unity, a unity that should be discernible in the church's tradition.[89]

---

86. Jenson, *ST* II, 282. For de Lubac's monumental work on this subject, see *Medieval Exegesis*.

87. Jenson's terminology is similar to John David Dawson's distinction between "figural" and "figurative." See Dawson, "Figural Reading," esp. 188. Cf. Frei, *Eclipse of Biblical Narrative*, ch. 1.

88. Jenson, *ST* II, 282–83. See Jenson's larger discussion here for the different "spiritual senses" available to medieval exegetes. Theological, specifically christological, readings of Scripture are finding new voice among some contemporary theologians. Aside from numerous instances of such reading throughout Jenson's corpus, see most notably his commentary titled *Song of Songs*, which does not shy away from historical-critical issues but eventually seeks (contrary to most critical scholarship) a theological interpretation of the book, a move justified by the rationale for its canonization and reception within the church. See especially the introduction for a clear articulation of and defense of his methodology. Also, for examples of the revival of theological readings of Scripture, see Fowl, *Theological Interpretation of Scripture*; Vanhoozer, *Dictionary for Theological Interpretation of Scripture*; Treier, *Introducing Theological Interpretation of Scripture*.

89. Returning to a previous point, it is sometimes assumed that Judaism's exegesis of Israel's Scriptures is more "literal" and therefore more credible than a christological-spiritual exegetical approach, which some see as imposing a foreign interpretive grid upon these texts. The point to be repeated here is that Judaism and the church have equal right to the interpretation of these texts since they emerged simultaneously in history.

At several points in our discussion of the authority of Scripture, we have nosed up against the necessity of tradition. We can no longer stave off directly addressing the authority of tradition, because it is only by the light of that authority that we can read the Scripture as a whole in the way we have outlined, or have Scripture at all. The unity of the Bible and our hope to be addressed by it in the present depend on some account of the authority of tradition.

The Authority of Tradition

We may begin our treatment of this second locus of authority (i.e., tradition) by gathering up again some key pieces from the previous section. For Jenson, the church's central task is to speak the gospel (whether to God in praise or to the world as promise). Since any speaking of the gospel to the world only occurs as it holds out a *promise* spoken toward antecedent hopes and fears, it cannot be a mere repetition, because each setting will have a different set of hopes and fears that must be addressed by the content of the gospel. Speaking the gospel must involve thinking about what to say in any given context so as Fto be saying what the apostles said. The necessary connection with the apostles who first spoke the gospel involves the gospel in a process of its own tradition, because the gospel does not come to us unmediated, but rather only through a chain of witnesses who in succession have spoken the gospel in their own time and place. Thus, we can say that the gospel "lives only in history." The historical nature of the gospel is rooted, for Jenson, in the gospel's character as promise, a piece of Pauline theology. It is the character of a promise to both open and enable a future. As such, a promise is an "impeller and enabler of history" and "*therefore* the gospel must itself have a history."[90] And while this history is enabled by a future, the process of tradition itself does not occur above the level of contingencies or embodied locality, which again highlights the importance of the visible church for Jenson. He says, "Because the church is the fellowship gathered around the story of the man Jesus, and because it possesses that story only by the *usual processes of historical tradition*, the church is a social, economic,

---

Judaism interpreted these texts with reference to *torah* and the church interpreted them with reference to Christ, who is their fulfillment. See Jenson, *ST* II, 284.

90. Jenson, *ST* I, 14–16. For more on the gospel as promise handed through tradition, see Jenson, *Story and Promise*, 6ff.; *Religion Against Itself*, 14–16.

and legal entity whether its members want it to be or not. It is bodies, not disembodied souls, that gather."[91]

Jenson repeatedly defines theology as "thinking about what to say to be saying the gospel," where the gospel is "whatever the apostles said to say, 'Jesus is risen.'"[92] Insofar as it occurs as an act of receiving a word and producing a new word essentially related to the old word, it is a hermeneutical enterprise. Further elaborating on the character of theology, Jenson states that "theology is reflection internal to the act of tradition."[93] In a more pregnant description, he asserts, "Theology, we have seen, may be described as the historically continuing discussion and debate internal to the mission of the gospel."[94] Anyone familiar with the philosopher Alasdair MacIntyre's now famous definition of tradition cannot help noticing the similarities. MacIntyre defines a living tradition as "an historically extended, socially embodied argument, and an argument in part about the goods which constitute that tradition."[95] Given the obvious parallels between Jenson's and MacIntyre's conceptions of tradition, it is remarkable that Jenson cites MacIntyre only twice in his two-volume *Systematic Theology*, and in neither case is it related to a discussion of tradition. But we have just seen that in this particular instance, Jenson makes his case from the nature of the gospel itself without reference to any particular theory of tradition. When we understand the event character of the gospel and that it does not become gospel until it is proclaimed to actual hearers, we are disabused of the notion that the gospel is merely static content to be repeated.

Theology has the character of discussion and debate because each new occasion for gospel proclamation emerges in new theologoumena.[96] Since theology has a founding reference point (i.e., apostolic theology), churchly theologians are interested in securing their place in a continuing deliberation even as they provide fresh interpretations. As we noticed earlier, they are tested by running up against other accounts claiming to participate in the same undertaking, and eventually are measured at the bar of their cor-

91. Jenson, *Religion Against Itself*, 77.

92. E.g., *ST* I, 32.

93. Ibid., 14.

94. Ibid., 32.

95. MacIntyre, *After Virtue*, 222

96. Jenson, *ST* I, 32. Elsewhere he describes the ongoing nature of theology as "continuing consultation." He states, "Theology is not the adding of proposition to proposition in the steady construction of a planned structure of knowledge. It is a discussion and debate that as it continues regularly confronts new questions, and from which participants drop out and into which new participants enter," *ST* I, 17.

respondence to apostolic theology witnessed in Scripture. Yet we must remember that, for Jenson, these apostolic writings are samples of the kind of activity we should be undertaking; we are not called to reproduce and adopt materially all the theologoumena found in the New Testament, which are marked by distances even among themselves. Within Scripture itself, we see that "continuing argument between different and sometimes incompatible proposals" is internal to the logic of gospel proclamation.[97]

Thus, Scripture in its role as a touch point for theology (as opposed to its liturgical use noted earlier) is not formally distinct from theology understood as tradition, but rather its founding instance. Tradition is of the same fabric as Scripture in Jenson's thought, only Scripture represents the foundational touch point of the continuing process of discussion and debate, and because of that it is demarcated by a separate label from tradition more generally. Certainly, many within the free church tradition would not be comfortable with such conclusions. For those who would desire to posit a formal distinction between Scripture and tradition, especially one based on some theory of inspiration, the burden remains to account for the theological diversity in Scripture as well as its unity. Jenson's account attempts to deal truthfully with both.

If Scripture and extrabiblical tradition are not formally distinct, does any authority adhere to such tradition, and if so, how? As we have seen, theology is a hermeneutical exercise that occurs in the transition from hearing to speaking the gospel. Jenson states that theology's logical form is, "To be saying the gospel, let us say 'F' rather than 'G.'" When this is spoken to the community by a member or members, the role of the theologian is in view. When it is spoken by the community to the members, the role of the church's teaching office is in view. This latter kind of teaching is called "doctrine." Some doctrines come to be recognized as dogma. Jenson observes that the increasing ecumenical distinction between doctrine and dogma revolves around the notion of irreversibility.[98] He seizes upon the ecclesiological implications for such a description:

> A dogmatic choice is one by which the church so decisively determines her own future that if the choice is wrongly made, the community determined by that choice is no longer in fact the community of the gospel; thus no church thereafter exists to reverse the decision. Therefore, to believe that the entity which now

97. Ibid., 32–33.
98. Jenson especially points to the work of George Lindbeck on this point. See "Papacy and the Ius Divinum."

calls itself the Christian church is the church of the apostles and to believe that the church's past dogmatic decisions were adequate to their purposes—not necessarily in every way appropriate to them—comes to the same thing. If, for example, the decision of Nicea that Christ is "of one being with the Father" was false to the gospel, the gospel was thereby so perverted that there has since been no church extant to undo the error.[99]

Clearly, in Jenson's view, the existence of the contemporary church as truly being church rises or falls on the legitimacy of historically achieved dogma, since it is according to its central dogma that the church has perpetuated herself for centuries now.

Canon as Dogma

How does tradition expressed as dogma actually exercise authority? There are many ways to begin to answer this question. For a free church audience with a history of overly idealistic notions of *sola scriptura*, one especially effective place to begin is to consider again the issue of the scriptural canon. Jenson maintains that the canon of Scripture *is* a dogmatic decision of the church. The canon of Scripture is the list of writings *together with* the instruction, "Take all these writings and none other as standard documents of the apostolic witness."[100] The "together with" in the previous statement is critical in Jenson's understanding of the canon. It indicates that the authority of the canon does not merely inhere in its status as a static norm. It has its authority by virtue of its traditioned character; that is, by virtue of the historical processes of deliberation and argument that led to this collection of writings and the subsequent *instruction* to take this collection as authoritative.

This process of deliberation and gathering must surely be understood as historically contingent in Jenson's view. He surmises that if we were only now beginning to gather a canon in light of the critical scholarship available to us, we might end up with a different list, adding some and excluding others that the ancient church chose to add.[101] What we have was what was *in*

---

99. Jenson, *ST* I, 17. Jenson states that there are few dogmas because there have been so few occasions when the church has found it necessary to speak in such a committed manner.

100. Ibid., 27.

101. Ibid., 28. We shall observe in chapter 5 that McClendon makes almost the exact opposite claim—that is, any faithful church in any time would arrive at just about the same collection of books. I will argue that McClendon's view on this matter reveals a

fact historically achieved and received. He states, "Within Christianity, what might have been is beside the point; contingency is for Christianity the very principle of meaning; it is what in fact has happened—that might not have happened—that is God's history with us, and so the very reality of God and us."[102]

To admit that canon formation is truly a historically contingent process is to admit there is a possibility that these writings are inadequate to the task of accurately representing the witness of the apostles. But if this is true, the church has been "irretrievably astray since the middle of the third century at the latest. Belief that the gospel is still extant includes belief that the canon is adequate. And adequacy is, as with dogma, all that is required."[103]

This way of affirming the *adequacy* of tradition avoids foundationalist attempts at securing Scripture's authority over against anything external to it (including tradition). Further, it introduces the notion of faith with respect to authority. To believe that Scripture is a proper locus of authority, we are led simultaneously to ascribe authority to tradition in a similar act of faith. As Jenson so ably puts it, "If we allow no final authority to churchly dogma, or to the organs by which the church can enunciate dogma, there can be no canon of Scripture. The slogan *sola scriptura,* if by that is meant 'apart from creed, teaching office, or authoritative liturgy,' is an oxymoron."[104] Free churches have not on the whole truthfully enough addressed this insight, though more free church theologians are now acknowledging its truth. Our ascription of authority to Scripture rests on the belief that the church is still the church, and one can believe this, says Jenson, because of faith that the Spirit works in the course of the church's history to bring her to her proper end.[105] To invoke belief in the Spirit at this point is not, for Jenson, a way to escape historical contingency in the process of canonization. The Spirit works precisely through the contingencies of history.

---

lack of commitment to genuine contingencies of history, something Jenson is eager to maintain here and in many other contexts.

102. Jenson, "Catechesis for Our Time," 144.

103. Jenson, *ST* I, 28.

104. Ibid.

105. Ibid., 27. Our faith that the church is still the church and that its gospel is truly the gospel is confirmed simply by our participation in the life of the church. But once we affirm by faith that the church is still the church, we have affirmed (intentionally or not) the adequacy (and no more) of the processes and instruments by which this church has come to us.

Confessional Dogma

Beyond the canon of Scripture as an instance of authoritative tradition, there is the issue of what authority attaches to tradition as embodied in the church's dogmatic teaching, most centrally represented in the ancient catholic creeds. Of course, this is the point at which many in the free church tradition explicitly balk, especially those who reject the creedal tradition in favor of the Bible alone. Jenson states forthrightly, "Claims to have 'no creed but Christ' either urge a tautology or are self-deception."[106] Unfortunately, it seems that the latter is the usual case within the free church tradition.

Jenson observes that the decisive event in the mission of the gospel is baptism. The process of initiation that baptism marks is naturally governed by an exchange of interrogation and confession. As a result, formulas carrying the content for such an exchange appear very early, evidenced already in the New Testament.[107] These developed into later "rules of faith"[108] and closely related baptismal confessions which were designed as basic instruction in the gospel. They provided the "grammar of the church's discourse within itself and with the world."[109] Rules of faith function as norms within the work of theology which seeks to "expand and purify an already existing network of such regulations, whose most stable components are the so-far established rules of faith." A creed, in its narrowest sense, is a more fixed confessional formula (or rule of faith) that carries dogmatic authority. As such, "It demands currency in the life of the church, and any legitimate member of the church must be able to join in." It demands currency because it sets the bounds for controlling the church's discourse about the content of its faith.[110]

---

106. Ibid., 35.

107. Ibid. While there is scholarly debate about particular occurrences in the New Testament, Jenson mentions the following as clear indications of such formulas: Rom 1:3–4; 1 Cor 15:3–5; Gal 1:4; 3:27–28; 1 Thess 4:14.

108. In patristic literature, the phrase occurs as "the rule of faith," which is accurate in terms of content. In reality the wording was fluid and so the rule existed in different (though similar) forms, so we can reasonably speak of them in the plural. "Rules of faith" were short summaries of the central content of Christian faith. For several examples, see Tertullian (*On the Veiling of Virgins,* i; *On the Prescription of Heretics* 13; *Against Praxeas* 2) and Irenaeus, the latter of whom uses the phrase "canon (or rule) of truth" (*Against Heresies,* 1.10.1; 1.22.1).

109. Jenson, *ST* I, 36. The usage of "grammar" here follows that usage made common by George Lindbeck in *Nature of Doctrine.* See *ST* I, 18ff.

110. Jenson, *ST* I, 36.

Jenson argues that an effective way of displaying how dogma functions authoritatively is to recount the church's creedal history, which he briefly does. The most notable feature of the early baptismal creeds is the three-article form reflecting the name "Father, Son and Holy Spirit" which was confessed at baptism. As Tertullian explained,[111] baptismal creeds were a fuller form of the specific deity's name being confessed at baptism. It was a way of instructing the neophyte more fully in the God into which they were being baptized by recounting the narrative of this God with his creation.[112] It is important to note that the triple naming of this God as Father, Son, and Spirit arises out of the church's central liturgical practices (seen especially in early habits of prayer and baptismal practice). This accords a foundational authority to such traditional liturgical practices as they served to regulate discourse about God from the beginning.[113]

With the First Ecumenical Council of Nicea in 325, something new is demanded of the church's authoritative statements of faith. Because of historical exigencies, the church had to speak in such a way as to exclude an entire mode of interpretation of the triple name (namely, one that reduced the deity of Christ by attempting to affirm the oneness of God). The fathers at Nicea took the basic structure of a baptismal creed and inserted theological test phrases to further clarify the church's confession as well as to eliminate the possibility of advancing an interpretation of Scripture that ran counter to this confession. Scripture alone could not suffice since competing parties were supporting their theology from Scripture. What seemed to be consensus at the time of the council emerged in a protracted period of conflict between competing factions, councils, and creeds. Through a long and

111. *On the Crown*, 3.

112. Jenson, *ST* I, 36–37.

113. For Jenson's discussion of the authority of instituted liturgy see ibid., 34–35. Jenson's point could be underscored more forcefully at this point (though he does so very briefly a bit earlier in this work, p. 13). It was precisely because churches were regularly baptizing in the triune name and that Jesus was an object of adoration and prayer within the liturgical context that these problems arose in the first instance for worshippers whose roots lay unequivocally in the worship of one God. The question was not whether, in view of established monotheism, they should be engaged in these particular liturgical practices. Rather, it was how to make theological sense of these practices, which seems to indicate a widespread, deeply rooted, and uncontestable liturgical tradition. What we observe in these early theological struggles is that theology was struggling to conform to liturgical practice rather than vice versa; thus, the ancient maxim *lex orandi, lex credendi*. That the church's central dogma developed in large part from these practices would seem to secure the ongoing and irreversible authority of such liturgical practices, to the degree the creedal dogma is received as authoritative.

complicated history, the ecumenical councils of Constantinople in 381 and Ephesus in 431 affirmed the faith articulated at Nicea (although its logic had been further clarified through the fire of debate). To speak with the unity of the church represented in ecumenical council *by this time* meant to speak of the Father, Son, and Holy Spirit as all being on the same side of whatever line divided divinity and humanity (i.e., controlling the grammar of God). How then to affirm the humanity of Christ while abiding by the Nicene logic became the next problem to struggle through, and a dogmatic statement was produced at Chalcedon in 451 affirming both the full deity and full humanity of Christ.[114]

The course of events of this pivotal period in Christian history (and Jenson's careful study of them) leads him to an important conclusion:

> We must note that it [dogma] emerges and functions within the continuing theological enterprise of the church. Dogmas mean what they mean only from their historical and systematic locations in the total theological tradition. Thus also that total tradition is in a certain way normative for theology. One cannot obey, for example, the christological decrees of Chalcedon if one knows nothing of the thinking of Cyril or Leo, or if one regards these persons as simply curiosities of the past.[115]

These words are carefully chosen and precise. First, dogma (i.e., irreversible teaching) *emerges* within an ongoing theological tradition of discussion and then becomes authoritative in that discussion. It was not at the time obvious that what emerged as "orthodoxy" would triumph.[116] But, like the canon of Scripture, once it emerges, it functions with authoritative weight. Second, dogma cannot be separated from *historical* emergence. It is what it is because of the specific historical debates that gave rise to it. It is not timeless

---

114. For this brief summary, see Jenson *ST* I, 37–38; *Canon and Creed*, 66–68.

115. Jenson, *ST* I, 38.

116. This is the general line taken by a number of leading patristic scholars today. For example, it is reflected both in the content and title of R. C. P. Hanson's magisterial volume which traces the immense complexities of the fourth-century debates, *The Search for the Christian Doctrine of God*. See also the collection of essays in R. Williams, *Making of Orthodoxy*. The general approach represented in these volumes is to be contrasted with both the tone of inevitability in John Henry Newman's theory about doctrinal development as well as with Adolph von Harnack's thesis which sees so-called doctrinal development as doctrinal degeneration spiraling away from the core of actual apostolic doctrine. For Newman's view, see *Essay on the Development of Christian Doctrine*; for von Harnack's view, see *History of Dogma*. For an early articulation of the more contemporary position taken between the extremes of Newman and von Harnack, see Turner, *Pattern of Christian Truth*.

teaching that transcends its occurrence in an ongoing tradition of debate, but from its inception it shapes all further debate. Third, as Jenson says, the total tradition is then *in a certain way* normative for theology. *In a certain way* indicates the total tradition does not carry the weight of the conciliar proclamations but must be attended to for properly reading and locating the conciliar decisions since the latter do not exist apart from the former. The authority of creedal dogma inheres in its historically embedded yet still irreversible character.

To say that the entire tradition is *in a certain way* normative does not mean that one must find agreement with all previous theologians. That would be impossible since theology is a tradition of discussion and debate, and to engage in this process is to choose sides at certain points along the way. Further, no one now can know the entire tradition, so one's interlocutors and theological choices demonstrate where one has entered the tradition of discussion and debate.[117] To ascribe a certain normativity to the tradition as a whole simply reminds us that we cannot abstract dogmatic teaching out from its context of debate.[118] We must attend to the whole even as we give special authoritative status to the achieved dogma within the stream of debate.

117. Jenson, *ST* I, 38.

118. There is a parallel here with the historical-critical study of Scripture. To use one of Jenson's examples earlier referenced, in the statement "Jesus is risen," the meaning of the term *risen* is not to be ascertained by just any way in which this term can be taken. It finds its Christian meaning within the semantic field of the Old Testament by which early Christians understood this proclamation. So also, some such phrase as "of one substance with the Father" must be understood against the backdrop and semantic field from which such a statement emerged. As Jenson states in his description of systematic theology:

> It must quickly be noted that also the internal coherence of the faith does not impose itself by mere analysis but rather in the historical course of the church. Thus the conceptual structure that the anti-Arian theologians invoked was discovered in phrases and practices of established liturgy. Therefore even the most "systematic" theology cannot refrain from exploring history, as will be superabundantly plain in the following" [i.e., his own systematic theology], *ST* I, 22.

And Jenson makes good on this promise. However contestable any of his readings of history may be, his constructive theology emerges out of an impressive range and depth of exploration in historical theology, both primary and secondary literature. He creatively weaves together insights from across the theological spectrum (East and West; Catholic and Protestant; ancient and modern), though he rarely engages thought from the free church tradition except to quickly dismiss things such as anti-creedalism. A. N. Williams traces a distinct development throughout Jenson's corpus, noticing a deepening and increasingly sympathetic relation to the church's tradition. Further, he notices an increasing move toward Thomistic theology across the breadth of Jenson's career, "The Parlement of Foules and the Communion of Saints."

Dogma as a Principle of Biblical Interpretation

Another way of demonstrating the authoritative function of tradition is to observe its role not only in canon formation, which we addressed above, but also its role in subsequent biblical interpretation. Jenson notes that long before Pentecost, the way in which Israel told the story of God with her was by the development of her history book through a process of writing, editing, commenting, etc. The early church continued that same tradition by gathering her own texts and positioning them with respect to the Old Testament according to the story she had been telling all along, whose drama centered on Christ. As Jenson observes:

> A narrative general interpretation of the documents that became
> the New Testament, in their relation to the Old Testament and to
> each other, was itself the principle of their gathering. The church's
> continuing practice of proclamation and prayer, and the collection
> of Scripture as it was gradually shaped, were simply versions in
> two media of the same story.

Each (i.e., Scripture and tradition) needed the other, a point the church learned explicitly, in part, from Irenaeus.[119]

We recall here the exegetical rules Jenson adopts from Irenaeus:

1. Scripture is a whole.

2. Scripture *is* a whole because and only because it is one long *narrative*.

3. To be able to *follow* the single story and grasp Scripture whole, we need to know the story's general plot and *dramatis personae*.

4. It is the *church* that knows the plot and *dramatis personae* of the scriptural narrative, since the church is one continuous community with the story's actors and narrators, as with its tradents, authors, and assemblers.

5. The church's antecedent knowledge of Scripture's plot and *dramatis personae*, without which she could not read the Bible as a whole, is contained in what Irenaeus calls the "rule of faith."[120]

---

119. Jenson, *ST* II, 274. The point of the reciprocity of the canon and the creed is Jenson's central point in *Canon and Creed*. He uses the image of notched puzzle pieces to express the notion that "each advances what the other holds back," 41.

120. Jenson, "Hermeneutics and the Life of the Church," 95–98.

It is the final rule in this list that we must observe carefully at this point. Irenaeus maintained that it was the traditional rule of faith, as it principally identified the *dramatis personae* (Father, Son, and Spirit), which gave the collection of scriptural texts their unified shape. As we just noticed Jenson saying above, "It was the principle of their gathering."

For Jenson, this leads to what he calls a drastic point: "Therefore there can be no reading of the unitary Bible that is not motivated by and guided by the church's teaching. We will either read the Bible under the guidance of the church's established doctrine, or we will not read it at all."[121] Scripture must be read within the scope of its organizing principle (the narrative structure embodied in the church's core teaching) or there is no unified book to read.[122] If this is true, we cannot affirm the authority of Scripture apart from the history by which it came to be, but only through this tradition, preserved in the proclamation of churches.

Putting a couple of pieces together from what we have ascertained from Jenson's account of Scripture and tradition, we come to this point: Because the church gathered its Scripture as a unified canon guided by its traditional rule of faith which eventually congealed into its central Trinitarian dogma, and because (as was earlier discussed) in a living tradition past and present are mediated by the continuity of a community's language and discourse through a process of discussion and debate, *then*:

> . . . historical honesty requires the church to interpret Scripture
> in the light of her dogmas. If the church's dogmatic teaching has
> become false to Scripture, then there is no church and it does not
> matter how the group that mistakes itself for church reads Scrip-
> ture or anything else. But if there is the church, then her dogma is
> in the direct continuity of Scripture and is a necessary principle for
> interpreting Scripture and vice versa.[123]

Those within the free church tradition must at least pause before Jenson's challenge concerning historical honesty. Is it historically truthful for those within the free church tradition to accept a canon of Scripture that took shape according to the ancient church's teaching tradition and yet not continue to ascribe at least some kind of hermeneutical authority to that

121. Ibid., 98.

122. Jenson, *ST* I, 59.

123. Jenson, *ST* II, 281. As an example, we can see how Jenson follows this conclusion in his interpretation of the Servant of the Lord in Isaiah. He relates this servant to Christ according to the logic of the church's christological dogma of the Word born to Mary being identical with the Word of the Lord to the prophets, *ST* I, 80–82; *ST* II, 281.

tradition? Jenson claims that honesty *requires* reading Scripture in light of the church's dogmatic teaching.[124] He quickly adds that such a claim does not mean that every piece of Scripture must be made to fit the dogma. This is because Scripture is not theologically homogenous and because a community's diachronic continuity does not emerge through "point-for-point unanimity."[125] What it *does* mean is that our reading of Scripture must be

124. We may contrast Jenson's strong assertion with what we will see in chapter 5 with McClendon. McClendon treats the dogmatic tradition more positively than have many within the free church tradition, but eventually cannot bring himself to commit himself to it in the same fashion in which Jenson commits himself. It seems to me that truthfulness lies with Jenson on this point.

125. Jenson, *ST* II, 281. Jenson draws another consequence at this point that I find perplexing. In asserting that not every passage of Scripture must be conformable to dogma, he also reasons that "this does not mean that historical study may not find that particular apparently dogmatic decisions of the church are unsupported by Scripture. If this happens, the church, bound by her faith in the Spirit's leading, will suppose that the dissensus is not fatal and can be overcome." As an example, he cites what he understands to be a reshaping of Chalcedonian Christology by later councils (for his account of this history, see *ST* I, 131–36).

Aside from whether Jenson's account of this particular instance is completely accurate, he seems by this statement to be in danger of sawing off the limb upon which he has been standing. It is not clear what he means by an "apparently dogmatic decision." According to his own logic, dogma is never "apparent" but has its character as being fully recognized as dogma and "just so" (to use his cherished phrase) irreversible. If we allow the statement just quoted, then his other statements lose their force, those in which he claims that if the church's dogmas are false, there is no church now extant to correct them. For instance, *if* (which if the foregoing argument is correct could not be the case) through historical study, it could be determined that the doctrine of the Trinity were incompatible with Scripture, then according to the logic of the statement above, we would not conclude that there is no church, but rather, that Trinitarian dogma was after all only *apparently* dogma. We see in this same statement that the real crux of Jenson's thought in these matters resides, as we have already seen, in the church's belief in the Spirit's leading, which of course would not be compelling if Trinitarian dogma turned out to be only *apparently* dogma. It seems that Jenson is attempting to leave himself an escape hatch, instead of fully opening himself to the consequences of his more programmatic statements concerning the nature of dogma.

Or perhaps Jenson is speaking specifically with an eye toward the particular "dogma" of the Roman church which presents seemingly insurmountable obstacles in ecumenical discussion. For example, he describes the Marian dogmatic statement of 1854 by Pious IX (the doctrine of Mary's immaculate conception) as having been made in "unilateral fashion." He then says that "it remains to be seen what status these definitions will have in a reunited church and so what status they now can have in the ecumene." He registers the ambiguity of the language of this doctrine (and even more so the ambiguity of the Marian doctrine of 1950), but then proceeds to exegete Scripture in such a way as to harmonize with the doctrine (for the entire discussion, see *ST* II, 200–204). It is almost as if what Jenson is saying here is, "If this is legitimate dogma, I will demonstrate a biblical exegesis in harmony with it. But it is somewhat ambiguous. And perhaps one day in a

guided by the shape the canon gives to each part included in it. The whole must govern the parts, as we saw with Irenaeus. And the whole, for Jenson, is Trinitarian in scope, according to the logic of the church's ancient rule of faith. He offers a Christian exegetical mandate:

> To read the Bible whole, that is to read it as Bible, demands that the questions we bring to any text or set of texts or tradition or redaction . . . must be trinitarian questions. And to read the Bible whole, we must presume in advance that the doctrine of the Trinity is true, and that it must therefore also answer the questions the Scripture raises for us.[126]

That is, we must depend upon the authority of the church's tradition as our hermeneutical key for knowing how to read Scripture properly.[127]

Tradition, as it is instantiated in the church's liturgical forms and its rules of faith, serves not only as an authoritative hermeneutical lens for interpreting Scripture but also as an authoritative touch point for carrying out the tasks of theology. Tradition provides a first-level rule for the church's discourse, and theology seeks to provide second-level rules[128] as it labors "to expand and purify an already existing network of such regulations, whose most stable components are the so-far established rules of faith."[129] Jenson is committed to the idea that theology is always in process *toward* something beyond itself. As theology is itself tradition, it moves forward by backward reference to its "most stable components" but also looking to push the grammar forward by providing clarity, expansion, etc. This is exactly what Jenson himself attempts in his own theology. For example, for reasons we have observed in this chapter, Jenson believes that theology must proceed

---

united church, the decision will be reached that these definitions were unwarranted, at which point, we will know they were only *apparently* dogma."

126. Jenson, "Hermeneutics and the Life of the Church," 99–100. Jenson provides an illustration of how he puts this "neo-Irenaean exegesis" to work. He demonstrates a reading of some difficult psalms in which the speaker of the psalms is the *totus Christus*, the second person of the Trinity and his community; see 100ff. As indicated earlier, his interpretation of Song of Songs rests on this commitment to a canonical reading along Trinitarian lines as well. In his most recent work, he provides three brief chapters exegeting the following three texts in light of the church's creed: Gen 1:1–5; Luke 1:26–38; Mark 14:35–36. See *Canon and Creed*, 89–115.

127. As Jenson puts it, the doctrine of the Trinity is "the church's encompassing hermeneutic," "Scripture's Authority in the Church," 33.

128. His terminology here is indebted to George Lindbeck's exposition of theology as grammar which we earlier noted. See again Jenson, *ST* I, 18ff.

129. Ibid., 36.

in obedience to the christological guideposts formulated at Chalcedon. But also as we have seen, Jenson develops a Christology that is anything but traditional, all in an attempt to "expand and purify" the church's received dogma.[130] He struggles with Chalcedon, but he will not proceed apart from it. It will be up to others to determine through debate whether his Christology is a legitimate expansion and purification, a point Jenson himself realizes.[131]

In the end, the church must have confidence that its liturgical and dogmatic tradition adequately preserves her continuity of faith with the apostles. What grounds such confidence? Jenson summarizes it nicely: "On one side, this confidence can only be legitimated by the entire tradition's success as hermeneutical principle in the church's use of Scripture. On another side, it is a simple act of faith in the Spirit's guidance of the church."[132] We are back again to *faith* that the church is still the church and that God's Spirit has not abandoned her along the way through the contingent processes of struggle and debate by which she has come to understand her faith more fully on the way to her proper *telos*.

The Authority of the Teaching Office

We come now to the third, and most ecumenically controversial, locus of authority: an episcopal teaching office. There is a general recognition that many of the ongoing problems in ecumenical discussions continue to revolve around ecclesiology, and within ecclesiology, the most problematic point of discussion (especially between Protestants and Roman Catholics) seems to be the question of ordained ministry.[133] To state Jenson's position

130. See esp. *ST* I, ch. 8.

131. Jenson states, "It is the fate of every theological system to be dismembered and have its fragments bandied about in an ongoing debate," ibid., 18.

132. Ibid., 39.

133. For evidence of this fact from ecumenical reports, see Jenson, *Unbaptized God*, 47. Jenson, however, likes to begin by underscoring the remarkable achievements of ecumenical dialogues in this area and asserts that within communion ecclesiology, there has emerged an ecumenical doctrine of ordained ministry. See also *ST* II, 228. The consensus achieved thus far in this area between Protestants and Roman Catholics does not include those from the free church tradition, who, as Yoder noticed, have been largely absent from such conversations. Jenson acknowledges the lack of this perspective in ecumenical dialogue and speaks somewhat condescendingly (even if perhaps truthfully) in saying, ". . . dialogue with sectarian Protestantism has not yet progressed beyond the most superficial level. Perhaps the situation will change somewhat when and if such groups do come seriously to grips; the present situation, in any case, is very little shaped by the magisterial Reformation's old controversies with anabaptists and so-called enthusiasts," *Unbaptized God*, 10.

up front, he argues for the ecclesial necessity of the bishop's office as well as an episcopal church structure. Further, and more surprisingly for a Lutheran, he argues for the necessity of a universal pastor for the church and that, pragmatically, the Roman bishop is the only viable candidate to occupy such an office. Having summarily stated Jenson's basic position, we will now briefly follow his line of argumentation toward these conclusions and in doing so demonstrate how they fit within his broader ecclesiology and Trinitarian theology.

The Rationale for an Authoritative Extra-Congregational Teaching Office

Jenson's argument, not surprisingly, begins with the Bible, specifically the Pastoral Epistles, where we see the initiation of officers in the church through a formal rite of prophetic address and the laying on of hands.[134] This rite performed upon bishops and presbyters bestowed a "charism." Initially in Paul's congregations, charisms were expressions of the Spirit's direct activity in the church governed by the Spirit's unpredictable choice. In the Pastoral Epistles, the charism in view is still a specific manifestation of the Spirit, but now its occurrence is attached to a communal ritual that constitutes a regular office. The content of the office clearly involves, at least in part, maintaining continuity between the church's teaching and that of the apostles, which necessarily includes taking a role in the appointment of successors to the office. After consideration of the Pastoral evidence and terminology, Jenson concludes that the charism of the pastoral office has mainly to do with "the unity, both synchronic and diachronic, of the community."[135]

It is true that the Pastoral Epistles do not state a universal command beyond the scope of its recipients. It was a "subsequent choice of the church" to apply this teaching to her own ordained ministry, "as this had continued to develop on the lines that there appeared." If the church was to endure after the apostles' generation and according to the promise of Jesus, then "such an office, particularly in its diachronic dimension, was the one strictly necessary office," even if the form it took was a historical contingency.[136] With regard

134. See 1 Tim 1:6; 1:18; 4:14; 5:22; 2 Tim 1:13; 2:1–2; Titus 1:5.

135. Jenson, *ST* II, 228–29. For a much earlier discussion of the authority of the teaching office, see Jenson, *Visible Words*, 188ff.

136. Jenson, *ST* II, 230. In another instance, Jenson asserts, "The *common* in any community is both diachronic and synchronic, but it is fundamentally diachronic and only derivatively synchronic," "God, the Liberal Arts, and the Integrity of Texts," in *Essays*

to the necessity of *a* pastoral office (not yet touching upon the form it should take), ecumenical consensus has been reached within multilateral dialogue, especially represented by *Baptism, Eucharist and Ministry*. According to this consensus, the charism of this office is essentially *pastoral*. Ordained persons are there "to provide . . . within a multiplicity of gifts, a focus of unity." Working from the consensual understanding that the church *is* communion (i.e., *communio* ecclesiology), the office that tends her unity must be "constitutive for the life . . . of the church" and those who tend to this unity "since very early times have been ordained." [137] Also, they are "representatives of Christ to the community" being set apart in the community to speak for Christ to the community. [138]

For Jenson, such an understanding of this charism enjoins upon its recipients primarily two specific functions. First, since the communion of the church is founded upon eucharistic communion with Christ, the one upon whom the Spirit has bestowed the charism of tending to the church's unity should occupy the place in the eucharistic celebration where Christ is most clearly represented, tending to the church's unity as the visible host of the meal, the representative of Christ. Second, since the initial impetus for the charism was to maintain diachronic unity with the apostles' teaching, those who have received the charism must have the authority to determine what teaching accurately reflects the faith of the church, an authority that has traditionally been labeled *magisterium*. [139] The mention of *authoritative*

---

in Theology of Culture, 209–15, esp. 209.

137. Faith and Order, *Baptism, Eucharist and Ministry*, i.8 (hereafter *BEM*). Jenson observes that *BEM* is more hesitant than are some bilateral dialogues to declare that ordination is a sacrament, but materially it says just that. For this analysis, see Jenson, *Unbaptized God*, 48ff.

138. *BEM*, i.11. In the prolegomena to his *Systematic Theology*, Jenson provides a brief defense for an authoritative teaching office along similar lines, drawing upon the Weberian distinction between *Gemeinschaft* and *Gesellschaft*. The church needs a voice by which she (as a community) speaks for herself to her members (taken as an association). This voice is the teaching office which, as an instrument of the Spirit, defends the biblical text over against its churchly interpreters as association. See *ST* I, 39–41. For a fuller treatment of the same argument, see Jenson, "God, the Liberal Arts, and the Integrity of Texts." Without a voice by which the community speaks to itself as association, there will be nothing but a collection of alternative interpretations by individuals within the association, 212. This is obviously a point to be considered carefully by those within the free church tradition who appear defenseless in the face of innumerable and competing interpretations.

139. Jenson, *ST* II, 232; *ST* I, 17. In substance, Jenson notes that these two points have largely been adopted in ecumenical dialogue, but there is hesitancy from Protestants at the word *magisterium* because of its usual association with the episcopal mode of the

teachers raises the hackles of many, especially from a free church tradition. But Jenson argues that this negative reaction to authority is based on a misunderstanding of its nature. For something to be an authority for me means that it determines my future *in some way*. Jenson proposes that this "in some way" will either be an attempt at domination or an opportunity for greater freedom. Since the gospel is promise, the authorities by which it is perpetuated must function as instruments of genuine freedom rather than tyranny.[140] It is this kind of authority that Jenson seeks to place firmly within the teaching office of the church, regardless of any kinds of tyrannical forms of authority that might have been exercised through that office in Christian history.

At this point Jenson raises the question of apostolic succession. The question has become thorny in ecumenical dialogue.[141] Briefly stated, Jenson argues, in continuity with many dialogues, that the phrase "apostolic succession" should not primarily refer to a chain of ordinations but to the apostolicity of the church's faith, which is essential to her being the church. Succession in office is one essential factor *within* this substantive understanding of the church's relation to the apostles' teaching.[142] It is what the

---

pastoral office. We have not yet arrived at the appropriate mode of the office. The argument has only affirmed the necessity of an authoritative teaching office.

Elsewhere, when Jenson lays out the same basic argument in favor of a *magisterium*, he concludes, "The argument could be attacked only by supposing that 'common confession' is not a necessary part of the flock's unity; groups who could faithfully take this position are outside the dialogues," *Unbaptized God*, 58. While this appears almost as an aside in Jenson's argument, it is centrally pertinent for our purposes. It demonstrates the logic by which this discussion must proceed for those within free churches. As long as suspicion remains about a "common confession," arguments in favor of an authoritative teaching office will be superfluous. It is only since some within the free church tradition have recently been more vocal about affirming the authority of ancient ecumenical creeds that one of the major questions of this study can have meaning within that tradition, namely, what then about a teaching office?

140. Jenson, *Story and Promise*, 196–97.

141. For his fuller account of the complicated discussions, see Jenson, *Unbaptized God*, 52–55, 71–75.

142. Jenson, *ST* II, 233. Mark Mattes criticizes Jenson's advocacy of the Catholic perspective here. He states, "It is the gift of the gospel as a linguistic reality, not its deliverers, that defines the church's life," *Role of Justification in Contemporary Theology*, 133. Many, if not most, free church theologians would likely agree with Mattes on this point. Mattes' critique, however, seems to lead toward a Platonizing of the gospel, removing it from the embodied character that Jenson's entire theology insists upon. As a linguistic reality, the gospel is a tradition, and any linguistic tradition is what it is because of *how* it has been received, maintained, and handed on. This necessarily involves speakers and those who exercise more influence than others in shaping the discourse.

Roman teaching office refers to as the embodiment of "catholicity in time."[143] It is what Jenson, following then Cardinal Ratzinger, calls the "necessary *personal* aspect of the church's total diachronic unity with the apostles."[144] This personal aspect is essential because the historical continuity of the church is personal communion and not merely historical perpetuation, and because in the continued practice of the rite of ordination as its "form of granting office, the church expresses faith that she is a creature of the Holy Spirit, who forever continues to live by his gifts."[145]

The Mode of the Teaching Office

The *communio* ecclesiology that Jenson espouses affirms different uses of the word *church*. In the New Testament, the church exists at three levels: a local fellowship; many such fellowships as a class; all such fellowships as one great fellowship.[146] Each is appropriately called church, both the one and the many. *Communio* ecclesiology affirms that "the church is *in et ex ecclesiis* and that the churches are *in et ex ecclesiae*."[147] In Jenson's argument, once it has been established that the pastoral office is essential to the church, then it follows (and is a necessary implication of *communio* ecclesiology) that each "level" of church must have a pastor or pastors specific to that expression of communion.[148]

To fill this out, Jenson turns his attention to the *form* of the pastoral office. He briefly recounts the history of the early emergence of the monarchial episcopate within the threefold ministry, first attested in the letters of Ignatius, in which a single bishop flanked by a college of presbyters and served by

143. Jenson, *ST* I, 41, citing the Roman Catholic official response to *BEM* in Thurian, *Churches Respond to BEM*, 6:31–33.

144. Jenson, *ST* I, 41, citing Joseph Cardinal Ratzinger, *Theologische Prinzipienlehre*, 256.

145. Jenson, *ST* II, 233–34, quoting Ratzinger, "Fragen zur Sukzession." See also Jenson, *Unbaptized God*, 71ff.

146. Jenson, *Unbaptized God*, 68. See, e.g., 1 Cor 1:2; 7:17; 12:28. I shall argue in chapter 5 that one of McClendon's weaknesses is that he allows the term *church* to apply only to the local, gathered congregation.

147. Jenson, *ST* II, 234. While much of the *communio* literature seems to indicate only two levels (local churches and the universal church), Jenson argues that the principle involved allows for groupings in between these that would be sufficiently labeled "church."

148. Ibid. Jenson is careful to indicate that by "level" here he does not intend a hierarchical sense but a topographical sense, n. 41.

deacons represents and enacts the christological focus of the congregation's unity, especially in presiding over the eucharistic meal. In time the bishop's jurisdiction widened to facilitate the unity of congregations within a region, and presbyters acted as the bishop's vicars in eucharistic celebrations.[149]

This form of the threefold ministry (now known as "episcopal") became the norm until the challenges of the Reformation. The ecumenically challenging question today is whether this form, having appeared and become the norm in history, is divinely mandated. Does the episcopacy, having emerged in a series of historical contingencies, have dogmatic force? In traditional language: is it *iure divino* or *iure humano* (mandated by divine law or human law)? Jenson seeks to answer these questions in two primary ways. First, he appeals to an argument we noticed earlier: if Scripture is *iure divino* (and surely all Protestants would agree that it is), then something can appear in the church's history that, once it appears, belongs to her foundation. If it *can*, how then do we determine if in any given case it is so? Jenson appeals to two conditions offered by George Lindbeck: "historically relative and conditioned" institutions may be taken as divinely instituted if a) they are "contingently but really necessary,"[150] and b) once instituted, they are irreversible.[151]

We will recall Jenson's description of irreversibility: it is a choice by which the church so determines her future that if it was wrong, there would be no church to reverse the decision.[152] Two very important points emerge from this for Jenson. First:

> Canon, creed, and episcopate were but parts of a single norm of faith, discovered in response to a single historical crisis; if one of the three is alienable, how are the other two not? It was precisely in their interaction that they were to guard the apostolicity of the church's teaching; what justifies separating one as dispensable?[153]

This is a pivotal question for the purposes of our study. We noticed in the second chapter that free church theologians are increasingly acknowledging

---

149. Ibid., 234–36. For more on the entire matter, see also Jenson, *Unbaptized God*, 61–75. Jenson observes that there is general ecumenical agreement now that the pastoral office is one office exercised at different levels of ministry.

150. This is what Jenson has expressed through the idea of dramatic necessity; that is, not predetermined but once there the very thing that had to happen. For this, he appeals to Aristotle's definition of dramatic coherence. See *ST* I, 64.

151. Jenson, *ST* II, 238. See Lindbeck, "Papacy and the Ius Divinum," 202–3.

152. Jenson *ST* I, 17.

153. Jenson, *ST* II, 239.

the way in which this triple authority operated to shape catholic teaching. Yet what has emerged out of this is a call to retrieve the church's ancient dogmatic tradition without a call to retrieve the mechanisms through which it emerged. Jenson's question is valid. It would seem, at the very least, that these free church theologians who have contributed so much in the way of turning their tradition toward the larger Christian tradition owe a fuller explanation on this point.

Second, Jenson returns again to his point that we are "left with faith in the Spirit's guidance of the church." But he fills this out toward a dogmatic end. To say that an irreversible decision of the church is one "on which the church bets her *future* self-identity" (emphasis added) points us, according to Jenson, in the direction we should look in making the judgment about the episcopate's dogmatic status. Since it was not in place from the beginning, we must look to the end to judge its narrative coherence, as is true for any coherent narrative. Jenson reminds us, "The church is what she is by anticipation of her transformation into God." To look to the future rather than the past in assessing the normativity of churchly developments does not diminish the past. Rather, "We look to the gospel's vision of fulfillment to provide clues by which to perceive precisely the dramatic continuity of the Spirit's leading in past history: for a way to tell how the church's past is authoritative for future decision, how past decisions guide future choices and can prohibit certain paths."[154]

There is, of course, no way to determine ahead of time what precise pattern of ecclesial structure would conform to the kingdom's fulfillment. But we can judge after the fact whether a particular development is "dramatically appropriate" and so be able to determine the Spirit's leading toward the future. And according to Jenson's fuller ecclesiology, we do know something about the future: the church's proper *telos* will be perfect inclusion in the triune life of God. Appealing then to one of the central convictions of *communio* ecclesiology (i.e., that the church's *koinonia* is rooted in its participation in the very *koinonia* of the triune life), Jenson proposes that what becomes normative for our judgment concerning church structure is that it be "differentiated, perichoretic, and reciprocally hierarchical." That is, the church's office will include different roles that find their substance only in interaction with the others, and these roles will be unequal in such a way that the direction of subordination is determined by the context.[155] Obviously, much of

154. Ibid., 239–40.

155. Ibid., 240. Jenson also grounds a hierarchical understanding of the church in the fact of Jesus' selecting of the twelve apostles as relayed in the Gospels. He says that

the force of this argument depends both on Jenson's argument that the end of the church is inclusion in the life of God as well as on his description of that triune God in whom the church will be included. If both of these hold, the argument has strength. To cap Jenson's argument, which ultimately empties again into faith in the Spirit's leading, observe the following:

> If the Spirit has been leading the church, then if the episcopate has been in fact established in the history of the church, and if this establishment *can* dramatically have been the leading of the Spirit, then we must judge that the establishment *was* the leading of the Spirit. And, as we have just argued, given the scope of the decision made as the episcopate became established, if this particular decision was in its time proper it is also irreversible.[156]

For Jenson to reach this conclusion is not to idealize this structural model. First, some other model could have emerged that equally satisfied the needed requirements, but that is beside the point. This is the one that did *in fact* emerge. Second, while Jenson affirms the dogmatic status of an episcopal structure, he also calls for its reform, specifically in two areas: a) Given the center of their function as maintainers of unity, bishops must be pastors of plausible "local" churches, actual eucharistic assemblies. Without this, those outside the episcopal system have no strong reason to join it. b) The bishop's central functions need to be steered away from administrative duties and back to sacramental and instructional concerns.[157] Jenson's suggestions for reform should serve to at least lower free church defenses. Jenson shows a remarkable concern for local churches, arguing in fact that it is from those actual eucharistic assemblies that a teaching office arises at all. Further, those within the free church tradition are often rightly concerned about how bishops behave and are perceived as authoritarian administrators. But the office poorly practiced does not negate the need for the office.

Jesus' community was never homogeneous in an abstractly egalitarian sense, but rather was hierarchical, marked by "concentric circles of differing responsibility." This structure remained even when the Spirit freed the church for its mission with "Peter, standing with the eleven" as he "raised his voice," *ST* II, 183–84. We will later contrast Jenson's understanding of hierarchy with McClendon's repudiation of hierarchy.

156. Ibid.

157. Ibid., 241. In this work, Jenson appears to go beyond his earlier discussions of the church's pastoral office. For example, earlier he produced much of what appears in his later work, but he did not assign dogmatic status to the threefold office. Rather, he argued pragmatically for it, saying that it is manifestly not mandated in Scripture, but that it has met the church's needs over time better than other structures, especially those of a congregational sort of polity. See Jenson, *Visible Words*, 188–203, esp. 196.

Jenson calls for its reform in ways that might be able to resonate for those within the free church tradition.

In the present, we cannot perceive the one great assembly of Christ. If we can only perceive the one body of Christ by demonstrable eucharistic openness toward other eucharistic communities, then an ecclesial structure that facilitates and *enacts* this openness becomes necessary for visible unity. This is what happens as the bishops recognize each other in visible eucharistic fellowship; they enact the "communion of communions" not just ideally but through actual fellowship in the Eucharist.[158] Jenson states, "The polity of the church, in so far as it is truly necessary at any time or place, is therefore nothing but the structures by which eucharistic fellowship is enabled and bounded."[159]

So what of churches without episcopal succession? Jenson appeals to the Roman Catholic designation "wounded" to describe them. He approvingly quotes an Orthodox commentator on these matters: "Not by episcopal succession alone, but certainly not without episcopal succession, can there be any discussion of the recovery of the true unity in the one Church."[160] Thus, Jenson calls for both healing of the dogmatic practice of episcopal structure and healing of the wound among those churches separated from that structure which facilitates visible unity primarily through eucharistic fellowship.

The Papacy

Jenson admits that the issue of the papacy may be the one obstacle in ecumenical dialogue that only a new and unexpected intervention of God's grace can overcome, but he finds this paradoxical. As he argues, the papacy presents few new problems beyond what has already been covered in theory within discussions of the episcopal office in general and the episcopacy in particular. This is especially true since the time of Vatican II, when official Roman teaching attempted to define the pope's role with reference to the bishops rather than vice versa.[161] At the beginning of his treatment of the papacy, he says very simply, "If the communion ecclesiology is anywhere close to the truth, then plainly the 'one church' of its slogans must have her

---

158. Jenson, "Church as *Communio*," 6, 9–11.
159. Jenson, "Church and the Sacraments," 218.
160. Jenson, *ST* II, 242, citing Stephanopoulos, "Lima Statement," 278.
161. Jenson, *Unbaptized God*, 76–77.

own pastor."[162] Thus, for Jenson, the argument for a universal pastorate has already been accomplished in developing a communion ecclesiology followed by the argument for the pastoral office in general.

The first major issue is to determine what can be said about this function. Much of the problematic language was set down at the First Vatican Council. While Jenson concedes that much of the language used at Vatican I was "bombastic," he argues that when the substance of what is actually said about the universal pastorate emerges, it is "unproblematic and even tautologous, if the universal church is herself real."[163]

Jenson briefly touches on some of the controversial terminology from Vatican I and attempts to read it sympathetically with the help of Vatican II interpretation along with recent commentators. For example, there is the debated teaching that the pope's "jurisdiction" is "ordinary" and "immediate." These terms get interpreted to emphasize that the pope's role is of the same *kind* as that of pastors in local churches; it is truly episcopal in character. The pope's operation emerges out of the same charism as that by which bishops do their work. He is a local bishop with universal responsibility.[164] And whatever some of the bishops at Vatican I thought, these terms cannot mean that all ecclesiastical authority is consolidated in the pope, since Vatican II determined that it is the episcopacy that is "invested with the fullness of this office"[165] and not simply the pope as such.[166]

Jenson devotes the majority of his discussion to the divisive issue of papal infallibility, the dogma notoriously decreed by the First Vatican Council. It states that when a pope speaks "*ex cathedra*" (that is, from the weight of his office in defining teaching for the entire church), he possesses "that infallibility which the divine Redeemer willed his church to enjoy," and these definitions are "irreformable in their own right [*ex sese*] and not by the consent of the church."[167] This statement has been subject to much discussion and debate. Jenson argues that it cannot mean that a pope cannot err when claiming to define doctrine, a position demonstrated by the overturning of the Monothelite doctrine formally defined by Honorius I, an overturning

162. Jenson, *ST* II, 242.

163. Ibid.

164. Ibid., 243, following the careful historical and interpretive work of Catholics Thils, *Primaut et infallibility*, 61–106, and Tillard, *Church of Churches*, 257–60.

165. *Lumen Gentium*, 26.

166. Jenson, *ST* II, 243.

167. *Constitutio dogmatic prima de ecclesia Christi*, iv, cited in ibid., 244.

that occurred in the sixth ecumenical council and was confirmed by a subsequent pope.[168]

Following the lead of prominent Catholic scholars, Jenson focuses his attention upon what conditions must be met for a genuine (and therefore infallible) *ex cathedra* pronouncement. While Vatican I declared that consent of the church is not a condition for papal infallibility, it may be that the consent of the church is a "necessary sign that those conditions are fulfilled." The Second Vatican Council adds to the teaching of Vatican I by stating that when a papal teaching is *in fact* irreformable, the "assent of the church cannot fail" to follow.[169] As Cardinal Ratzinger (now Pope Benedict XVI) said, in clarifying the teaching of Vatican I the bishops of Vatican II declared:

> It is now said that the work of the teaching office always takes place on the background of the faith and prayer of the whole church. Yet at the same time it cannot be restricted only to the expression of an already established common opinion but . . . must under certain circumstances take the initiative . . . over against the confusion of a church without consensus.[170]

Jenson then argues that this must in fact be true of any pastorate, with the proviso that presbyteral pastors or bishops cannot declare what *the* church teaches in such a way as to settle a matter; that belongs to a specific authority of the universal pastorate.[171]

Jenson's reading of infallibility relies heavily on the assent of the church. He grounds this eventually in the fact that what is being said about the pope is true of universal councils. He states, "The decisions of the ecumenical councils—found to be ecumenical by the assent of the church!—have all along provided our model and rationale of strictly dogmatic teaching." To the question of whether a council can err, Jenson answers in the affirmative. And once again, we see his pneumatological rationale. If a council errs, "This will be discovered, if the Spirit guides the church, and the church's assent 'cannot fail' to be refused."[172]

---

168. Jenson, *ST* II, 244.

169. *Lumen Gentium*, 25. The precise meaning of this phrase has been hotly contested among Catholics, but it at least officially opens the door for a less totalitarian reading of the teachings of Vatican I than is sometimes given either by its supporters or detractors.

170. Ratzinger, *Theologische Prinzipienlehre*, 247, cited in Jenson, *ST* II, 245.

171. Jenson, *ST* II, 245.

172. Ibid., 246. He points to the famous "Robber Council" at Ephesus as evidence.

In displaying Jenson's appreciation both for the role of the hierarchy and for the crucial role of the laity and the ways in which they should mutually benefit each other

Having argued for a universal pastor and having offered a sympathetic defense of a certain line of Catholic interpretation of that role, Jenson addresses the question why this office should be located in Rome. Pragmatic answers have been recognized in ecumenical dialogue. In official Anglican-Roman Catholic dialogues, it was agreed that the ancient church recognized Rome as a principle center regarding things related to the universal church, and that since Rome is the only see that makes any claims to universal primacy, it is appropriate that if the church finds visible unity in the future, the Roman see should hold a position of primacy. Jenson supports such pragmatic reasoning. He states:

> It is clear that the unity of the church cannot in fact now be restored except with a universal pastor located at Rome. And this is already sufficient reason to say the churches now not in communion with the church of Rome are very severely "wounded." Just so it is sufficient reason to say also that the restoration of those churches' communion with Rome is the peremptory will of God.[173]

Jenson then provides a brief (and seemingly halfhearted) attempt at legitimizing Roman primacy through a "historical initiating understanding" of its ancient development based on the fact that it was the church in Rome, rather than the Roman pope per se, which held primacy as a touchstone of fidelity to apostolic teaching. But he concludes tentatively, "Probably we must judge: identification of the universal pastorate with the Roman episcopacy is not strictly irreversible. On the other hand, hard cases make bad law."[174]

For Jenson to support the mandate for a universal pastorate (and to a lesser degree its location in Rome) is not to say that Jenson is uncritical of its practice. Indeed, Jenson takes seriously Pope John Paul II's proclamation in a 1995 encyclical that the exercising of the primacy is "open to a new situation." The pope then invites Christians who are in "real but imperfect communion" with Rome "to engage with me in patient and fraternal dialogue on

---

in sacrificial love, I am reminded of a similar portrayal by John Henry Newman in a remarkable little book he wrote amidst the controversial pronouncements of the First Vatican Council, *On Consulting the Faithful in Matters of Doctrine*. Newman believed no portion of the church could be *safely* neglected in matters of doctrine (104) and that while there was a necessary *kind* of authority in the teaching office, the laity provided a unique witness to the tradition that must be attended to by the teaching office, but which could not operate alone. He considered the *consensus fidelium* to be "a sort of instinct, or φρόνημα, deep in the bosom of the mystical body of Christ" and "a direction of the Holy Ghost," 73.

173. Jenson, *ST* II, 247.

174. Ibid., 248.

this subject."[175] Jenson believes this challenge should be taken up, and he has taken steps in that direction.[176]

Jenson concludes his discussion of the church's teaching office by drawing attention back to the church as communion. If one focuses on his discussion of office and authority to the exclusion of his broader ecclesiology and its images (e.g., polity, body of Christ, etc.), he believes one would come away with a distorted view of his overall ecclesiology. He takes Orthodoxy's vision of the hierarchy as *itself communion* as his final word (though in his view it is perhaps least realized in the Orthodox churches): a communion modeled on the triune God, in which authority and hierarchy are marked not by domination but by love and sharing. Since the church exists by anticipation of full inclusion in this "differentiated, perichoretic and reciprocally hierarchical" triune life (to use a phrase noted earlier), it will repeatedly fail at all levels to realize this perfectly, but this must continue to shape its vision and remain its hope.[177] If the church is seen merely as an institution resulting from Christ's foundation apart from the establishing role of the Spirit at Pentecost, the church will slip into institutionalism, and the only escape will be to run to the opposite problem, individual spiritualism. Institution and charism must be seen in their mutuality, as reflecting the mutual and distinct Trinitarian roles in establishing the church.[178] Those within free churches should appreciate Jenson's appeal to the Spirit to protect against rigid institutionalism, but they should also heed his warning about sitting light with regard to the institution and devolving into the kind of individualistic spiritualism that the free church has been so successful in producing.

175. John Paul II, *Ut Unum Sint*, 95–96.

176. Carl Braaten and Jenson edited a collection of essays from a broad spectrum of ecclesiastical perspectives, precisely in response to this invitation by the pope, *Church Unity and the Papal Office*. For his own responses and challenges to the pope, see *ST* II, 248, and his response in "The Future of the Papacy."

177. Jenson, *ST* II, 249. Gabriel Fackre challenges Jenson's "episcopocentric" and "subordinationist" arguments for the church's structure in favor of a structure derived from a commitment to the priesthood of all believers where office holders and laity are mutually submissive, a view that is in turn based on a symmetrical understanding of Trinitarian relations of mutual submission. He asserts that Jenson argues for both symmetrical and asymmetrical Trinitarian relations and so is inconsistent, "Lutheran *Capax* Lives," 101. Fackre does not seem to appreciate the nuance in Jenson's Trinitarian thought or the weighty role he gives to the laity, as we have observed. Further, one must wonder how an office holder could exercise *any* authority in a relationship that was completely symmetrical.

178. Jenson, *Unbaptized God*, 135. See also *ST* II, 280.

Conclusion

In 2003, Robert Jenson together with Carl Braaten assembled an ecumenical group of scholars to address the widely recognized problem that the ecumenical movement had stalled out. The result (*In One Body Through the Cross*) was a published proposal for Christian unity that attempted to reinvigorate the agenda of the 1961 New Delhi statement with its urgent call for visible Christian unity. In their preface, Jenson and Braaten assert that this endeavor was undertaken with the firm conviction that ecumenism is not simply a trend with which Christians may or may not choose to involve themselves. Rather, based on the priestly prayer of John 17, it is a mandate for authentic Christian faith. In trying to rekindle ecumenical energy, they recognize the need to invite new players onto the ecumenical field, especially those who have been left out, such as evangelicals and Pentecostals, groups which often see ecumenism as a waste of time or a distraction from the task of evangelizing. These groups must be brought into the discussion, not only because they are among the fastest growing Christian groups in the world, but also because evangelization is impeded when visible unity is not displayed.[179]

The Princeton Proposal recognizes widespread complacency concerning ecclesial division and states that one of the reasons for division is that Christian traditions tend to nurture their distinct identities and special distinguishing marks ahead of the one communion of Christ.[180] As we observed in the second chapter, even those within the free church tradition who are calling for a deep engagement with the church's wider tradition often do so with the express concern to prop up whatever specific traditions they belong to. Throughout the course of his career, Jenson has increasingly been willing to place the unity of the one body of Christ ahead of the maintenance of his Lutheran tradition, and has often suffered within his own ecclesial context as a result. Those within the free church tradition who press questions of unity and authority much further could suffer the same fate within their own tradition.

Jenson's theology is compelling largely because of its insistence on visibility and embodiment. Surely, Jenson's theology is at key points shocking to those with traditional sensitivities, and while we may not follow Jenson

179. Braaten and Jenson, *Ecumenical Future*, vii–viii. The attempt to reach out to these thus far sidelined voices is evident in the inclusion of Telford Work's essay titled "Speaking for the Spirit in the Time of Division."

180. *In One Body Through the Cross*, 32.

in his more radical proposals, he challenges us to take the incarnation with full ontological seriousness.[181] He challenges us to think about why participation in the life of the triune God through the *incarnate* Christ must not be overspiritualized, a challenge greatly needed within the free church tradition. As a result, the visibility of the church receives its full weight. The actual practice of the Eucharist ("visible words") finds its place in the center of an actual and embodied gathering which is established in communion precisely through its sharing of Christ, who is embodied in the community through the visible loaf and the cup.

Based on his firm commitment to the church as the visible body of Christ, Jenson is able to honestly acknowledge that the gospel has from the beginning been tied to a gathered and witnessing community that sees to the speaking of the gospel, the gospel that has been mediated through a complex process of tradition. This tradition has involved instruments of authority that seek to maintain the unity of the church and its proclamation across time. Jenson has argued that while Scripture has been at the heart of this authority, it never has and cannot function apart from the church's larger tradition and a living teaching office. Nonetheless, his arguments do not mask over the difficulties involved with observing the complex of authorities that have been at work in mediating the gospel. We recall that for Jenson, neither any one of these instruments nor all of them taken together can guarantee the faithfulness of our proclamation. Rather (as we have seen several times), the church operates from faith that the church is still the church, and if this is true, then we may believe that the Spirit has seen to the church's historical continuity through these structures.[182]

Jenson's confidence in these instruments has to do with the present existence of the church, which he ascribes to the Spirit's work drawing the church through history toward its final end in the triune God. For Jenson, this is not to say that these instruments are perfect or that things could not have happened differently. It is only to argue that they are *adequate* and that this is *in fact* the way the church has been preserved thus far. They have proven *useful* in the hands of the Spirit, and so we can take them as legitimate and, in hindsight, necessary instruments of authority.[183]

181. David Hart equally appreciates this aspect of Jenson's work, even while radically disagreeing with much of his work, "Lively God of Robert Jenson," 33–34.

182. Jenson, *ST* I, 25.

183. Jenson likes to speak of these instruments as "gifts" of God, "Theological Autobiography, to Date," 52.

One is left wondering why Jenson remains within the Lutheran church, given his increasing move toward a Roman Catholic position on these matters (largely supplemented by contributions from Orthodox theology). In the preface to *The Catholicity of the Reformation*, a book they coedited, Robert Jenson and Carl Braaten claim that "catholicity" was the intent of the Reformation, which sought to renew the one church of the creeds. Following Ignatius, they define catholicity as "wholeness," and this wholeness includes many things such as Scripture, apostolic tradition, sacraments, ecumenical creeds, worship, and the ministry. Jenson and Braaten then say that there are "degrees of catholicity" with full catholicity being an eschatological reality. In some ways, the groups that descended from the Reformation have resulted in a "diminishment of catholicity" (e.g., loss of episcopal office).

With this understanding in view, "catholicity" is not to be found *only* in the Roman Catholic Church. It may be diminished in certain ways among certain non-Roman groups, but that does not mean it is not diminished in certain ways within the Roman church herself, especially if the church exists only in anticipation of its fullness. And if there is a certain "degree" of catholicity in different Christian groups outside of Rome, then to abandon these groups and "go to Rome" is to abandon catholicity in those groups and move to a church that is still not yet completely whole, partly because it is not in communion with other Christian communities. Perhaps because Jenson can still perceive (to some significant degree) the one church of the creeds in his Lutheran tradition, he believes that a move to Rome would be from one wounded church to another, even if the latter is less wounded. Perhaps he believes the way to wholeness is not abandoning one wound in favor of a lesser wound, but in seeing that someone needs to remain with the greater wounds for the wholeness of the entire body, until such a time as the wounded limb is determined to be dead. Apparently, he has not made that judgment about his own tradition.

4

Rowan Williams on Unity and Authority

Introduction

WE NOW TURN OUR attention to Rowan Williams, who currently serves as the archbishop of Canterbury, the preeminent seat of ecclesial authority within the worldwide Anglican Communion. Prior to his move to Canterbury, Williams served as the bishop of Monmouth and then as the archbishop of Wales, finally assuming his role as archbishop of Canterbury in 2003. Williams brings to his pastoral role a distinguished career in academic theology that culminated in taking up the prestigious position of the Lady Margaret Professor of Theology at Oxford in 1986. Williams's sprawling corpus covers a bewildering range, both in content and style. He is widely recognized for his intellectual acumen as well as for his daunting and sometimes impenetrable academic writing. Although he is no systematician,[1] his work consistently renders the portrait of a man who does theology from within the church and who has an unflagging commitment to working toward the visible unity of the one body of Christ.

There are several things that make Williams an attractive yet challenging conversation partner for those within the free church tradition. First, as with Jenson, Scripture occupies a central position in Williams's work. His

1. The nonsystematic nature of his work is partly to do with the often occasional nature of his work, but it also has to do with some basic methodological convictions. For his clearest statement about his theological method (to the degree that he acknowledges one), see the prologue to his collection of theological essays titled *On Christian Theology* (hereafter *OCT*). Here he briefly offers a very nonfoundational methodology in which he locates three modes or styles of theology: the celebratory, the communicative, and the critical. Despite the unsystematic nature of his work, there are discernible and regular themes. For a very good introduction to the general terrain of Rowan Williams's theology, see Higton, *Difficult Gospel*.

understanding of the nature of Scripture may cause discomfort for many within conservative free church settings, but they can at least affirm his insistence that all Christian discourse must emerge from and return to Scripture. Second, while Williams ultimately cannot subscribe to a free church model, the "local" church receives a strong emphasis within his theology.[2] Third, Williams's theology strongly challenges certain tendencies or commitments often found within the free church tradition, especially individualism, biblicism, primitivism, and congregationalism. As we will see shortly, these latter challenges arise especially from Williams's firm insistence on the inescapability of historical contingency and linguistic exchange in the process of human knowing (an insistence that is at odds with what sometimes seems to be an inadequate attention to historical contingency within the free church tradition, which I shall argue in chapter 5 is the case with McClendon's work). As a result, at the core of Williams's thought is a strong emphasis on the principle of mutuality, along with its attendant virtues of truthfulness, self-critique, and apophatic reserve.

While Scripture is of central importance for Williams, in his view its authority is bound up with its relation to the church's tradition and its teaching office. Further, because of his great commitment to the principle of ever widening levels of mutuality, Williams eventually argues for an account of visible ecclesial unity expressed through a web of global relationships among local churches, with the local churches represented to each other primarily by their bishops. The central force of the web image, in contrast with the Roman hierarchical model (advocated by Jenson) as well as the fragmented free church model, is the acknowledgment of dependent yet decentralized relationality. Jenson and Williams have much in common with which to challenge those in the free church tradition, but Williams's theology will add to Jenson's strengths some important questions about mutuality and truthfulness and how they impinge upon visible unity. And in turn, we shall see that Jenson's theology presses back with questions of its own. I do not intend to primarily place Jenson and Williams in tension with each other but to use them together to create a space for conversation within the free church tradition.

2. In Williams's usage, "local" usually refers to a province of parishes gathered around a bishop rather than to a single worshipping congregation as it generally indicates within the free church tradition.

History, Knowledge, and Truthfulness

Inseparable from Rowan Williams's theology as a whole are some deeply held convictions about history, language, and knowledge, convictions that ultimately impinge upon his understanding of ecclesial unity and authority. A central conviction detectable across the breadth of Williams's career is that knowledge and language cannot be separated from historical contingency. One of his earliest books already sounds this note loudly, developing it from within Christianity's own historical resources. A primary goal of this early work is to demonstrate how differing conceptions of history have affected various Christian understandings of spirituality. If Christians affirm that meaning and reality are only accessible by reference to a series of historical events around the man Jesus of Nazareth, they close off the possibility that reality is somehow accessed through a flight into timelessness and away from the particularities of history.[3] Much in the Gnostic and Greek world of thought tempted some early Christians toward an understanding of knowledge and salvation that depended on abstracting away from historical contingency, but there has been a steady stream of Christian spirituality from the beginning that resisted this move, despite the complexities involved with embracing contingency as part of the salvation process.[4]

Williams's emphasis on historical contingency developed from theological resources is complemented by his philosophical indebtedness to Ludwig Wittgenstein, whom he labels "the greatest of twentieth-century philosophers."[5] Williams credits Wittgenstein (and Dietrich Bonhoeffer) with unmasking the illusion of an inner authentic self living "inside" a body, an illusion promulgated by the so-called masters of suspicion (e.g., Freud

---

3. R. Williams, *Wound of Knowledge*, 11–12.

4. See especially his account of Gregory of Nyssa, who resists the false distinction between a timeless soul and imprisoning body. In Gregory's view, change through the contingencies of life become the soul's only security as it moves constantly and restlessly toward God, ibid., 62–72.

5. R. Williams, *Why Study the Past?*, 90. Williams's indebtedness to Wittgenstein brings him within the proximity of other recent theological approaches, most notably the so-called postliberal approach. James McClendon, who will figure prominently in the next chapter, is closely associated with the postliberal approach, so this brief overview will help provide a general orientation to McClendon's theology as well. But, as I will argue in the next chapter, while some of McClendon's strengths emerge from his engagement with this general philosophical approach, some of his key weaknesses emerge, perhaps, from not following through with its implications thoroughly enough. Williams's work may provide some needed augmentation to McClendon's valuable contributions to the free church tradition.

and Marx). By contrast, Wittgenstein locates the human self at the level of the "profundity of surfaces," according to which selves are constructed through cultural/linguistic engagement with what is "other." He (and Bonhoeffer) "presuppose that to interpret the symbolic, linguistic, and behavioral complex that 'addresses' us in the human world is to have one's own pattern of speech and action conditioned (not determined) by it."[6]

The self (or "soul" as Williams leads us to call it) is *made*. It is "not fixed or obvious, not the result of a neutral, natural process, but is the deposit of choices, accidents."[7] Even inward feelings and desires are shaped by the language and practices we have learned through negotiation with others. Such a view challenges a timeless, authentic interiority to which appeal can be made as a center of unchallengeable authenticity.[8] The rejection of such a timeless interiority puts some serious questions to those within the free church tradition for whom "inner experience" is often considered an uncontestable court of appeal, barred off as it supposedly is from historical contingency or dependence on any frame of reference outside itself aside from the Bible, which is read and interpreted individualistically.

These Wittgensteinian observations address not only *how* we know anything but also *what* knowledge actually is. Since being human is bound up with involvement in language and culture, knowledge turns out to be the creative reordering of what is given. Williams argues:

> [Humans are] looking for *and* creating meaning: patterns of order, schemes of communication in which the confusing experience of life in the world to which we belong (and to which we did not choose to belong) is drawn into language, into the ever-extending web of sharing perception, experience, selfhood itself, that constitutes human being as human.[9]

Williams's use of the web as a metaphor for knowledge is significant, and I will later return to this image as I attempt to draw a direct connection between Williams's epistemological and ecclesiological commitments. Rather

6. R. Williams, "Suspicion of Suspicion," in *Wrestling With Angels* (hereafter *WWA*), 186–202, esp. 197. Increasingly, Williams came to recognize these same themes in Hegel. See, for example, "Logic and Spirit in Hegel," in *WWA*, 35–52; "Between Politics and Metaphysics," in *WWA*, 53–76.

7. R. Williams, *Lost Icons*, 111. The idea of the social construction of the soul is central to this entire book. It is especially prominent in the fourth chapter.

8. Ibid., 103, 141. See also "'Religious Realism,'" in *WWA*, 228–54, esp. 234, 251, n. 18.

9. R. Williams, "Nature of a Sacrament," in *OCT*, 197–208, esp. 197–98.

than knowledge being about conclusions or a fixed and unmediated correspondence between inner conceptual representations and outward reality,
it is bound up with receiving and extending connections made in specific
times and places. Summarily, "We learn by being reminded; we understand
by chains of association, not by the delivery of a self-standing concept."[10]

A natural question at this point concerns the possibility of arriving at
truth, an important issue for any discussion of ecclesial unity and authority.
Does a cultural/linguistic approach such as Williams advocates lead us inevitably toward relativism? While Williams admits that his approach entails
that perception is always incomplete, that in no way suggests that there is
no possibility for a truthful relation between speech and reality. Knowledge
is a *process* of generation and re-presentation. What is "real" is active rather
than static, a moveable *pattern* where one generative form of life in one place
can be repeatedly taken up and "lived again" in another place. As Williams
says, "Re-presentation assumes that there is excess in what presents itself for
knowing."[11] As we shall see, these observations will bear fruit within Williams's understanding of revelation, tradition, and how the church comes to
know what it knows.

What follows for Williams from such an understanding of history
and knowledge is an intense interest in truthfulness that pervades every
aspect of his writing. While Williams is not afraid to discuss truth and reality, he is more often concerned to urge his readers to account for their
own truthful*ness* in the knowing process, a challenge those within the free
church should face without fear or defensiveness. Humans must actively and
repeatedly acknowledge their own limited perspectives as they attempt to
seek for meaningful connections and coherence.[12] The result is a truthfulness marked primarily by the willingness to self-critique and to take time
with the strange other, since it is only through such relational and historical
processes that we become what we are.[13] The ecclesiological implications
of all the foregoing are far-reaching. It is possible to argue that some free
church accounts of knowledge, especially as it relates to revelation, are an
attempted flight from time and historical contingency, an impulse that has

10. R. Williams, "Unity of the Church and the Unity of the Bible," 6–7. See also *Grace
and Necessity*, 137.

11. R. Williams, *Grace and Necessity*, 137–40.

12. R. Williams, *Lost Icons*, 138.

13. R. Williams, "Suspicion of Suspicion," in *WWA*, 199–200. In a footnote on this
point, Williams quotes Wittgenstein: "This is how philosophers should salute each other:
'Take your time!'" 202, n. 60.

been a perennial struggle within the Christian faith, but one that the church has regularly felt the need to resist for theological reasons. If such accounts are resisted, the kind of individualism and nonnegotiated ecclesial identity that the free church tradition has promulgated thus far comes in for some serious questioning.

One particular expression of Williams's concern with truthfulness is his strongly apophatic theological impulse, or what in traditional language is termed the *via negativa* (the negative way; or "negative theology"). He absorbed this impulse largely from his engagement with Eastern theology, especially as it was mediated to him through the work of the Orthodox theologian Vladimir Lossky.[14] For Williams, the apophatic impulse does not mean that truth is completely beyond human perception. It functions, rather, as a check against the human tendency to control its subjects through its words and images, especially when the subject is God.[15] A commitment to apophatic reservation does not mean words are unimportant or have no real reference to truth.[16] Our words matter. We should not "romanticize idle inarticulacy or take refuge in the 'ineffable' quality of our subject matter."[17] Yet, negative theology is always aware of its location in an ongoing and incomplete process of linguistic debate and exchange, the "hermeneutical spiral." It is a *metanoia* (repentance) of the intellect.[18] It is a proper humility that results from taking both one's locatedness and the otherness of God seriously, a willingness to open one's words and ideas to judgment. Williams's apophatic reserve greatly influences the way he speaks of doctrinal "truth" and how it functions authoritatively. It is also likely to be one of the most uncomfortable aspects of Williams's theology from a typical free church perspective.[19]

14. Along with Williams's doctoral dissertation, "The Theology of Vladimir Niko-laievich Lossky," see also an essay-length treatment of Lossky's construal of the *via negativa* in "Lossky, the *Via Negativa*," in *WWA*, 1–24; and "Eastern Orthodox Theology," 506.

15. See *Christ on Trial*, 40.

16. Christian apophaticism is always rooted in the concrete life of Jesus Christ. Williams, "Deflections of Desire."

17. R. Williams, "Theological Integrity," in *OCT*, 3–15, esp. 15.

18. R. Williams, "Lossky, the *Via Negativa*," in *WWA*, 2. He takes this idea from Lossky, *Mystical Theology of the Eastern Church*, 37–39. See also R. Williams, "Trinity and Revelation," in *OCT*, 131–47, esp. 146.

19. For an overview of apophaticism in Williams's theology as well as some questions from a theologically conservative viewpoint to which someone from the free church tradition might be able to relate, see Moody, "Hidden Center." With regard to the questions he raises near the end of his treatment of Williams, I believe Moody has not read Williams carefully enough, though that is admittedly a challenging task for anyone.

The Church as the Body of Christ

Before we proceed to consider how Williams articulates the related authorities of Scripture, tradition, and the teaching office, we will briefly sketch his vision of the church's nature and calling. The reason for doing so is that, for Williams, authority is recognizable and legitimate only in relation to certain goals. In this view, we do not begin by determining what is authoritative by virtue of some essential quality it may possess. Rather, we must begin by asking, what are these loci of authority authoritative *for*? Only when we have the Christian vision properly before us can we begin to speak about what is authoritative and how it is authoritative for promoting that vision, a vision that, in Williams's theology, is most centrally about visible social unity.

The Social Body of Christ

For Rowan Williams, the Christian vision points to an *essentially* social reality embodied in the church. To say this already puts on alert any conception of the church as a voluntary association that is instrumental to helping individuals pursue worthy goals, a conception that has been the functional ecclesiological model for many within the free church tradition.[20] In fact, the church's good news is most centrally that a new kind of humanity is possible, one rooted in peace and unity rather than hostility and division, a social reality that is the direct result of Jesus' resurrection (Eph 2, Col 1:20).[21] It is not enough simply to say that the event of Jesus' life, death, and resurrection provides an external model to be imitated. We must say that Jesus' life, death, and resurrection *constitute* new possibilities for relationship both with Jesus (and thus with God) and with each other.[22]

The newly constituted relationships that the event of Jesus' life makes possible are to take on a specific shape, that of mutual *gift*. Williams regularly

20. R. Williams regularly denounces such a conception. See, for example, "Being a People," 11; "Lutheran Catholic"; "Mission-Shaped Church Conference—Keynote Address."

21. R. Williams, "Incarnation and the Renewal of Community," in *OCT*, 225–38, esp. 233; "Resurrection and Peace," in *OCT*, 265–75, esp. 265.

22. R. Williams, "Trinity and Pluralism," in *OCT*, 167–80, esp. 172; "On Doing Theology," 4–5. Williams resists accounts, such as the "incarnationalist" account, that see the value of the incarnation as "filling up" the natural systems of relation found in the world. Rather, the Christian message is that of radically new possibilities resulting from a common sharing in Christ's paschal event. This is the basic argument in "Incarnation and the Renewal of Community," in *OCT*.

appeals to the notion of mutual *gift* to describe the Trinitarian life of God, the life that ultimately provides the impetus and rationale for new relations in Christ.[23] Contrary to relationships marked by competitive self-interest and control of the other, relations in Christ are to be marked by creative generosity and compassion that revelation teaches us is "the most basic reality there is."[24] This most basic reality is revealed most clearly in the life of Jesus of Nazareth, who "gives himself up" for his people (Eph 5:25).

Because Williams sees *gift* as being at the very heart of the Christian vision, he regularly gravitates to Paul's description of the church as the body of Christ. Paul describes the church as a body, a system of differentiated and interdependent parts working harmoniously for the building up of the entire body (1 Cor 10:23; Rom 14:19), where one's acts are gifts for the deepening of faith in others.[25] Moreover, Paul's understanding of "building up" entails that believers are involved in *constructing* each other's humanity by bringing them more fully into the shape of Christ's life, an activity that is their "fundamental form of relation."[26] It is a social vision where one's particularity and a common life do not exist in a threatening competitive relationship but in generous interdependence. To return to our focal image, Williams can speak of the "web of gifts, which is Christ's church."[27] Such a social vision of essential interdependence challenges any understanding of the church that sees membership in it as voluntary, merely supportive of an individual's personal and immediate relation to God.

23. R. Williams, "Incarnation and the Renewal of Community," in *OCT*, 226. Rhys Bezzant expresses concern over Williams's application of "social trinitarianism." Aside from scant evidence of such a move in Scripture, the doctrine of the Trinity was designed to affirm the deity of the Son and the Spirit and should be used with caution in applying it to anything it was never designed to address, "Ecclesiology of Rowan Williams," 23–24. As should become apparent throughout the rest of this chapter, Bezzant appears to miss what view of Scripture and dogma would allow Williams to make such a developmental move with integrity. Williams, however, does acknowledge in an interview that he regularly has to rein in his urge to apply the "social Trinity" model too quickly. See Cunningham, "Living the Questions," 26.

24. R. Williams, *Ray of Darkness*, 140.

25. R. Williams, "Nobody Knows Who I Am," in *OCT*, 276–89, esp. 285.

26. R. Williams, "Incarnation and the Renewal of Community," in *OCT*, 232–33. See also "Archbishop's Lecture Given at the Pontifical Academy of Social Sciences, Rome."

27. R. Williams, *Resurrection*, 37–38.

The Visible Body of Christ

To declare that the Christian vision is essentially concerned with a social reality is not quite enough, especially in light of the idea of the "invisible church" which (as we noticed in chapter 1) has often been used within the free church tradition to account for the unity of the church. Williams, by contrast, never turns to the concept of the "invisible church" to flesh out the church's essential unity. He writes:

> [God] calls into being a tangible human community, whose common language is the carrier of its common relatedness to Christ's invitation. Move away from this, and the visible reality of the Church becomes something almost optional, in a way that makes more abstract the interdependence of believers on one another— their interdependence precisely as visible, material, historical and language-using subjects.[28]

As we have seen, it is the flight away from history and into abstraction that Williams regularly resists. "God's way is to be incarnate, fleshed out, in Jesus and in the friends of Jesus. Our way too is forward and into the flesh, not away from it; the love of bodies is the condition for learning, sharing and growing."[29]

At one point, Williams states that one of the most basic definitions of the church is that it is the place where Jesus is *visibly* present in the world.[30] To say that the church is the body of Christ is to say that, precisely in its mutual dependence of parts, it is his tangible presence in the world.[31] One of the reasons for insisting on the visibility of the church relates to the church's role as a witnessing community, as "essentially missionary."[32]

To highlight the visibility of the church, Williams often reverts to terms such as *people* (in the political sense of *laos*) or *nation*, drawing especially on the language of 1 Peter 2:10. He suggests that the term *community*

28. R. Williams, *Why Study the Past?*, 109.

29. R. Williams, *Ray of Darkness*, 36. See also *Resurrection*, 93, where Williams again roots the visibility of the church in the incarnation.

30. R. Williams, *Tokens of Trust*, 128.

31. R. Williams, "Trinity and Pluralism," in *OCT*, 172. See also *Resurrection*, 56; "Theology and the Churches," 13–15. Williams is careful to indicate that this does not mean that the church exhausts Jesus' identity or activity. See, for example, "Between the Cherubim," in *OCT*, 183–96, esp. 189.

32. R. Williams, "Judgement of the World," in *OCT*, 29–43, esp. 31. This resonates with certain free church theologians who are giving greater attention to the visibility of the church, as we noticed in chapter two.

can be too ambiguous. The church is not just a collection of like-minded people who have some inner sense of connectedness; rather, "There is a given common ground for the identity of Christian believers that is more like belonging to an ethnic or linguistic group than anything else and that has a public structure that manifests this common ground."[33] Williams argues that if the church is called to be a very real, tangible "nation" existing as a public witness to a new way of being human, it needs practices and life patterns that remind the church of its distinctive calling. He says, "A church which does not at least possess certain features of a 'sect' cannot act as an agent of transformation."[34] The public and political structure of this "people" is bound up most centrally with its distinctive, self-identifying acts of sacramental fellowship (reading certain texts, baptizing, and eucharistic fellowship) by which the church takes perceptible shape and receives its identity as a community of *gift*.[35] It is possible, however, for such practices to become severed from their essentially communal purpose. Williams says that "the most lethal distortion of baptism," for example, is what William Stringfellow called its "privatization." When this occurs, baptism no longer signals entry into a new citizenship that relativizes all other commitments; rather it (among other things) merely indicates individual commitment to Christ. He specifically attaches this truncated understanding of baptism to

33. R. Williams, "Being a People," 11–12. See also "The Lutheran Catholic." The visibility envisaged here is evidenced in part by the tensions between early Christian communities and the surrounding societies because the Christian society refused the authority of prevailing accounts of status and power, "Nobody Knows Who I Am," in *OCT*, 284–85.

34. R. Williams, "Incarnation and the Renewal of Community," in *OCT*, 233. In arguing for the church having "certain features of a 'sect,'" he is in sympathy with George Lindbeck, who argued for the importance of churches as "communal enclaves" concerned with socialization and mutual support (Lindbeck, *Nature of Doctrine*, 126–27). Williams, however, is also concerned with what he believes to be the church's responsibility to restore "an authentically public discourse" in its social setting, or else the church will be relegated to the position of a stylistic preference in a pluralistic culture. He says, "The communal enclave, if it is not to be a ghetto, must make certain claims on the possibility of a global community, and act accordingly." See "Judgement of the World," in *OCT*, 36. One could attribute such a statement merely to the fact that Williams speaks within the context of an established church, a reality that is clearly in view in this essay. However, it is primarily a *theological* conviction for Williams that the church exists to announce in word and deed a new humanity of universal significance. In doing so, it brings the onlooking world to a moment of "judgment," a moment of decision for or against this new humanity of peace.

35. R. Williams, *Wound of Knowledge*, 31; "Resurrection and Peace," in *OCT*, 273; "Trinity and Ontology," in *OCT*, 148–66, esp. 164.

"most Churches practicing believers' baptism."[36] Whatever the theological merits of believer's baptism movements in history, it is not too difficult to recognize the truth of Stringfellow's observation within much contemporary free church practice. The language of "personal commitment" and Jesus as one's "personal Lord and Savior" often occlude, or eliminate, any meaningful sense of living within a new social context. And to state matters more directly than Williams, often in contemporary expressions of the free church tradition, baptism plays more of a peripheral role than a central role even in the process of making one's personal commitment.[37]

Authority within the Body of Christ

If the Christian vision is inseparable from the visible display of a new humanity founded in peace, then the urgency for visible ecclesial unity is heightened. Once the necessity of attending to visible unity arises, the discussion of authority naturally follows. If visible unity matters, then some things simply are not options, and these things are largely determined by reference to authorities. As Williams says, "Authority, in the most basic sense, has to do with precisely this limiting of options. . . . What is 'authoritative' clarifies the distinction between the essential and the peripheral, and persuades me of the superior *significance* of certain features of the matter."[38]

As the source event for Christian faith, the root of authority is the life and death of Jesus Christ.[39] The issue then becomes a matter of discerning what derivative authorities mediate the central authority of the Christ event.

36. R. Williams, "Being a People," 15–16. The reference to Stringfellow is from Stringfellow, *Keeper of the Word*, 159–62. Williams also acknowledges here that another distortion of baptism conceives of it in terms of "familial piety and resignation in the structures of existing society (where infant baptism is practiced)." Elsewhere, he says, "The more Christianity ceases to be a distinctive communal life to which adult persons choose to commit themselves, the more this tension is eroded" (i.e., the tension between the churchly society and its surrounding worldly society), "No One Knows Who I Am," in *OCT*, 285. These are interesting observations for an archbishop of Canterbury to make, given the established nature of the Church of England. Obviously, he is providing a certain level of self-critique. If he is right in his assessment of baptism here, it seems he owes a more thoroughgoing defense of the practice of infant baptism. Secondly, while it is true that believer's baptism has often become an individualistic affair, the roots of believer's baptism in the Anabaptist tradition might offer a closer parallel to the vision he is recommending here than contemporary Anglican approaches.

37. This is more or less true depending upon which free church community one assesses.

38. R. Williams, "Authority and the Bishop in the Church," 90.

39. R. Williams, "On Doing Theology," 6.

Like Jenson, though with different accents, Williams locates authority in the classical trio of the Bible, the church's tradition, and the episcopal teaching office of the church.[40] Williams also attaches authority to the church's central sacramental actions, but since in his theology (as with Jenson's) these are bound up so integrally with the teaching office, we will consider them together under our discussion of the teaching office.

The Authority of Scripture

Revelation and Scripture

Williams is resistant to theology that treats revelation as the communication of otherworldly propositional truth in a fairly unambiguous way (what he calls "veil lifting") and that does not occur within the ordinary processes by which we learn speech. Such theology tends to treat revelation as the communication of something that is finished and fixed, a static given that one attempts to possess.[41] The free church tradition has tended to operate with an understanding of revelation precisely along the lines of what Williams is critiquing here.

Taking a cue from Paul Ricoeur's work on revelation and poetics,[42] Williams argues that revelation has to do with what is *generative* in our experience—generative of new frames of reference, new language for speaking about God, new possibilities for living and for new debate. The major biblical examples he adduces are the exodus, the giving of Torah, and the appearance of Jesus.[43] These foundational and generative events are not revelation in the way of closed and fixed content to be endlessly repeated. Rather, as

40. R. Williams, *Anglican Identities*, 2.

41. For example, see R. Williams, "Trinity and Revelation," in *OCT*, 131–33. Williams indicates here that such an ahistorical understanding of revelation is illustrated not only by outdated propositional accounts of revelation but also liberal theology that seeks to appeal to some ahistorical core behind all historical contingency. He also criticizes Barth's account of revelation which appears early in *Church Dogmatics* in which Williams claims Barth isolated the revelatory event from historical conditions by arguing that revelation occurs *in*, but not *as part of*, history. For his most sustained examination and critique of Barth's account of revelation, see "Barth on the Triune God," in *WWA*, 106–49. He argues that Barth is too concerned with certainty of knowledge in the theological enterprise. He tempers his assessment of Barth in a more recent reflection. See "Author's Introduction," in *WWA*, xv–xvi.

42. See especially Ricoeur, "Toward a Hermeneutic of the Idea of Revelation," in *Essays on Biblical Interpretation*, 73–118.

43. R. Williams, "Trinity and Revelation," in *OCT*, 133–36.

events with universal relevance, they must be able to fit and extend any human enterprise of finding meaning, and the result may not be described in advance. The significance of these events must be "learned" over time within the community that is formed by these events. Thus, revelation has to do not only with foundational generative events but also with the subsequent hermeneutical enterprise to extend the universal and unending potential of these events.[44] We can already begin to see at this point how Williams's account of revelation strains against a narrow adoption of the *sola scriptura* principle that has generally marked the free church tradition. If revelation is not primarily to do with fixed content but foundational generative events, then not only are the primitive responses to these events important, but so is the interpretive tradition that arises out of engagement with the foundational events as mediated through its first respondents. Here is one of the several reasons Williams eventually ascribes a certain authority to tradition.

How, then, does this understanding of revelation affect Williams's understanding of Scripture and the kind of authority it exercises within the body of Christ? Because Christian faith is rooted in foundational historical events, Williams is not bashful about affirming the "central and decisive" authority of Scripture, since Scripture is "the unique witness to those events."[45] Further, Scripture uniquely informs its readers about the nature of faith, about which we would know nothing apart from its witness. Across its breadth, Scripture lays out the story and content of God's call and demonstrates the nature of faith as a response to that call.[46] So along with being the normative witness to the foundational events, Scripture is the "normative story of response to God".[47]

While Scripture is uniquely authoritative in the Christian community, it is not unambiguously so. Williams certainly rejects accounts of Scripture that treat it as a well-defined container of fixed and easily unified content,

---

44. Ibid., 142–43, 147. Elsewhere, Williams contends, "The words in which revelation is first expressed are not solid, impenetrable containers of the mystery; they are living realities which spark recognition across even the deepest of gulfs between cultures, and generate new words native to diverse cultures which will in turn become alive and prompt fresh surprise and recognition," "Service to Celebrate the Bicentenary of the British and Foreign Bible Society."

45. R. Williams, "On Doing Theology," 7. Williams's deep commitment to the authority of Scripture is charmingly recounted by Oliver O'Donovan: "'Why, oh why,' he groaned, when wrestling with yet another ill-judged offering from the Liturgical Commission, 'will they not use the *Bible*?'" "Archbishop Rowan Williams," 6.

46. R. Williams, "On Doing Theology," 7–9.

47. R. Williams, "Theological Integrity," in *OCT*, 7.

accounts that have often been characteristic of many within the free church tradition. He also expresses concern over a more recent theological approach to Scripture, which at first glance bears resemblance to his own—particularly, the program of George Lindbeck. Part of Lindbeck's "postliberal" agenda is to challenge the liberal propensity to translate Scripture into contemporary categories, where the contemporary idioms and categories are the driving force of the interchange. Lindbeck believes it should work the other way around. As he puts it, "Intratextual theology redescribes reality within the scriptural framework rather than translating Scripture into extrascriptural categories."[48] Although sympathetic to Lindbeck's critique of liberalism, Williams expresses discomfort with the "territorial cast" of Lindbeck's expression which too simplistically conceives of Scripture as a bounded framework into which things are inserted. Williams responds, "The 'world of scripture,' so far from being a clear and readily definable territory, is an *historical* world in which meanings are discovered and recovered in action and encounter. To challenge the Church to immerse itself in its 'text' is to encourage it to engage with a history of such actions and encounters."[49] How God's people "learn" is not to be abstracted from the normal ways of learning through the processes of historical contingency, and this applies to the people we find producing Scripture as well.

This brief critique of Lindbeck opens the door for us to consider more fully Williams's own more complex understanding of Scripture which attends carefully to both its inner tensions and its continuities. How one deals with each of these has implications for how Scripture is to function authoritatively within the believing community and for how the unity of the church may be conceived. We will first address Williams's treatment of the complexities and tensions within Scripture. We will then demonstrate how Williams suggests we discern unity within Scripture: always, of course, in a way that aims at truthfulness.

History and the Literal Sense of Scripture

As mentioned in the previous chapter, recent years have seen an increasing swell of challenges against the long established hegemony of historical-critical methodology in the field of biblical studies. Critiques and alternative proposals have ranged far and wide, including proposals for returning to

48. Lindbeck, *Nature of Doctrine*, 118.
49. R. Williams, "Judgement of the World," *OCT*, 29–30.

"precritical" forms of exegesis.[50] Williams, however, has reservations about some of these proposals. He wonders how certain of these reactions against historical-critical modes of interpretation make room for a crucial component of precritical exegesis, namely, the primacy of Scripture's *sensus litteralis*. As contemporary interpreters grow more suspicious of looking for interpretations revolving around the normativity of authorial intent (a suspicion many within the free church tradition have not yet caught up to), or as they grow increasingly suspicious of the whole notion of normative meaning at all, what room is there for an authoritative level of reading that is bound to history, which is what precritical exegesis understood the *sensus litteralis* to be?[51] As we have seen, Williams will in no way countenance an interpretive strategy that sits light with respect to history.

To help in arguing for the primacy of the literal sense, Williams displays the distinction between literal and nonliteral senses of Scripture through the use of the corresponding terms *diachronic* and *synchronic*. A diachronic reading follows the text in a "dramatic" way, reading it on a time continuum as a sequence of changes and repeated patterns, a process likened to a performance of a drama or music. A synchronic reading treats the text as a "field of linguistic material" that functions as a closed system in which signs cross reference each other in any direction, an interpretive process more like analyzing the surface of a picture. In the diachronic approach, the unity of the text emerges in time. In the synchronic approach, unity occurs in something more like space.[52]

In Williams's view, the primary flaw with synchronic readings (allegorical, existential, etc.) taken alone is that they tend toward premature harmonies and unities by ignoring the inner historical processes of production by which the text comes to be, and ultimately this is not truthful. A diachronic reading "takes time" with the text, following sequentially its inner connections, progressions, conflicts, and contradictions.[53] Such a histori-

50. For examples provided by R. Williams, see "Discipline of Scripture," in *OCT*, 44–59, esp. 44; "Historical Criticism and Sacred Text," 217–19.

51. R. Williams, "Discipline of Scripture," in *OCT*, 44–45.

52. Ibid., 45. Williams's account of diachronic readings that search for patterns within Scripture is very similar to what is traditionally labeled "typology," and what, as noted in the previous chapter (see n. 87), Dawson labels "figural" as opposed to "figurative." We can see the similarities between Williams and Jenson at this point.

53. R. Williams, "Discipline of Scripture," in *OCT*, 46, 55. Earlier, we saw this emphasis on "taking time" in connection with his epistemology. Here we see it with explicit reference to the interpretation of Scripture. For Williams, Scripture reveals a historical process of learning, not disconnected from the general ways in which humans learn

cally oriented reading must be given a controlling force, since, as Aquinas argued,[54] the literal sense is whatever the author intends (which in the case of Scripture is God), and God's intention is primarily revealed in historical events, not in the text itself. Thus all readings must be answerable to the literal sense which is inseparable from history.[55] A dramatic mode of exegesis that takes the history of production seriously does not see "understanding" as a "*moment* of interpretive perception,"[56] as if Scripture were a finished body of information to be mastered. Rather, it follows the historical developments and negotiations within and among texts as meaning is sequentially (i.e., historically) produced.

It is because of his great concern for the historical processes of Scripture that Williams insists it would be naïve to try to discard the insights that have come from critical scholarship. A text is a *product*, not a neutral archaeological site. Scripture clearly expresses its own "produced" character as it reveals an inner literary history of cross-referencing and rereading of earlier texts.[57] So we seek the meanings of God not apart from but "with an eye to tensions within the text, to the voices on its edge, to what it opposes or suppresses, so far as we can discern."[58] Historical critical tools are essential for Williams, because they help enhance a diachronic reading of Scripture by clarifying the movement *between* texts. It is important on a good first reading to clarify as much as possible the "world of the text" in order to see how

---

within a linguistic world. For examples of the kinds of conflicts within Scripture that Williams has in mind, see 53–54.

54. Williams locates the first unambiguous defense of the primacy of the "literal sense" in Thomas Aquinas, *Summa Theologiae*, I.1.ix–x.

55. R. Williams, "Discipline of Scripture," in *OCT*, 46–47. Williams is careful to distinguish his (and Aquinas's) use of "literal" from what has become common among fundamentalism. Even Aquinas did not believe that the literal sense meant that all scriptural statements were a detailed description of real states of affairs. He made room for the different genres within Scripture and their different functions. According to Williams, fundamentalism correctly indentified the "literal" with the "historical" (in concert with traditional understandings) but made the mistake of associating the "historical" with exact representations of "fact," 48. For a similar assessment, see Frei, *Eclipse of Biblical Narrative*, ch. 1.

56. R. Williams, "Discipline of Scripture," in *OCT*, 49.

57. R. Williams, "Historical Criticism," 221. Williams calls "theologically wrongheaded" any postcritical theology that ignores the critical moment and seeks to find a way around mediation and history. Historical-critical work reminds interpreters that, even if history will not settle issues of meaning, interpretations that are incompatible with history lead us away from the "difference" of the text, and therefore are not truthful, 228. See also "On Doing Theology," 11.

58. R. Williams, "Historical Criticism," 223.

the text establishes its frame of reference and conditions for its meaningfulness. And, of course, no text is able to do this fully for itself, so critical tools become useful for this kind of work.[59]

Williams, however, is also quite sympathetic to the recent chastening of critical methodology. While he admits its insights are crucial to a truly diachronic reading of Scripture, he sees its contribution as a part of a more holistic process of interpretation. The problem with historical-critical methodology as it has developed has been its tendency toward either genealogy (i.e., the earlier is the authentic) or evolutionism (i.e., the later texts in the developmental narrative are the complete and definitive ones).[60] Williams's criticism of the genealogical tendency in much of historical criticism touches also upon an impulse that has been inherent in much of the free church tradition, namely, the tendency toward primitivism. While many in the free church tradition would not support an exegetical strategy that looked upon the earliest textual traditions within Scripture as conveying greater authenticity than later texts, they might argue that the New Testament witness taken as a whole provides a view of "the primitive church" that is to be the unambiguously authentic model for all future generations. For Williams, such a view does not account seriously enough for inner textual tensions and developments.

The Unity of Sacred Scripture

The degree to which Williams attempts to portray the Bible as a product of historical debate and negotiation may trouble many within the free church tradition who operate with a less complicated understanding of revelation as it relates to Scripture. Some might conclude that Williams seems *most* interested to undermine the unity of Scripture by pointing up and even searching for its inner tensions and contradictions, but that would miss Williams's intention, which is aimed ultimately at discovering the deep unities within Scripture. It is not that Williams is suspicious of unity within Scripture; it is that he is suspicious of easily achieved unity that is not truthful about historical processes and contingencies involved with knowing anything, including the things of God.[61]

59. R. Williams, "Discipline of Scripture," in *OCT*, 52. See also "Historical Criticism," 228.

60. R. Williams, "Historical Criticism," 222.

61. Williams says that the Bible itself "warns us against a simplistic account of what unity we may reasonably hope for in the Church," "Unity of the Church and the Unity

As *a* text, Scripture displays the same kinds of characteristics and contradictions involved with any text. For Williams, however, the unity (or unities) of Scripture emerges from considering the further question, "What is a *sacred* text?" He describes a sacred text as follows:

> A sacred text, I suggest, is one for which the context is always more than the social-ideological matrix. This cannot be established, of course, by historical study or phenomenological analysis. It arises from a reading context that assumes a continuity between the world of the text and the world of the reader, and also assumes that the reader and text are responding to a gift, an address or a summons not derived from the totality of the empirical environment. In other words: what the text represents is not only the conversation between writer and social-ideological environment, but also a conversation with a presence that is not a rival speaker, a participant in the exchange and negotiation of empirical speakers (which makes it a very strange conversation, of course).[62]

We encounter in this statement two central emphases of Williams with regard to Scripture. First, for the Bible to be read as a sacred text assumes a reading community (i.e., the church) that affirms (indeed assumes) a continuity between the world of the text and the reading community. Second, to read the Bible as a sacred text assumes that God somehow addresses the readers of Scripture as they engage Scripture. We will examine these two points under two consecutive headings.

Analogy and the Unity of the Bible

Williams's belief in the continuity between "the world of Scripture" and the world of subsequent readers of Scripture receives special focus through his appeal to *analogy*. Central to the literal reading of Scripture is a commitment to what Williams labels *analogia durationis*: a recognition that the duration of the text is familiar to us and is like the way we experience movement and production in our own lives.[63] The principle of analogy affirms that "this life *now* can have *that* kind of structure."[64] I especially emphasize this

---

of the Bible," 19.

62. R. Williams, "Historical Criticism," 224.

63. R. Williams, "Discipline of Scripture," in *OCT*, 52, 56.

64. R. Williams, "Unity of Christian Truth," in *OCT*, 16–28, esp. 23. See also "Judgement of the World," where Williams uses the phrase "*This* can be the source of *that*," in *OCT*, 30.

particular formulation, because it bears close resemblance to the reading strategy proposed by James McClendon,[65] which we will consider in the next chapter, but in a way that leads to some different conclusions from those that Williams deduces from his own vision of analogical reading, especially with regard to issues of tradition and catholicity.

Williams derives the principle of analogy partly from Scripture itself. He argues that unity is articulated in both Old and New Testaments through analogy, according to which "diverse events, persons, patterns of behavior are reconstructed in writing and in the editing processes of canonical formation so as to manifest a shared form, a family resemblance."[66] Already within the Old Testament itself, we see the community's understanding of its relationship to God worked out through analogy. As one example, we see moments in Israel's textual history when the community is represented as Israel in Egyptian captivity or as Israel in the wilderness wanderings. This *method* found within the Jewish Scriptures then provides an analogue for what is done in the New Testament. The New Testament writers draw out analogies ("family resemblances") between Old Testament paradigms and the experiences of those initial followers of Jesus.[67]

Beyond finding the principle of analogy already in Scripture, the possibility of such analogies and continuity within Scripture rests also upon the prior conviction of God's unity. Williams asserts that the meaning of "God" in Jewish and Christian history "has to do with the historical realities of transformation or renewal of such scope that they can only be ascribed to an agency free from the conditions of historical contingency." We should then expect that God's actions should be consistent. Consequently, the community that arises out of the actions of this God should display some "unifying points of reference," including reflective speech which seeks to articulate the divine consistency.[68] We see exactly this in the Old Testament layers of

65. McClendon's central interpretive strategy is summed up in his phrase "This is that; then is now," *Systematic Theology*, 1:32–33.

66. R. Williams, "Unity of Christian Truth," in *OCT*, 22.

67. Ibid., 22–23. For a shorter and more current treatment of this material, see "The Bible Today: Reading and Hearing." He states here that the twofold canon instructs us to read in such a way as to trace connections and movement. He strongly affirms his belief that the unity of the entire canon is "real and coherent, even if not superficially smooth."

68. R. Williams, "Unity of Christian Truth," in *OCT*, 21. There is an obvious contrast here between Jenson and Williams on the issue of historical contingency in relation to the life of God. Williams argues, rightly I think, that God's consistency can only be relied upon if God is free from the conditions of historical contingency. For the possibility of Scripture's unity being rooted in the self-consistency of God, see also "Paper for Seminar 'Scriptures in Monotheistic Faith.'"

textual tradition reworking earlier reflection in the attempt to work out the unity of God's actions in and through the overcoming of ruptures in Israel's history. Subsequently, we observe writers in the New Testament working diligently to assimilate God's actions in Christ with the unity of God's actions as displayed in the Old Testament (creation, covenant, exodus, etc.). Williams suggests that the diversity of the New Testament indicates that there is no systematic resolution to constructing the relation of God's actions in Christ to the diverse history of God's actions with Israel, but this is at least the *kind* of work that needs to be undertaken. In that case, the New Testament is "less a set of theological conclusions than a set of generative models for how to do Christian thinking," giving us methodological guidance for our own thinking and speaking.[69]

While the unity of Jewish and Christian language is grounded in a prior commitment to the unity of God, the unity of God is in turn discovered and spoken of in relation to the unity of possible patterns of human life opened up through discourse that witnesses to the foundational events of the confessing community.[70] As Williams says, "The meanings of the word 'God' are to be discovered by watching what this community does—not only when it is consciously reflecting in conceptual ways, but when it is acting, educating or 'inducting', imagining and worshipping."[71] What *Christians* mean by "God" is to be discerned around a pattern of life marked by holiness, a pattern disclosed most fully in Christ and made available to humans through him.

Williams's steady concern for locating patterns of holiness can be linked directly to his understanding of the goal of being human. Like Jenson, Williams has been an ardent promoter of *theosis* as the proper *telos* of humanity. So central is *theosis* that Williams thinks of the major fourth-century Trinitarian developments as being fundamentally a defense of this position. He firmly asserts that "any Christian theology worth the name will need a doctrine of 'deification'. . . ."[72] As we will shortly see, there are some ambiguities in Williams's account of Scripture that might cause discomfort for many in the free church tradition, but we might suggest here that the less

69. R. Williams, "Unity of Christian Truth," in *OCT*, 22. On this point there is an important parallel with Jenson, "On the Problem(s) of Scriptural Authority," 243.

70. R. Williams, "Unity of Christian Truth," in *OCT*, 23.

71. R. Williams, *OCT*, xii.

72. R. Williams, *Wound of Knowledge*, 59. See also 23–24 where Williams states that the end of the believer's life is knowledge of God, where knowledge of God is understood not in terms of conceptual grasp but primarily as a reference to union, sharing what God is (e.g., 1 John 3:2; 2 Cor 11:2; Eph 5).

one is inclined to give a central place to some version of *theosis*, the less likely one will be able to follow Williams toward some of his conclusions about Scripture. Free church theologians have not generally nurtured a soteriology heavily rooted in *theosis*, so this might make hearing Williams's account of Scripture more difficult. It is a theological theme some free church theologians are beginning to engage, as I will observe in the conclusion.

One of the primary questions, then, in thinking about the authority of Scripture and *how* it functions authoritatively has to do with the question, why do we read this book? We should not simply ascribe "authority" to the Bible as if it were an essential quality inhering in these texts. Rather, we ask what they are authoritative *for*. For Williams, the proper end for reading this book is directly related to the proper end of humans—holiness, being transformed more and more fully into the image of Christ toward full union with God (*theosis*). The Bible is central both to worship and to providing criteria for holiness, and it does not operate as a "bare text of reference" apart from these functions.[73]

It is not clear how Williams, or anyone, would discern which patterns of holiness were normative. Williams insists, though, that Christians must discern patterns of holiness that find their point of unification in Christ, most centrally the cross and resurrection. Here we find Williams's central hermeneutical principle; it is Luther's axiom, which Williams cites often: *crux probat omnia*. The unifying themes of Scripture are not simply decided on by its readers. Rather, they should emerge from what is understood by all as unifying the community, namely, the cross of Christ (thus, the importance of *gift* in Williams's theology). This does not mean we begin with Christ and then "scour the text for iconic types" (this would be more akin to what Williams calls synchronic reading). Rather, "The scriptural *history* has to be told, has to be followed diachronically or literally, *as it leads to* Christ and the cross of Christ."[74] *That* Christians must read the Bible around Christ

---

73. R. Williams, *Why Study the Past?*, 42.

74. R. Williams, "Discipline of Scripture," in *OCT*, 56. See also "Unity of the Church and the Unity of the Bible," 18. This hermeneutical strategy allows Williams to deal with some of the more difficult parts of Scripture. Scripture is a record of contest and wrestling with God. The Bible is full of exclusivism, condoned violence, sexism, etc. Scripture is not simply transparent to the mind of God. Rather, revelation comes to us in the midst of brokenness and fallibility. We must read the Bible around Christ, because in Christ, there is no distortion of God's gift. It is the gift of God perfectly given and perfectly received. Rather than blind adoption of every word of Scripture, or dismissing the authors as "benighted savages," we see in them our own weakness as we, like them, are caught up in God's gift but often misapprehend it. We read trusting that our own confusions and uncertainties, like theirs, will be taken up into God's triumphant work, *Ray of Darkness*,

is a given for Williams. But he admits *how* this occurs at the level of details is not always easy.

For Williams, the prospect of unity is not about *simply* referring to Jesus, as if Christians could easily find unity through mechanical obedience to or unmediated imitation of Christ.[75] Because theological unity is perceived through continuities of holiness that demonstrate the *effects* of Jesus in a variety of lived responses over time, the search for theological unity involves heavy engagement with Christian history, with all its complexity and difficulties.[76] One of the important implications of this view of Scripture is that, for Williams (like Jenson), Scripture does not seem to be *essentially* different from the history of Christian living in general. The narrative of Scripture is certainly normative for reflection and provides a "grammar of human possibility,"[77] but its record of responses to God does not exhaust human possibilities for holiness; thus, the heightened importance of the Christian tradition in Williams's theology.

Observe that Williams's understanding of what Scripture reveals is related to some of his epistemological convictions we outlined earlier. We come to understand things by "chains of association." Truthfulness then is something that unfolds as that which is generative opens up to new and endless expressions. There is "excess" in the foundational narratives of the Christian faith. Thus, Williams is perennially concerned about avoiding "closure." The meaning of Jesus' life is not yet exhausted, and we discover the unity of Christian truth by tracing the contours of patterns of holiness emerging through reference to Christ.

What does all this mean for how Rowan Williams actually reads Scripture? John Webster has rightly observed that there is fairly little sustained exegesis in Williams's work. He refers to Williams as a conversational rather than commentarial theologian. That is, Williams does not view the Bible as a "bordered territory" simply to be mined by the theologian. Rather, texts (even the biblical text) "open the world," and their meanings are discovered as we attend to their afterlife, what they make possible beyond themselves. For Williams, "exegesis is not the end of theology." He is always looking for

---

134–37.

75. Cf. Bonhoeffer, *Discipleship*, 82.

76. R. Williams, "Unity of Christian Truth," in *OCT*, 23ff. The theme of patterns of holiness as central to reading the Bible is pervasive in Williams's work, but this is perhaps the fullest description of it in one place.

77. R. Williams, "Theological Integrity," in *OCT*, 7.

patterns across the biblical text that "stimulate reflective expansion."[78] Williams says that good biblical interpretation must always seek to locate unities and anologies; in Dietrich Ritschl's phrase, to "try with overall outlines." But this must occur without smoothing over the real and particular history within the texts of Scripture. It must be marked by "slowness and strain" to avoid "empty piety or archaic biblicism."[79] While exegesis might not be the end of theology, it would seem that Williams could probably stand to perform more sustained exegesis in his work, a practice he could learn from both Jenson and many within the free church tradition, including McClendon.

For Williams, then, Scripture is authoritative mainly in that it witnesses to the foundational events of faith which are generative of patterns of holiness leading toward *theosis*. Revelation is "not in the possession of solutions but in the almost 'marital' promise to abide with this language and framework for our growing."[80] Williams suggests that one of the primary ways for abiding with the language of Scripture is through the "performance" of Scripture, by "taking time" with its literal sense through dramatic reading. This especially happens through the use of scriptural lectionary which is designed to "bring our time and the time of the canonical narrative together."[81] For Williams, the hope for realized unity rests partly on the church's submission to this discipline of reading. In his words, "The vision of unity in our context, and perhaps in every Christian context, is more likely to emerge by way of a newly critical and constructive reading of scripture—the revived 'analogical' skills of a base community."[82]

78. Webster, "Rowan Williams on Scripture," 106. Williams's book *Resurrection* is one sustained example of Webster's characterization. Williams states in the introduction that his concern in this book is not sustained exegesis of the resurrection narratives. Rather, he is looking for "significant patterns" that emerge across these accounts. While there is certainly diversity in the accounts, a point regularly emphasized by New Testament exegetes, Williams wants to show that the resurrection did not mean radically different things to different communities, xi-xiii.

79. R. Williams, "Theological Integrity," 14–15. The reference to Ritschl is from *Logic of Theology*, 92.

80. R. Williams, *Anglican Identities*, 80–81.

81. See R. Williams, "Discipline of Scripture," in *OCT*, 50–51. Williams follows Nicholas Lash's account of the "performance" of Scripture found in "Performing the Scriptures," in *Theology on the Way to Emmaus*, 37–46. He also shows indebtedness to Hans Urs von Balthasar for this idea in "Balthasar, Rahner and the Apprehension of Being," in *WWA*, 86–105, esp. 96. For a brief treatment of the theme of "performance" in Williams's understanding of Scripture, see Barton, "New Testament Interpretation as Performance," 187–90.

82. R. Williams, "Unity of Christian Truth," in *OCT*, 27.

God's Relationship to the Bible

Of course, the account of Scripture we have seen thus far would raise great concerns among many within the free church tradition. It appears to be an account that has left out any substantial reference to God in relation to the production of this text. Even leaving aside stringent accounts of inerrancy which often dot the landscape of free churches,[83] does Williams have *any* working notion of inspiration? Or is the Bible simply a record (albeit a privileged one) of where others have been in their responses to God's summons in Christ?

The notion of inspiration does not figure large in Williams's treatment of Scripture. But it is present, and it is worth mentioning briefly because of what it does convey. Williams does not ascribe inspiration to the text of the Bible *per se*. Rather, inspiration has to do with the divine *use* of Scripture. He says that two mistakes have typically characterized Western views of Scripture: either Scripture is seen as a mere historical record, or it is seen as an oracle, but one that is disconnected from the presence of the living Christ. The latter view more closely resembles typical free church approaches to Scripture. Williams attempts to avoid both of these pitfalls by arguing that it is the divine presence that points to the written word of the Bible. In reflecting on Christ Pantocrator, the icon in which Jesus is holding open the Bible, Williams says, "And when we approach the Bible, we must approach it as if it were, as in this icon, held open before us by the living Christ."[84]

Elsewhere, Williams regularly associates inspiration with the Holy Spirit's use of the Bible. The Spirit makes possible an analogical reading, the root of which is a faith that Christians are in the one body of Christ together, in one network of relations. Historical awareness simply will not let us smooth over that which separates us from figures in the Bible. Yet:

> Whatever tradition stands behind the stories we have, it is ineluctably part of what makes us who we are as believers, and we must

83. To illustrate this, one has only to run an Internet search of statements of faith published on the Web sites of various evangelical congregations. Most often these statements of faith begin with a strong statement of the inerrancy of Scripture, even prior to articles on God! This illustrates the degree to which their theology rests foundationally upon an understanding of Scripture as divinely fixed content.

84. R. Williams, *Dwelling of the Light*, 77–78. This is an important statement in the face of John Webster's criticism that for Williams, Jesus is more of a resource and a pattern than a present and perfected transforming agency. It might be true that Williams sees more potential in Christ's life as he comes to his fullness in the church, but it is inaccurate to suggest that in Williams's thought Jesus is only a historical pattern. See Webster, "Rowan Williams on Scripture," 12–13.

expect as we labour with the text to find ourselves caught up in some kind of recognition. The inspiration of Scripture, as some modern writers have said, is not a matter of the Holy Spirit holding a writer's hand as a book is written; it is the *present* reality of a divine mediation that makes recognition possible as we now encounter the strangeness of the story.[85]

If inspiration refers to the Bible, it refers to its capacity to be used by the Spirit to make Jesus present in the reading, such that his invitation becomes immediate in the hearts and minds of the readers.[86] Williams reminds us that the Reformation appeal to Scripture assumed that reading Scripture was not merely a literary undertaking, but that its readers are actively being engaged by God in the process as he continues to call his people.[87] It is in this sense that Williams can occasionally refer to the reading and preaching of the written word as a sacrament, since it mediates the presence of the Holy Spirit.[88]

The recognition of the Holy Spirit's role in using the text leads Williams to argue that Scripture is first and foremost to be read *in company* (and as we shall see, this includes the tradition of its reading). The Reformers would have been puzzled by the individualistic appropriation of Scripture that has resulted from their protest. If the Bible is seen primarily as a single book to be approached and interpreted by individual readers, it is easy to become consumed with issues of its reliability in every sense. This obsession, however, is relieved somewhat if the Bible is seen primarily as a collection of texts which the Holy Spirit consistently uses to "renew and convert the Church" as it gathers for worship. Any individual appropriation of Scripture must flow from a communal reading.[89]

We have seen that, for Williams, the authority of Scripture in the church is not bound up with some inherent quality of the Bible itself as a divinely orchestrated product that now serves as a finished text of reference. The goal of Bible reading, then, is not primarily to discover "the truth" in each part of Scripture through historically oriented exegetical methods. Rather, the authority of Scripture is bound up with its purpose in shaping humans toward their final goal of union with God (*theosis*). Its authority does not depend upon smoothing out apparent contradictions or historical

85. R. Williams, *Why Study the Past?*, 29.

86. R. Williams, *Tokens of Trust*, 122.

87. R. Williams, "On Doing Theology," 8.

88. R. Williams, "Word and Spirit," in *OCT*, 107–27, esp. 124.

89. R. Williams, *Tokens of Trust*, 124.

tensions. Its authority is related to the conviction of faith that behind all of its diversity, offensiveness, and tensions, there is one God at work, which can be discerned through the hard work of discerning patterns of holiness, patterns that extend outward from Christ's life. Its authority is also related to the conviction that the Holy Spirit uses Scripture to enable an analogical reading of these texts, so that recognition is possible across the historical divide. The Holy Spirit's use of these texts occurs primarily in the church as it gathers for worship, so the reading of this text comes to life principally through a commitment to read in company, in a web of relations which is the goal of all things, peaceful union with God and with others.

From a free church perspective, perhaps one of the great concerns about Williams's approach is its tendency toward indeterminacy. And this concern is not limited to those within the free church. John Webster (a fellow Anglican) offers several critiques of Williams's understanding of Scripture, but they all turn around this problem of indeterminacy. He sees Williams's articulation of Scripture as a seemingly endless process of eschatological deferment. He is concerned whether Williams believes much of anything can be said at all.[90] Christopher Seitz accuses Williams of "enjoying the ambiguous." He points out that Williams warns us away from too literalistic a reading, on the one hand, and away from looking down on Scripture, on the other. Seitz concludes that "this is simply too apophatic an appeal to Scripture's plain sense to be useful. . . . Gone is the joy of actual recourse to 'the lamp unto our feet.'" In his view, Williams erodes Scripture's capacity to speak clearly (what has traditionally been called Scripture's perspicuity).[91]

These critiques do pose serious questions to Williams's work. They especially begin to bear down with regard to the contemporary debates over homosexuality in the Anglican Communion. It becomes increasingly difficult to know how visible unity could ever be realized when Scripture is read in such a way as to be slow about making clear and definitive statements about boundaries. This does not mean that Williams advocates a "peaceful co-existence in an undemanding pluralism." That is too easy a solution (and ultimately untruthful). But he is more patient of the existence of conflict than are some others. A "literal" reading of Scripture as he articulates it alerts us to the fact that unity is "learned or produced only in *this* kind of history, the history of counter-claims and debate." Such a reading is clearly in

90. Webster, "Rowan Williams on Scripture," 120ff.
91. Seitz, "Canterbury and Unity," 13.

tension with an account of the literal sense of Scripture which sees Scripture as a "resource for problem-solving clarity."[92]

Ambiguity still remains, however. As Williams acknowledges, this way of reading Scripture is not easy in the details.[93] Some might wish to argue for an account of Scripture that is capable of more clarity for the sake of truth and unity. But before they rush to such arguments, they must be aware that much of what is motivating Williams's own understanding of Scripture has to do with his commitments concerning history, language, and knowledge as well as his refusal of a monolithic "world of Scripture." If there is to be an argument against Williams's view of Scripture, it must be prepared to deal with these issues in *truthful* ways. It is partly because of the ambiguity of his approach to Scripture that tradition and a teaching office take on a heightened importance in his ecclesial vision. It is to the authority of tradition that we now turn.

The Authority of Tradition

Williams has published numerous books and articles that deal not only with the idea of tradition, but that actively and creatively engage the thought of a vast range of voices from across the breadth of the church's tradition. His treatment of the past is never simple; it is always attuned to patient listening, a point beautifully evidenced by his highly acclaimed academic contributions addressing the dizzying complexity of the fourth-century Trinitarian debates.[94] We will first notice how Williams argues that tradition is something to which believers are accountable. We will then focus more specifically on how Williams deals with the issue of doctrinal development and the sense in which historically negotiated dogma is authoritative for the church's life and teaching.

92. R. Williams, "Discipline of Scripture," in *OCT*, 57–59.

93. Perhaps some of the ambiguity could be helped by more often providing sustained exegetical examples alongside his theoretical discussions dealing with scriptural interpretation. But if his theory is anywhere close to correct, scriptural interpretation is simply going to involve ambiguity.

94. Aside from numerous articles related to this subject, his most recognized work in this area is *Arius: Heresy and Tradition*.

Why Must We Attend to Tradition?

In his book *Why Study the Past?*, Williams argues for a particular understanding of history that steers between two mistaken conceptions. As he labels them, the traditionalists do not expect to be surprised by the past, and the progressives do not expect to be interested or questioned by it. Both suffer from "misplaced certainty." The traditionalist option is overly confident that the past is in essence the same as the present. There is nothing distant or strange about the past. The progressivist mistake assumes that the faith of the past is a faith of its age, and the gulf between now and then is too great to be negotiated in any way in which the past could be significant or authoritative for the present.[95] The problem with both the traditionalists and the progressives as he has described them is that neither group takes history seriously enough. According to Williams's definitions, the free church tradition includes both traditionalist and progressivist elements, often fusing them together. What he calls traditionalism has often been expressed as primitivism within free churches. The progressivist impulse assumes that the faith of later ages was so time-bound as to be unhelpful at best and corrupted at worst, the latter of which is probably the more common account among those in the free church tradition. Williams leads us to think about Christian history as involving the inevitability of both continuity and change.

There are several points of rationale discernible in Williams's work for the church being accountable to its tradition. I will mention four. They are highly interrelated, so the dissection is for purposes of analysis only. A first reason Williams gives for the necessity of attending to the Christian tradition has to do with the historical nature of Christian faith. Churches have always been "conserving" communities, because they have an understanding of salvation that is attached to a particular person in a particular time and place. So there is intense concern about being linked with *that* particular history.[96]

In a remarkable essay titled "Does It Makes Sense to Speak of Pre-Nicene Orthodoxy?" Williams demonstrates, by observing the behavior of early Christian communities, the historical impulse that undergirds a proper understanding of the church's tradition. In contrast to those who see "orthodoxy" as a result of centralizing political pressure which suffocated the early pure and ahistoric essence of the gospel, Williams demonstrates how early

95. R. Williams, *Why Study The Past?*, 3, 88–89. We may note that these are roughly the same poles both Jenson and Williams seek to avoid in their interpretation of Scripture.

96. Ibid., 91.

Christian communities were greatly concerned about historical, time-bound connections.[97] They did not focus on timeless principles or individual experiences resulting in an abstract spiritual union. Rather, they were concerned with being in a new kind of society, with belonging in actual communities marked by discernible patterns of relation and behavior. Williams demonstrates this by observing the great amount of epistolary correspondence between churches that would become "orthodox" churches, not only in the New Testament but well into the second century (e.g., the letters of Ignatius). Such correspondence testifies to a sense of mutual accountability for faith and practice among what were perceived to be comparable communities, even communities that were in conflict.[98]

This "almost obsessional mutual interest and interchange" stands in striking contrast to Gnostic groups (the primary form of "heterodoxy" during that period) for whom we have virtually no evidence of anything comparable. Williams suggests that the primary reason for the lack of a comparable "epistolary spider's web" among the Gnostic groups is that historical origins were of little consequence in their religious outlook that focused on timeless identity. For the "orthodox" groups, one was initiated into a new world of relations rooted in the foundational narrative of Christ. To ensure that any telling of the foundational story was the *same* story creating continuities of Christian practice, canons of authorization became important. Certainly Gnostics were interested in mission and conversion, which necessitated some chain of historical mediation, but the "catholic" perspective held that the believer *continued* to be formed through historical mediations (gospels, canon, sacraments, episcopal succession, debate, etc.), with all the difficulties this involves. Bauer was right to deny an oversimplified narrative of an early singular mainstream tradition. But the history of frequent exchange of letters between local churches indicates that "there were features *within* the task of communicating about Jesus" that facilitated the development of a "normative" (though not homogenous) Christian faith prior to Nicea.[99]

A second rationale for accountability to tradition arises from the first; it is that the church is inevitably involved in a process of historical formation

97. R. Williams, "Does It Make Sense," 4. Williams's explicit target is Walter Bauer's influential thesis set forth in *Orthodoxy and Heresy*.

98. R. Williams, "Does It Make Sense," 11–13. Williams makes the important observation here that very few (if any) analogues for the canonical epistles exist from the ancient world, so the fact that these were handed on as "canonical" is indicative of their formative role in nascent orthodoxy.

99. Ibid., 11, 14–18. For a similar account of early developments toward "orthodoxy," as well as for the concurrent development of "heresy," see R. Williams, "Defining Heresy."

and self-understanding. From the earliest times, we see churches working out their identities through debate and exchange with other churches. This observation complements Williams's cultural-linguistic approach to epistemology we outlined earlier in this chapter, but here, Williams is applying these insights to the church as a whole and not just to individuals.[100] Since the Christian community is a historical *human* community, "its identity is in process of formation rather than unproblematically given in a non-historical 'nature.'"[101]

As noted above, many within the free church tradition believe that the Bible gives immediate access to the foundational events of faith. Williams strongly and regularly repudiates this kind of naïve confidence. In his view, the Bible's address will inevitably be reflected through the history of prior engagements with Scripture. As a result, "We have a certain kind of responsibility to them as well as to the bare text of the Bible."[102] Mature persons need to put aside all the crippling illusions of independence. Rather, "I depend on the past, and it is part of me; to deny it is to deny myself. I *am* my history."[103] We must attend to tradition because "only tradition makes thinking possible."[104]

From this angle, the authority of tradition has to do with the necessity of attending to it for the purposes of truthful self-awareness. It has to do with a kind of recognition that the past is inevitably part of the present. Williams says that such "recognition entails a move beyond the idea that my good, my interest, has a substantial integrity *by itself.* . . . I have learned from others how to think and speak my desires; I need to be heard—but that means that I must speak into, not across, the flow of another's thought and speech." What lies beyond such recognition is "a commitment to the charitable conversation that has in fact always and already included me."[105] The notion of speaking into and not across the flow of another's thought is a helpful

---

100. This is an important point, because as I shall argue in the next chapter, it is precisely at this point that McClendon fails to carry out consistently enough his commitments to a cultural-linguistically rooted epistemology. Simply put, McClendon does not apply to the church what he applies to individuals.

101. R. Williams, "Resurrection and Peace," in *OCT*, 272. See also *Resurrection*, 23–24.

102. R. Williams, "On Doing Theology," 9–10. More assertively, he says, "We cannot be Christians without the Bible or without the history of its reading," *Why Study the Past?*, 105.

103. R. Williams, *Ray of Darkness*, 49.

104. R. Williams, "What Is Catholic Orthodoxy?" 12.

105. R. Williams, *Lost Icons*, 93.

way to put the matter. I will suggest in the next chapter that perhaps some engagements with the extrabiblical Christian tradition among free church theologians, such as James McClendon, seem to be marked by a latent desire to peer over the heads of the bearers of tradition in an attempt to get back to the foundational events as recorded in Scripture. It can sometimes appear that they are trying to speak across rather than into the flow of speech that has carried the gospel to them, which is not truthful.

While Williams strongly believes that tradition is the church's "charismatic memory"[106] energized by the Holy Spirit, he just as strongly believes that the church's tradition is not monolithic. A consistent theme in Williams's treatment of tradition is that the church's tradition is organic. This theme is, in fact, the subtext of his book *Arius: Heresy and Tradition*, as indicated by the epigraph borrowed from Alasdair MacIntyre: "Traditions, when vital, embody continuities of conflict."[107] Because the tradition is not monolithic, attention to tradition should not be by way of uncritical repetition. Mere repetition fails to risk genuine dialogue, which is more dynamic than repetition.[108] For Williams, the way to think about the church engaging the tradition is in terms of "conversational skill."[109]

Scripture may be foundational for the church's life, but more is needed. The events to which Scripture witnesses are generative of a new way of living, but Scripture does not exhaust the potential expressions of its vision.[110] It is not just the Bible, but the Bible as it has been read and lived out thus far that is inherited by the contemporary church. "The urgent issue," says Williams, "is how we speak truthfully of a material life that includes among its material activities a self-representation that is ventured in the community of other speakers, a material life that somehow *represents* the duration in which it lives."[111] So if the church is going to be truthful, it must not only appeal to its foundational texts, it must also consciously locate itself in the duration of those texts as they have been appropriated over time through exchange and debate.

A third rationale for being accountable to tradition is more directly theological in nature, and it has to do with the unity of God. We noticed

---

106. R. Williams, *Why Study the Past?*, 92. He borrows this phrase from Florovsky, "Work of the Holy Spirit," 49–64.

107. MacIntyre, *After Virtue*, 222.

108. R. Williams, *Truce of God*, 52–53.

109. Shortt, *Rowan Williams*, 73.

110. R. Williams, "On Doing Theology," 10.

111. R. Williams, *Lost Icons*, 138.

earlier how Williams used the concept of *analogy* to argue not only for the unity among Scripture's diverse texts but also for the unity between Scripture and its contemporary readers. What undergirded this account of analogy was a commitment to the unity of God (i.e., if God is one, we should expect to see consistency in the actions of God over time). Williams extends the principle of analogy to include the church's tradition.[112] Christians must let the past be strange, but they cannot allow the past to be completely other because of the belief in the unity of God's action in the one body of Christ that includes believers in one community unrestricted by time, space, language, and culture.[113] For the Christian, careful conversation with the past goes beyond the kind of mature self-awareness that results from knowing that one's self is bound up with what is given in other selves, though as we have seen in the previous point, it does include that. "Such a conversation," says Williams, "is the sign of belonging in one network of relations, organized around the pivotal relation with Jesus and his relation with God, into which Christians are inducted. Historical understanding is not a luxury in such a context."[114] The last sentence is crucial. If one is convinced of the unity of God's action in Christ, then attention to the Christian tradition becomes more than added value; it becomes a theologically rooted means by which the church comes to understand itself in the present.

For Williams, the conviction of the unity of God also prohibits the move to write off most extrabiblical history as irrelevant or "fallen." He states:

> If we were to say that all or most conceptions of the human vocation developed by earlier Christian generations were *fundamentally* misconceived or superseded, and that we were authorized to re-imagine the shape of Christian humanity from scratch, we should again be settling for a plurality of contingent projects, radically vulnerable to the distortions of history, with no inherent critical elements to keep them in motion and dialogue: the "salvation" of the medieval peasant and of the twentieth-century bourgeois would operate in mutually inaccessible frames of reference. There could be no engagement, critical or affirming, between them; only the blanket dismissal modernity is usually happy to pronounce. If this is problematic in the contemporary context, the same holds across the historical divide.

112. Wiliams, *Why Study the Past?*, 102.

113. Ibid., 8–10, 26–27. Recall that Jenson made an almost identical argument, *ST* II, 279–80.

114. R. Williams, *Why Study the Past?*, 29.

> The focal problem here is not simply that this makes it dif-
> ficult to talk about "a" Christian community in any more than a
> rather formal and boring sense, but that it makes it difficult to talk
> about *God*.[115]

If Williams is correct on this point, then the burden should not be on those
arguing for the importance of engaging the church's broad tradition. Rather,
the burden should fall upon those who believe that the church's tradition is
devoid of anything critical to the present church's self-understanding. To
deny the validity of the Christian tradition as an indispensible theological
resource is to put a question mark over the unity of God's consistent action
in Christ and his body. This is a compelling argument that free churches
should engage more often and perhaps more truthfully.

Finally, Williams offers a fourth discernible rationale for the church
being accountable to the Christian tradition that arises naturally out of the
theological rationale just discussed. It has to do with Williams's conviction
that the church is fundamentally a community of mutually dependent gifts.
We have already seen how important the concept of gift is in Williams's theology. In this context, it emerges in a robust account of tradition. If God's
action in Christ is consistent, and if the body of Christ is one, then we should
expect the exchange of gifts to occur between the living and the dead. Williams argues that it is because the past is always capable of bearing its gifts
within one common body that renewal movements regularly arise out of
reengagement with tradition.[116]

After considering the previous four points, we must immediately
remind ourselves that Williams does not see the appeal to tradition as an
unproblematic or uncomplicated process. Agreeing with B. F. Westcott,[117]
Williams affirms that God revealed himself in such a way that did not spare
us labor. Returning to the notion of gifts, Williams says:

> And accepting the labour of having to live with a history that in-
> sists upon our involvement is one of the challenges of believing
> not only in a revealed religion but in one that sees each of us as
> indebted to all. If it isn't an option simply to discard our history, we
> are bound to this demanding conversation, this mutual question-
> ing of past and present, in which we discover more fully what we
> are as a community and who we are as baptised Christians.[118]

115. R. Williams, "Unity of Christian Truth," in *OCT*, 20–21. Cf. Jenson *ST* I, 17.

116. R. Williams, *Why Study the Past?*, 26–27, 97.

117. *Lessons from Labour*, 148.

118. R. Williams, *Why Study the Past?*, 112.

To appeal to Scripture as the sole authority and ignore the Christian tradition because of the complexity and variety of its witness does not get us anywhere, because if Williams is correct, Scripture presents us with the same kind of complexity within itself. In fact, he leads us to read the tradition very much like he leads us to read Scripture, which highlights again for us that for Williams, while Scripture is foundational, it is not a fundamentally different *kind* of thing from tradition. The inspiration of Scripture

> is the *present* reality of a divine mediation that makes recognition possible as we now encounter the strangeness of the story. . . . *So it is* with the history of the Church. We are not dealing with a holy text, but with a very untidy history of how the holy text has been read and lived out. But *the same challenge is there*: to be ready for recognition as we give full weight to what is strange. We are not allowed to come at this subject as if it were a series of displays behind glass. This is our world too.[119]

The authority of tradition in Williams's thinking does not have to do with mere repetition of words, formulas, ethical norms, etc. It has to do with understanding that the unity of the church will not be recognized more fully without sustained attention to its past, done in the conviction that genuine conversation and recognition are possible across the gaps. Williams does not simply argue for an analogical unity among the various parts of Scripture or between Scripture and its present readers. He argues also for an analogical unity perceived *through* (not around or in spite of) the tradition which has carried Scripture to the present both as a book and as a variously lived reality.

The Nature of Doctrinal Development and Its Authority

Everything said above applies to the necessity of the present church being accountable to the broad Christian tradition. But do all parts of the tradition carry equal weight? What of the notion of Christian "orthodoxy" and dogmatic statements such as we find in the classic creeds? At the heart of Williams's understanding of orthodoxy, as it is reflected in traditional dogmatic formulae, is the conviction that we cannot seek the meaning of these formulas in abstraction from the historical contexts of debate in which they emerged. Just as with Scripture, Williams wants to steer clear of conceiving of dogma primarily in terms of propositional content that somehow floats

119. Ibid., 29–30.

above historical contingency both in its emergence and ongoing function within the church.

Williams has provided numerous instances of just the kind of exacting historical work he says is crucial to theology. His widely acclaimed *Arius: Heresy and Tradition* is perhaps the best place to witness his method in practice. One of his primary goals in this work is to demonstrate how orthodoxy emerges through conflict. In his view, a proper understanding of orthodoxy (and heresy) has long been occluded by a strategy of demonization employed by those who eventually came to be recognized as "orthodox" against those who became known as "heretics." The regular demonization of heretical positions tends to result in a conflict-free account of orthodoxy which often speaks in terms of "conserving" or "defending" a clear deposit of faith. In contrast, Williams argues that orthodoxy has a *real* history. Much of the language and imagery of heresy makes its way into orthodox expressions as the debate proceeds. Such a dialectical process leads us to understand orthodoxy as something still future, which emerges through historically contingent conflicts. In Williams's striking phrase, "Orthodoxy continues to be made."[120]

To think of orthodoxy as something that genuinely emerges through conflict opens the very idea of orthodoxy up for attack. For instance, it has become fashionable to argue that doctrinal development can be reduced to ecclesial power struggles.[121] Williams does not deny the political forces at work in the making of orthodoxy; that is part of the messy business of history.[122] He denies, however, that doctrinal formulation can be reduced to negotiations of power interests. There are genuine theological issues at stake, and it is part of the burden of a book like *Arius* to uncover the theological matters involved in all their historical locatedness.

After the "distorting glass of Athanasian polemic" is removed, we see that the fourth-century debates that resulted in the Nicene expression of

120. R. Williams, *Arius*, 25. For Williams's introductory overview of these matters, see 1–25. Elsewhere he says doctrine was "learned, negotiated, betrayed, inched forward, discerned, and risked." He makes this observation in critique of John Milbank's theological vision which appears too much "achieved" for Williams's taste, "Saving Time," 321.

121. We have already noted one early and influential expression of this in Walter Bauer. See also "Maurice Wiles and Doctrinal Criticism," in *WWA*, 275–99, in which Williams responds to a similar position articulated by Maurice Wiles.

122. He states, "Doctrine is implicated in power if it is implicated in history," "Maurice Wiles and Doctrinal Criticism," in *WWA*, 282. For example, Williams acknowledges that Athanasius was sometimes unscrupulous in his tactics and sometimes treated his opponents with brutality, *Arius*, 239.

faith were less about a struggle between "heresy" and "the church," and more about what kinds of continuity were possible and necessary in the language the church used to speak of God. Arius was a conservative concerned to preserve traditional and biblical themes and terminology, but because of increasing theological ambiguities at his time, he saw the need to systematize them in a way that pressed them to logical conclusions not present in earlier theology.[123] By the middle of the fourth century, it was generally agreed that returning to pre-Nicene language was no longer an option. The question then was what *kind* of innovation would be required to faithfully transmit the tradition of the church in a way that not only responded to the need for intellectual clarity but also maintained the coherence of the ongoing worshipping experience of the church. Despite his lamentable tactics, Athanasius demonstrated how what might appear to be a break in the continuity of tradition (e.g., the introduction of the controversial term *homoousios* into Trinitarian language) is "a necessary moment in the deeper understanding and securing of tradition; more yet, it is to persuade Christians that strict adherence to archaic and 'neutral' terms alone is in fact a potential betrayal of the historic faith."[124]

And surely, for Williams, this realization of the occasional necessity of new language and conceptualities is part of the theological payoff for the kind of historically critical appropriation of doctrine he advocates. The very process by which doctrinal formulae came into being is a story that warns against the mere repetition of formulae for theological continuity. The uncritical repetition of even the most cherished formulae will produce continuity and unity at nothing more than a formal level. Like Scripture, traditional dogmatic definitions need to be read in such a way that highlights their historical strangeness and difficulty, so they can be read more truthfully in the present.[125] The church should continue to discern what such language made possible in its own context and what sorts of developments it makes possible for contemporary speech about God.[126] Orthodoxy, then,

---

123. R. Williams, *Arius*, 177–78; 234–35. Williams points out that what made Arius controversial was eventually his radically conservative theological impulse combined with a very un-conservative ontology, 232.

124. Ibid., 235.

125. Ibid., 236. Elsewhere, Williams uses the term "hobbitry" to refer to "a fascination for the quaint and *folklorique*, on the grounds of supposed antiquity and/or catholicity." See "Imagining the Kingdom," 12. This description might accurately describe some initial forms of contemporary free church engagements with the ancient tradition, which sometimes appear less like relations of accountability and more like romantic interests.

126. R. Williams, "Beginning with the Incarnation," in *OCT*, 86–92.

is a "tool," rather than an end in itself; a "means of access to the generative, creative events at the source of a community's life."[127]

Classical dogmatic definitions were themselves designed to keep things open more than close things down, according to Williams. In fact, what the early church called heresy was often the church's language made too tidy, too drastic a narrowing of its range of meaning, a "destructive longing for final clarity, totality of vision,"[128] Earlier we noticed that Williams described authority as that which limits options. This might seem incompatible with his view that the dogmatic definitions served to keep things open, but in the case of the dogmatic definitions, it was precisely by keeping things open that the dogma limited the option of conceptual closure. The theological definitions of the fourth and fifth centuries were a set of warnings designed to mark out space rather than exhaust meaning.[129] In large measure these statements represent an attempt to warn against overdetermining the metaphorical and narrative modes of speaking of God, modes that were richly embedded in the church's scriptural and liturgical tradition.[130] Doctrinal definitions func-

127. R. Williams, "What Is Catholic Orthodoxy?" 13–14.

128. R. Williams, *OCT*, xii–xii; "What Is Catholic Orthodoxy?" 16, 25. At this point, we should register a difference between Jenson and Williams. By Jenson's own admission, he has had little engagement with Williams's work beyond reading the collected essays in *On Christian Theology*, which he reviewed. After a few predictable remarks of appreciation for Williams's work, he turns to his criticisms, the chief of which has to do with Williams's distrust of closure and his treatment of what dogmatic language accomplishes. In response to Williams's argument that through the formulation of dogmatic statements the Fathers were trying to keep essential questions alive, Jenson contends that their answers certainly resulted in further questions but they also "*thought* they were *settling* certain essential questions" and "did not suppose that the purpose of their formulations was to keep alive the debates that brought them to the meetings." See Jenson, "Review of *On Christian Theology*," 368. I suggest that some of the significant differences between Jenson and Williams (e.g., their doctrines of God, their understandings of ecclesial polity) can be traced back, in part, to the way each understands what language is actually capable of. Williams's apophatic reserve is a good reminder of the need for intellectual humility and the limitations of language, especially when discussing God. Jenson, however, may provide a needed push back in the other direction to emphasize that perhaps we can have a bit more confidence in language than Williams seems sometimes to allow. Free church theologians can and should enter into the space between these two theologians to think carefully about the nature of language in general, and specifically about theological language.

129. R. Williams, *Why Study the Past?*, 42. In an interview, Williams says that the doctrine of the Trinity is "the 'least worst' way we've found of talking about something very disturbing and inexhaustible." See Cunningham, "Living the Questions."

130. R. Williams, "Maurice Wiles and Doctrinal Criticism," in *WWA*, 285. Williams argues that contrary to claims that Nicea moves closer to mythical irresponsibility, it is actually an important step in the demythologizing of Christian discourse, "The Nicene

tion (then and now) as a regulative grammar "warning against canonizing in theology the tempting idioms of human personal interaction."[131] This "set of rules" did not claim a conceptual grasp of divinity itself. In fact, these definitions actually reinforce the apophatic impulse by providing a formal structure for speaking about this God whom we cannot speak of *substantively* but only in relation to the narrative of redemption, yet in such a way that gives the narrative intellectual coherence.[132] Doctrine teaches us that we can never speak adequately of God, but nonetheless we can speak truthfully of him, and without recognizing both of these points, doctrine can become sterile and oppressive.[133]

The beginning point, then, for dogma is not a desire for conceptual neatness that arises from a historical assessment of the person of Jesus. Rather it arises out of some form of the question:

> What is to be said of a human life that is creative and definitive of a new frame of reference in speaking of God and the world by establishing a new social reality in which God is spoken of—a human life which is believed, rightly or wrongly, to be present and active, still being lived, for and in the Christian, a life not perceived as something that can be talked of as an episode in the past?[134]

Heritage." See also R. Williams, "Redeeming Sorrows," in *WWA*, 255–74, esp. 268ff.

131. R. Williams, *Arius*, 267. While it is common to speak of doctrine as grammar, we should be attentive to Williams's particular understanding of what this entails and how it is distinct from other accounts. For example, George Lindbeck has famously used this terminology in *The Nature of Doctrine*. Benjamin Myers has argued, however, that Lindbeck's account of doctrine is essentially rationalistic in contrast to Williams's constructivist proposal. In Myers assessment, Lindbeck distinguishes between the essential, ahistorical core of doctrine and its historically contingent *form*. Williams rejects such essentialist accounts and sees doctrine's development as thoroughly historical, with conflict playing a more central role than Lindbeck's view allows. Myers also demonstrates how Williams's view differs from that of T. F. Torrance and Kathryn Tanner. The former has a generally progressivist view in which there is really nothing new in doctrine; it is simply the "unfolding of the immanent logic of Christian truth." Tanner, like Williams, strongly emphasizes the historical constructedness of doctrine but in such a way that doctrinal continuity is perceived as a formal rather than a substantial continuity. Williams's view is sophisticated enough to hold together a constructivist understanding of doctrine as well as a concern for truth emerging from the historical process of doctrinal formation, "Disruptive History," 48–50, 62–64.

132. R. Williams, "Nicene Heritage," 47. As a contrast to Jenson, see Williams's discussion about the theological misstep of projecting the "achieved" character of the union between Christ and the Father on to eternity, "Trinity and Ontology," in *OCT*, 160–61.

133. R. Williams, "Creed and the Eucharist in the Fourth and Fifth Centuries." See also R. Williams, *Christ on Trial*, 37.

134. R. Williams, "Maurice Wiles and Doctrinal Criticism," in *WWA*, 292. Williams

In other words, in the New Testament and beyond, the pressure toward doctrinal definition was initiated by an *experience* of union with the risen and present Lord, in such a way that *subsequently* their language of God necessitated certain kinds of revision and expansion.[135] And as the quote above indicates, the experience in view here is not simply an inward, subjective experience, an important point to underscore in contrast to the individualism that often marks the free church tradition. Rather, the move toward doctrinal definition grew out of an experience rooted in a newly constructed social order orchestrated around union with the risen Christ.[136]

When we see that the generative moment for dogma is one of a socially disruptive and transformative union with Christ, we are brought back around to Williams's emphasis on *theosis* as being at the heart of the Christian vision; it is "what the church hopes for." Athanasius's argument against Arius hinged largely on keeping open the possibility for deification, a transformative union that can be accomplished by nothing less than God himself. A mediator cannot enable union with the divine (although "Arians" believed they were taking *theosis* as seriously as Nicenes).[137] It was the *experience* of such a "new creation" and "union with Christ" that was largely motivating speech about God in the New Testament, in early liturgy, and in the debates

---

says that what initiates belief is not the "raw event" of the historical Jesus but the event of Jesus "as witnessed to—as already mediated," 291.

135. This is the basic thesis of Williams's essay "Beginning with the Incarnation," in *OCT*, 79–92. Elsewhere, Williams asserts that the gospel is communion before it is information. It *effects* the restoration of community without prescribing an entire range of conclusions. The New Testament and early Christian history demonstrate that the implications of this experience of communion only slowly resulted in linguistic and conceptual clarification, and only then through trial and error, *Ray of Darkness*, 230. See also "Trinity and Ontology," in *OCT*, 161; *Why Study the Past?*, 42.

136. See also R. Williams, "Maurice Wiles and Doctrinal Criticism," in *WWA*, 290; "Incarnation and the Renewal of Community," in *OCT*, 231. Sometimes the New Testament emphasis on life in the spirit has been interpreted to indicate an inward experience as opposed to the outward life of the flesh, but Williams point out that life in the spirit (Spirit) is a designation of rightly ordered relations in *koinonia*, "To Stand Where Christ Stands," 2.

137. R. Williams, *Arius*, 240–41. For *theosis* being at the heart of these doctrinal developments, see also "'Is it the Same God?'" 206–08. Williams argues that without *theosis* as the central soteriological concern in the fourth-century debates, the Trinitarian developments were superfluous. Athanasius's argument that the Word cannot deify if he is not God represents the central concern, *Wound of Knowledge*, 59. In my own studies of the fourth-century debates, I came to the same conclusion before I discovered Williams's clear statement of the matter.

of Nicea and its aftermath.[138] Arius's argument pressed for conceptual relief at the expense of keeping an eye on the kinds of transformative encounter that generated Christian faith in the first place and that undergirded traditional (though not systematic) theological and liturgical language about God.

We arrive, then, at the question of the authority of orthodoxy, especially as it is expressed through classical dogmatic definitions. First, Williams claims that there is a certain "hermeneutical charity" appropriate when testing dogmatic statements, a generous assumption that there is something to look for with regard to a truthful telling of the gospel. Second, he addresses the question of whether these classical statements such as Nicea and Chalcedon should have a privileged and protected status within the church's larger tradition such that they articulate the conditions for subsequent theological definition. He answers tentatively in the affirmative: "I suspect that something like this may be true," but not in a way that is "unhelpfully positivistic" or "short-circuits the details of doctrinal discussion." These dogmatic statements must always function in a way to renew the same kind of fidelity and answerability to the present judgment of Christ that gave rise to the dogma in the first place. We must not settle into arguments for the truth or falsity of phrases such as "*verus Deus, verus homo*" in isolation from the historical concerns that prompted such speech in the first place.[139] Again, somewhat tentatively, he states, "If we want to be faithful to the fundamental impulse of dogmatic speech, we may well, I believe, have to say that the classical dogmatic tradition has served to keep the essential questions alive."[140] Eventually, the essential questions kept alive by dogma are concerned with a vi-

138. R. Williams, *Arius*, 242–43. See also "Beginning With the Incarnation," in *OCT*, 92; "Unity of the Church," 10

139. R. Williams, "Beginning With the Incarnation," in *OCT*, 89. Williams says that both revisionism and positivism are misguided by not attending to the *role* the formulae were intended to play in articulating the direction of Christian life. Some brands of feminist theology, for example, attempt to write off classical dogma on the basis of its patriarchal language. Williams does not deny the patriarchal bent of the period but argues that the dogmatic language was more interested in protecting the notions of "generator" and "generated" than maleness. We simply have not developed any terms beside *Father* and *Son* that can convey these meanings, but Athanasius and others knew the point in all this was not gender. Conversely, Williams rejects positivists who argue that God *specifies* his name through the revelatory events. He specifically names Robert Jenson in this connection, and calls this move "worse than unsatisfactory," "'Is It the Same God?'" 213–16, 217, n. 15. This is a good example of Williams's careful exegesis of the tradition. It would be nice to see him (in his writings) regularly display the same kind of exegetical attention to Scripture.

140. R. Williams, "Beginning With the Incarnation," in *OCT*, 92.

sion for human life. And for Williams, commitment to the Trinitarian creed (including an understanding of its historical formation) is "a precondition for doing what Christians should do"—namely, witnessing to a comprehensive and healed human community "because of what happened to specific human beings and their relationships in connection with the ministry, cross and resurrection of Jesus."[141]

Benjamin Myers helpfully summarizes Williams's understanding of the authority of orthodoxy: "If the interpretive strategy of 'orthodoxy' finally emerges as a normative authority, this is not because orthodoxy has articulated a timeless truth that preceded the conflict, but rather because it has decisively *constituted* the community's proper identity through a new form of creative fidelity to the past."[142] While this process is bound up with historical contingency, Williams denies that his view involves a "wholly relativist view of doctrinal truth."[143] He is deeply concerned with continuity that is not merely formal but that truthfully mediates the invitation of Jesus Christ.[144] In his view, the dogmatic tradition represents instances of truthfulness as Christians of the past answered to the disruptive event of Jesus within their own contexts. In this way, orthodoxy becomes a normative resource for engaging the foundational events of Christian faith and for effective proclamation in the present that emerges in a distinctive way of life. "The actual Christian 'norm,'" says Williams, is not a completed metaphysic but "the continuing labour of engagement between the disruptive narrative and the conventions making for historical intelligibility."[145] What developments this may involve in the future are impossible to know ahead of time, and in this sense orthodoxy has an unfinished character; it is a project before us.[146] But commitment to the past, understood as continuities of conflict, is

---

141. R. Williams, "Trinity and Pluralism," in *OCT*, 179.

142. Myers, "Disruptive History," 58–59. Cf. Jenson, *ST* I, 17.

143. R. Williams, *Arius*, 25. See also, "What Is Catholic Orthodoxy?" 15, where he states that the claim to "some kind of access to reality" is not naïveté or arrogance; it is observed in the continued human effort at speech and meaningful action, "living significantly."

144. R. Williams, *Why Study the Past?*, 83.

145. See R. Williams, "Defining Heresy," 335. Williams contends that orthodoxy is "cumulative," because "its coherence is shown in a constantly expanding network of narratives, biographies," "What Is Catholic Orthodoxy?" 17.

146. While we have seen Williams tentatively affirm the privileged status of the classical dogmatic statements, the nature of orthodoxy as unfinished keeps him from treating that period (or any other) as a golden age. There is too much special pleading that must occur to privilege one age over another. See *Why Study the Past?*, 102–5.

the only way in which the church can proceed with coherence. And in this sense, the project of orthodoxy is not unlike any other tradition. It does not bypass normal paths of knowing and dialectical construction of communal identity. It is distinct from them not in process but in where it locates its center, in the socially disruptive and transformative Christ event and what that event makes possible.

The Authority of the Teaching Office

Williams's account of Scripture and tradition as it has been laid out in the previous sections opens the door for some pressing questions, especially perhaps from a free church perspective. If the present is an occasion for newness and potential construction to the degree that Williams suggests, how are Christians today to remain recognizable to each other over time? Wouldn't such a seemingly ambiguous account of what Scripture and tradition actually deliver lead to an increasing plurality and eventual incompatibility of projects as contemporary churches attempted to perform in new contexts what they perceived to be the discernible patterns in Scripture and the tradition? Wouldn't a decreased emphasis on truth understood primarily as relatively fixed content jeopardize the church's identity over time? All of these questions are significant and should not be taken lightly. It is in the face of these kinds of questions, however, that we must observe the place of an extra-congregational teaching office in Williams's ecclesiological vision. As we might expect, while his account of the teaching office delivers perhaps less than some want (and perhaps more than others might desire), it nonetheless provides a way of responding to these and other important questions.

Williams is not idealistic or overly confident about what the teaching office actually provides the church. One would search in vain to find any place in which Williams argues clearly that the church in any way is essentially dependent on such an office or that a visibly unified teaching office is the only or even primary answer to the church's problems of visible disunity. As he is the archbishop of Canterbury, however, it is not surprising to discover that he argues for an episcopally structured church that resists the kind of centralization marking the Roman church. How could he do otherwise after all? Yet there is more to say than that he is compelled to legitimize the Anglican polity by virtue of his ecclesial position.[147] We should be attentive

147. According to Rupert Shortt, Williams strongly considered joining the Roman Catholic Church and entering Catholic monastic life. Ultimately, his decision to join the Anglican Communion rather than the Catholic Church had largely to do with the issue

to *how* he articulates the need for a web-like, episcopally ordered polity and not simply assume that his reflections on this matter are predetermined to move toward an inevitable conclusion.

The Freedom of God and the Sacraments

A spring from which naturally flows most of what Williams has to say about the church's ordered life together is the central Protestant insistence upon God's freedom and the gratuity of God's act. No church structure in itself can guarantee the effectiveness of God's promise and act without abrogating the freedom of God.[148] One of the major questions the Reformation puts forward, then, is whether it is possible to conceive of the issue of ecclesial unity as rooted in the priority of God's gracious act rather than visible church structures. This is not to say that structures are ultimately unimportant to unity. It seeks only to locate them properly. Following Reformation teaching, Williams argues that unity is *given* by God in baptism, and any other starting place for a consideration of unity compromises the foundational conviction of the freedom of God's act. Baptism is "the gift of a charismatic identity in Christ," and the Eucharist is the "regular renewal of this charismatic identity." Both of these human acts "necessarily and centrally" bear witness to what humans cannot do and to God's free initiative in granting this gift. Because God's free initiative must be protected, "it is possible to define the unity of the church *first* in relation to this pattern of corporate activity."[149]

Whatever Williams has to say about church structures arises largely out of this understanding of the church's identity as rooted most centrally in the gratuity of God's act, an identity most visibly constituted and reconstituted through the church's ongoing sacramental practice. As we have seen, Williams contends that the church is fundamentally created to be a "shared life of gift" made possible by its participation in Christ. To belong to the church is to submit to the decisive authority of the paschal symbol. The event of Jesus' death and resurrection is the "ultimate and decisive symbol

---

of ecclesial polity, *Rowan Williams*, 25–26.

148. R. Williams, *Why Study the Past?*, 66–67.

149. Ibid., 82–84. For baptism and Eucharist understood as the announcement of and reappropriation of the unity already given in the new humanity in Christ, see also "Sacraments of the New Society," in *OCT*, 214. Although unity is given in baptism, Williams also affirms that the full perception of unity is an eschatological reality. As with Jenson, though, Williams says, "this is no alibi for the *labour* of discerning or nurturing unity in the Christian community." See "Unity of the Church and the Unity of the Bible," 14, 19.

of undefeated compassion and inexhaustible creative resource," a symbol that calls for response and generates new life. According to Williams, "the simplest and most central 'authority' in the Church is the authority of the *symbol*." The central paschal symbol, entered into through baptism and ritually renewed in the Eucharist, is authoritative in that its force limits human options within the church. It shows that violent power is judged and that grace and mutuality are shown to be at the center of God's life.[150]

Williams eschews accounts of the Eucharist that are focused upon sacralized objects over sacramental actions. Following Aquinas,[151] Williams contends that what makes sacraments distinct is what they are *for*; it is what the church intends and signifies in these actions that matters. They are "performed" as a means by which worshipers become transparent to the converting sign of Jesus; they are the "modes of receiving" the life of God in Christ.[152] The sacramental act identifies the church by pointing to where the church looks for its source and self-understanding. The source event becomes present again and so becomes a resource.[153] And it becomes present through the necessarily material presence of Jesus signified as bread and wine which are the "fullest available embodiment and effective sign" of Christ's gracious giving and re-creating grace which is the foundation for the church's common life.[154] In receiving Christ's life, the church is called and

150. R. Williams, "Authority and the Bishop," 94–95.

151. See Thomas Aquinas, *Summa Theologiae* III.lx.2c and ad 1.

152. R. Williams, "Nature of a Sacrament," in *OCT*, 197, 205–6; *Anglican Identities*, 2–3, 15–16.

153. R. Williams, *Resurrection*, 52.

154. Ibid., 100. Williams insists on the material presence of Christ in the Eucharist elements though without, contra Jenson, necessitating this as some form of the physical body of Christ. The Eucharist is a real sharing (communion) in the "life" of Christ because he is able to "lend" to material objects "the significance of his own personal will and being." That material things *can* become charged with the life of Jesus provides hope for the entire material world, *Resurrection*, 101–4. When Jesus says, "This is my body," it is as if he is saying, "This *too* is my body; this is as much a carrier of my life and my identity as my literal flesh and blood." It is an "extension" of the reality of Jesus' presence. By eating and drinking the bread and the wine, believers receive the action and power of Christ that was operative in his physical body, his "life." This "extension" of Jesus' identity does not occur through any kind of magic, but by the action of the Holy Spirit, as the Eastern tradition emphasizes in its Eucharist prayer, *Tokens of Trust*, 116–17.

As the body of Christ, the church is not a mere "continuation" of Jesus or "undialectical extension" of him. The Eucharist serves to both identify the church with Christ and confront the church with Christ as he is materially available. The church must remember this to avoid conceiving of the resurrected Jesus as something within its control, *Resurrection*, 76, 82.

empowered to display in its communal life God's nature as mutual gift, and in doing so becomes itself a sign (or sacrament) of the self-gift that initiates the church. It is understandable, then, why the most self-identifying acts of the church from its beginnings are signs of the paschal event.[155]

We recall at this point that what allows for the kind of analogical reading of Scripture Williams advocates has largely to do with patterns of holiness discernible over time as people respond to the gracious call of God expressed in the form of Christ's life.[156] Williams locates the Eucharist at the very heart of such patterns of holiness. The sacraments are *for* "making human beings holy,"[157] drawing them into Christ's pattern of life. We might say that for Williams, then, the Eucharist makes reading the Bible (coherently) possible.[158] It quickly becomes apparent how centrally important the Eucharist is in Williams's ecclesiology. Theo Hobson writes, "The core of Williams' ecclesiology, to put it rather naively, is the fact that he really believes in the Eucharist."[159] This statement would be admirably precise without its central qualification.

Catholicity and the Teaching Office

Thus far, Williams's account of the Eucharist could possibly elicit support from a free church constituency, especially those with deep sacramental commitments. Taken alone, one could even develop it in support of a specifically free church polity. From such a perspective, one might argue that if sacramental practice and resultant lives of holiness and sacrificial love are occurring, which are the central concerns in Williams's view, then it really does not matter how the church organizes itself. Williams admits this is a "*very* tempting viewpoint," especially in the face of innumerable problems which have swirled around various ecclesial institutions. A simple solution

155. R. Williams, "Nature of a Sacrament," in *OCT*, 204. Elsewhere, Williams argues that the church is a "sign" most clearly in its central actions (including prayer and the reading and preaching of Scripture), because these actions "*name* and interpret the deepest direction and growth of human life as being *in* Christ and *towards* the Father," "Word and Spirit," in *OCT*, 124. For the church as a sacrament, see also *Truce of God*, 29–31.

156. R. Williams, "Unity of Christian Truth," in *OCT*, 24–25.

157. R. Williams, "Nature of a Sacrament," in *OCT*, 197.

158. See R. Williams, "The Bible Today." Here Williams argues that the Eucharist provides the context in which Scripture should be read. The meaning of the Bible has most centrally to do with the movement from rivalry and self-assertion to a community of mutual gift and peace, a life of shared dependence on God's gracious initiative.

159. Hobson, *Anarchy, Church and Utopia*, 48.

is the "retreat into the Small Group," but this "runs against all that the idea of 'catholicity' has positively meant in the Church."[160] Of course, a simple appeal to "catholicity" would not likely persuade many free church theologians. Even if they are willing to embrace the term *catholic*, we need to observe how Williams uses the term in such a way that renders the free church option a problematic ecclesial arrangement. We will notice in the next chapter that McClendon develops the term *catholic* in a way that does not call the free church polity into question and indeed justifies a free church polity. I will draw upon Williams's account to argue that McClendon's understanding of catholicity is insufficient.

Catholicity is a steady theological concern for Williams. His concern for catholicity arises from the church's proclamation that there is one human destiny, one pattern of life, grounded in relation to Jesus Christ, and that the vision for this unified humanity cannot be perceived without "communion," a deep and abiding involvement with each other.[161] If Jesus is Lord, then there is no place in which he is impotent or irrelevant, and thus we confront the possibility of meeting Christ in every place, people, and language.[162] Catholicity has to do precisely with this universal significance of Christ. The word *catholic* means "universal," but not merely in a geographic sense. In Greek, it connoted something "of general application." The term carries within itself the idea of wholeness, in the sense of continuity within the tradition but also in the sense of being relatable and adaptable to the whole range and unending variety of human experience.[163]

With such a conception of catholicity in view, Williams construes any local church's catholicity most centrally as its *mutual critical openness* to the entire range of believers past and present.[164] We can see how Williams's understanding of the church as a community of gifts and mutuality is funding

160. R. Williams, "Authority and the Bishop," 93.

161. R. Williams, *Truce of God*, 27. Again, rejecting any notion of the church as a voluntary association, a notion commonly found within the free church tradition, Williams declares that there is no such thing as a private and unstructured experience of new life in Christ prior to engagement with other believers. Association with other humans in Christ is not an afterthought to the gospel of salvation. A "catholic" faith is clear about this, "The Lutheran Catholic."

162. R. Williams, *Truce of God*, 31.

163. R. Williams, *Tokens of Trust*, 127; *Resurrection*, 57–58; *Truce of God*, 31. It is important to emphasize that for Williams, catholicity is antagonistic to globalization because it is concerned with wholeness on every level, including the wholeness of local culture and language. See "One Holy Catholic and Apostolic Church."

164. This theme is pervasive in his writings. See, for example, R. Williams, *Resurrection*, 57–58; "Authority and the Bishop," 93; "What Is Catholic Orthodoxy?" 22–23.

his understanding of catholicity. If we understand the church as a network of mutual interdependence, and if we believe that Christ's significance is universal in scope and that no local expression exhausts the significance of Christ's life, then catholicity, in the sense of mutual critical openness to the other, matters. And with another turn of the screw, "If catholicity matters, structures of authority matter."[165] It is the ordained ministry that "focuses the Church's catholicity," representing the particular gift of the local community to the wider fellowship.[166] Someone from a free church should be able to appreciate Williams's central concern for the integrity of the local church. Williams's account of catholicity, however, presses hard against the very heart of the free church identity, especially its emphasis on local autonomy. Autonomy ("localisms and self-assertive separatisms") not only serves to isolate local churches but also to imprison them. Localism as a final principle is "the most effective cultural captivity of the modern Church."[167]

Since catholicity has to do with a mutually shared vision for a universal and unified humanity, it is inextricably bound up with the Eucharist, the place where this vision is most concretely displayed. If the most central authority in the church is the authority of its governing symbol (i.e., the death and resurrection of Christ), mediated most centrally through the eucharistic symbol, then the persons believed to exercise authority in the community are those most closely associated with the enacting of its self-identifying symbols. In early Christianity the teaching authority of the bishop was inseparable from his role as the one who presides over the Eucharist. In this role the bishop (or his delegate) is a focal point for the church's catholicity, understood as the incorporation of the many into one.[168]

Because the bishop's authority is tied to his eucharistic role, the bishop's authority is primarily an authority to unify. It is not an authority to squelch all conflict but "to refer all sides of a debate to the unifying symbol" so that opponents or strangers are able to recognize Christ in each other.[169] It is not

165. R. Williams, "Authority and the Bishop," 93.

166. R. Williams, *Resurrection*, 59.

167. R. Williams, "The Lutheran Catholic."

168. R. Williams, "Authority and the Bishop," 96. Williams traces the early Christian history in which the authority of the bishop was often in tension with authority being claimed by martyrs and ascetics. The debate was primarily about where Christ was most discernibly present, because surely that is where authority was to be found. See "To Stand Where Christ Stands," 8ff. This says something about the connection of the bishop's authority to the Eucharist, where Christ was believed to be most clearly present.

169. R. Williams, "Authority and the Bishop," 98. As we have seen, for Williams, authority has primarily to do with setting limits. His claim here that the bishop's authority is primarily the authority to unify is not incompatible with the authority of setting limits

the power of a solitary representative of the people before God, or the power of an individual to ensure a change in the sacramental elements.[170] It is not authority in the sense of "ruling over," where a "teaching body" possesses power and knowledge that it passes on to a "learning body." The primary mode of the teaching office's authority is symbolic; it is the authority of invitation and manifestation, as the bishop serves as a symbol of the church's unity and catholicity.[171] If the bishop is there to *show* something (i.e., the catholic unity of the church as it gathers around the presence of Christ in the Eucharist), then the lack of such a personal focus is not so much a defect in the "validity" of the Eucharist as it is a defect in intelligibility with regard to this symbolic proclamation of the gospel.[172] The ministry gains its intelligibility in relation to its sacramental function as "the effective present symbol of continuities," a symbol (derivative from the eucharistic symbol) with the power to free the worshipping community from the prison of the local perspective.[173] Living in responsible communion means being liberated from what is merely local or self-concerned. The historic sacramental ministry is an expression of mutual recognition and responsibility, and the continued

---

as we shall see shortly.

170. R. Williams, "Being a People," 17. Williams insists that the sacramental transformation involves the community in its entirety.

171. R. Williams, "Authority and the Bishop," 97–99. Williams is favorable to the notion of the *epiphanic* understanding of the bishop found especially within the Orthodox Church. In this view, the primary function of the ordained ministry is to *manifest* the meaning of the eucharistic assembly, namely, its unity with the Easter event and its character as mutuality in and beyond the local context. But he offers a strong warning against the epiphanic model. Taken alone, it can serve to legitimate abuses of power by the clergy that do occur and have occurred in history. The office of ordination does not always manifest what it is called to manifest. There are times when the church's ordained ministers need to be spoken to prophetically when they betray the gospel. See R. Williams, "Theology and the Churches," 16, 20–23. As an example, Williams portrays Teresa of Avila as challenging certain ecclesial practices and the church's method of exercising authority. Her challenge comes "in the name of what the Church itself 'authoritatively' does and says," *Teresa of Avila*, 218.

172. R. Williams, "Theology and the Churches," 16. This is why, in Williams's view, the bishop should be the "normal celebrant of the sacraments," *Resurrection*, 59. Lay administration of the sacraments fails to demonstrate how any particular congregation is organically related to the catholic church, *Why Study the Past?*, 106. To argue for ministerial administration of the sacrament is not about differentiation between those who are active and those who are passive. But there is an appropriate differentiation of *roles* in the church, which reminds us what kind of social reality we were called into, unity expressed through differentiation of gifts, "Being a People," 18–19. See also "The Lutheran Catholic."

173. R. Williams, "What Is Catholic Orthodoxy?" 23–24.

pursuit of "full visible unity" in ministerial communion remains significant in spite of the difficulties involved.[174]

It is at this point that Williams can make use of the notion of apostolic succession. For him, succession relates directly to this task of the bishop to "unveil the catholicity of the local church." To perform such a task, "he cannot depend for his ordination only on the local and contemporary, he must visibly belong in a community extended in space and time and beyond the local."[175] But Williams stops short, in this context, of articulating what conditions should be specified to satisfy the demands of succession. We see only its logic in his overall presentation of catholicity and the Eucharist.

Is the bishop's authoritative role limited specifically to his eucharistic function? No, but his role cannot be severed from his eucharistic function. Because his primary authority is the authority to unify and draw all parties to find Christ in each other, he must make judgments concerning whether there are occasions in which certain people or responses are incapable of being bearers of Christ because of their incompatibility with the church's goals. Of course, this kind of judgment is risky, but it is an essential task.[176] Because of its universal vision for humanity and the pattern of life that entails, the church must have some authority to limit the options of what styles of life are compatible with the church's vision it proclaims in word and symbol.[177] Thus, the bishop's role as a symbolic focal point for the catholicity of the local church has centrally to do with his indispensible connection to the church's central paschal symbol and with the authority to nourish the kind of teaching and moral life that keeps the church open to its source and open to the gifts that all other believers in time and space have to offer.

A Via Media: The Church as a Web

To insist that catholicity leads the church to stretch beyond the local in no way diminishes the importance of the local church in Williams's estimation.

---

174. R. Williams, "One Church, One Hope."

175. R. Williams, "Authority and the Bishop," 100. Elsewhere he states, "The personal focus of worship and proclamation in the community is one who has publicly and demonstrably received, by a network and sequence of specific relationships, the word and power of the first witnesses," "The Christian Priest Today."

176. R. Williams, "Authority and the Bishop," 98. See also "The Christian Priest Today," in which Williams states that although the priest's work does not stop with the eucharistic celebration, all other tasks derive their energy from it.

177. R. Williams, "Authority and the Bishop," 93.

Both the universal and the local are crucial in his ecclesiology. The local is to be cherished for its *particular* gifts. Authentic communion is the unity of genuine differentiation, with the Trinitarian life as the model and ground of such a possibility.[178] Yet, to highlight the local church's unique identity is not to lobby for its self-sufficiency. Williams is far more interested to speak in terms of the local church's particularity than the local church's autonomy. The language of local church autonomy (which is at the heart of the free church tradition) indicates a defensive posture against intrusion.[179] The language of particularity, on the other hand, opens itself up to the image of the church as a universal humanity rooted in the mutual exchange of differentiated gifts.

If local churches are responsible to each other and their visible unity is mediated primarily through episcopal representation, a major question is whether the church needs a universal pastor as an ultimate focus of the church's unity. Across the span of his academic and pastoral career, Williams has resisted hierarchical centralization. In his view, one of the strengths of the Anglican (and Orthodox) ecclesial polity is that it avoids the excesses and dangers of both the independent congregationalism of the free church tradition and the tight centralization of Rome. Williams admits the plausibility of the argument that the pope is the effective symbol of global unity, but he has several critiques of the papacy. First, if the bishop's role in the community derives centrally from his sacramental function, the rationale for the pope becomes problematic. Does the pope have a sacramental function in relation to *all* the churches? If so, does this not risk de-catholicizing the church by implying that the *true* bishop of every church is the pope? Second, neither the Catholic historical argument for Roman primacy nor the argument for a special charism handed on to Peter's successors (i.e., the bishops in Rome) provide any foundation for concluding that the pope has an authority definable in individual terms (differing from other bishops) or that other bishops derive their authority from him.[180] Third, for Williams, the most problematic aspect of the supposed individual charism of the papacy has to do with the doctrine of papal infallibility.[181] For someone who believes that truth only emerges through historically contingent negotia-

178. R. Williams, *Tokens of Trust*, 136–37. He does warn here against the danger of thinking of God and the church as two examples of life in communion.

179. R. Williams, "Archbishop's Presidential Address to the 14th Meeting of the ACC."

180. R. Williams, "Authority and the Bishop," 105–7.

181. See R. Williams, "Debate on the Gift of Authority"; "Authority and the Bishop," 108; "Less a Roman Holiday."

tions, the doctrine of infallibility produces almost insurmountable hurdles. Appeals to personal infallibility tend to work against the grain of processes that Williams would consider truthful, even if these latter processes are far messier than what individual infallibility seems to deliver. In the end, he believes that it is important to challenge the unsacramental and individualistic ways in which the papacy has been conceived.[182]

It is interesting to note that for Williams, individualism is a common critique both of the free church polity and the centralized hierarchical polity as it is expressed in Roman Catholicism. In his view, the exercise of authority must always be consonant with the professed goals of the group involved, thereby connecting means and ends.[183] Here, then, is one of his most serious critiques both of excessive local autonomy and excessive universal centralization. Both models obscure rather than manifest the heart of the Christian vision which is a new humanity marked by mutual interdependence through exchange of gifts and in which the members necessarily take responsibility for one another (per Paul's description). Jesus Christ alone (i.e., not the pope) can represent the whole of this new humanity. After that is acknowledged, what is left is the work of mutual dependence of churches around the only one who can represent the whole.[184] Further, as we have seen, Williams wants to root the shape of ecclesial life in the shape of God's Trinitarian life. In a description of Sergei Bulgakov's work, which complements Williams's own perspective, Williams states that Bulgakov was reticent about christocentrism in ecclesiology. When the church's identity is seen only in relation to Christ, the church will tend to try to locate functional substitutes for Christ (e.g., an infallible pope or inerrant Bible) or encourage *individual* relation to Christ (as is typical in the free church tradition). Instead, the church should look primarily to the Trinitarian life marked fundamentally by *kenosis* for the shape of its own life.[185]

Williams advocates, then, an ecclesial polity that represents a *via media* between localism and centrism. But it is not merely a pragmatic middle way aimed at avoiding the excesses of these two extremes. In his view, a

182. R. Williams, "Authority and the Bishop," 108.

183. Ibid., 92.

184. R. Williams, "One Church, One Hope."

185. R. Williams, "Eastern Orthodox Theology," 504. Seeing the church as the image of the plurality-in-unity of the divine life is a common theme in modern Orthodox thought where it is often tied to patristic theology. Williams argues, though, that although this may be a legitimate development of patristic ideas (and surely Williams thinks that it is), it is not a clearly discernible theme in the Fathers and owes more to nineteenth-century Russian thought than to the Fathers, 510.

non-centralized, episcopally oriented polity itself witnesses to the kind of mutual dependence that is the Trinitarian life and that is fundamental in the economy of Christ.[186] In contrast with both a hierarchical and congregationalist position, he describes his own position as "conciliarist."[187] His favored descriptive metaphor for such a position is a web,[188] which structurally highlights the nature of the church as "a network of mutual dependence and mutual acknowledgement."[189] Williams's main concern is that structures of authority should display the fundamental nature of God and the church rather than obscure it.

While Williams's argument for a non-centralized, episcopally oriented polity is not merely pragmatic, it does have recourse to pragmatic considerations. Such pragmatic considerations are especially clear in an essay in which he recommends certain aspects of the theology of Richard Hooker. In contrast with the Roman position, Hooker does not argue for the *necessity* of the episcopal office (in the abstract) as essential to the church's identity (and certainly not the papal office). It is not directly a divine institution, and to insist upon its necessity would threaten the Reformation principle of the absolute freedom of God that is so central to Williams's own theology. In contrast with most of the free church tradition, however, Williams shows how for Hooker, the episcopacy is a "reasonable and defensible self-disposition of the Church, originating in the immediate wake of the apostles." We should at least be able to say that since orthodoxy has been proclaimed within this structure (especially in the formative years of doctrinal definition), it at least has not prohibited God's free action. However else it might have been, bishops have been part of the historical development of Christian identity, so the burden should be on those who would argue against an episcopal structure rather than on those who argue for it. As Williams summarizes Hooker, "The removal of bishops assumes that we have access to the mind of God valid for all time, through the pages of Scripture. . . . Better to trust our history where it does not appear actively to mislead us."[190] Williams can appeal to these kinds of pragmatic considerations more directly in his own voice. He states

186. R. Williams, "One Church, One Hope."

187. E.g., R. Williams, "One Church, One Hope"; "Less a Roman Holiday."

188. Williams's dependence upon the web image is especially pronounced in this statement where he speaks of "the bishop as a central figure in—and I choose my words advisedly—a 'web' of congregations of worshipping communities." See "Archbishop's Contribution during the Presentation on 'Episcopacy in the Church of England.'"

189. R. Williams, *Why Study the Past?*, 107. See also "Sermon at the 350th Festival Service of the Sons of the Clergy Corporation."

190. R. Williams, *Anglican Identities*, 37–38.

that in the abstract there may be ways of signifying the network of mutual relations fundamental to the body of Christ other than the church gathered around the ordained minister at the eucharistic table. As a matter of fact, however, it is the established way that churches have been able to recognize each other through most of history.[191]

The Anglican arrangement is not the only legitimate ecclesial arrangement in Williams's view. In fact, he is clear that no single tradition will be able to embody the fullness of the Christian vision. Nevertheless, he is confident that some kind of episcopal structure has a crucially important role to play in perpetuating the catholic vision.[192] If it is granted that a cross-cultural awareness among churches is central to their health, then structures are needed to facilitate such awareness and accountability so that local churches do not simply capitulate to preferences of the surrounding culture. "An isolated church," says Williams, "is less than a complete church."[193] Williams does not say than an isolated church is not a church but that it is an incomplete church. This is in contrast with the official Roman Catholic position since Vatican II, where free churches would not be called churches but "ecclesial communities."[194] If the free church tradition is going to be able to hear a challenge against its very identity, it will likely have to be a challenge willing to give free churches the status of "church," willing to recognize who they are and have been as recognizably Christian. Since Williams's theology places emphasis on "patterns of holiness," with ecclesial structures serving this goal, he is able to see the legitimate gifts of free churches while still considering them deficient in some important ways.

What is there in practice to recommend Williams's *via media*? Williams says that, historically, both Anglicanism and Orthodoxy have prized the integrity and independence of local churches.[195] Indeed, Williams himself seems to reflect this locally oriented perspective in an early essay when he states that supra-local structures should not basically be viewed as decision-making bodies. Rather, these structures are primarily consultative (not legislative) in nature and serve to keep the catholic perspective before the bishop. They serve to remind the bishop that he should not act without such global consultation, but ultimately decision-making authority rests

191. R. Williams, *Why Study the Past?*, 107.

192. R. Williams, "The Goal of Visible Unity," 13; "The Lutheran Catholic"; "Who Are You Looking At?"

193. R. Williams, "The Challenge and Hope of Being an Anglican Today."

194. E.g., Congregation for the Doctrine of the Faith, "Declaration '*Dominus Iesus*.'"

195. R. Williams, "Debate on the Gift of Authority."

with the bishop in consultation with the local church. In this early essay, Williams commends the Lambeth Conference (one of the chief Anglican "instruments of communion") for not binding decisions but nurturing general perspectives.[196]

This system, however, has been severely tested in recent years, especially amid the debate over homosexual practice and ordination of homosexual clergy. Does this *via media* eventually reach a point of strain that makes the Roman or congregational options the only functionally legitimate options for achieving meaningful communion? Will it turn out that John Henry Newman was correct in his assessment of the Anglican *via media*, namely, that this "middle way" has validity only on paper?[197] Prior to his enthronement as archbishop (and especially in his academic role), Williams advanced reflection that was sympathetic to faithful homosexual unions (and ordination), himself agreeing to the appointment of a practicing homosexual bishop of Reading in 2003 before he was pressured into backing away from the decision.[198] In the final years of his pastoral role, his emphasis shifted more toward facilitating unity. He has tried to stave off ecclesial division over this issue by encouraging Anglicans to try to recognize in those with whom they have deep moral disagreement a common "grammar of obedience." He encourages a deep attentiveness to them, trying to discern in them a gift of Christ. This shared "grammar of obedience" has primarily to do with a willingness to be self-critical in the presence of a common attention to Scripture, tradition, engagement with the wider community of believers, and the sacraments.[199]

Such language is still largely typical of Williams. He is always interested in keeping the conversation as open and unfinished as possible in order to keep Christians addressing each other in the context of eucharistic encounter. As archbishop, however, it seems that Williams increasingly began to recognize that more practical measures are needed to maintain a truthful communion and visible unity among churches. The problem, especially for conservatives, is precisely over who is a legitimate participant at the eucharistic table of mutual exchange. Decisions on such matters cannot be endlessly

196. R. Williams, "Authority and the Bishop," 101–3, 107.

197. See Newman, *Via Media of the Anglican Church,* 16 (this reflects the original pagination provided by Weidner rather than the pagination of Weidner's own text).

198. See Wilkins, "Anglican Schism?" For Williams's most celebrated reflection on sexuality which opens an avenue of reflection sympathetic toward the so-called inclusivist position, see "The Body's Grace."

199. For an example of this style of reflection typical of R. Williams, see "Making Moral Decisions," esp. 9–14.

deferred by somewhat ambiguous calls to Christians in deep disagreement to be attentive to each other, and as archbishop, Williams advocates following the general mind of the church in disallowing the blessing of homosexual practice in the church. He thinks his arguments from his days as a professional theologian still have merit, but as archbishop he is responsible for facilitating the church's broad discernment, and "there are no arguments that are winning the majority of Christendom over to a new position" from the historically consistent denouncement of homosexual practice.[200]

Williams has clearly denounced the American Episcopal Church for electing a practicing homosexual, Gene Robinson, as bishop. Despite his own views, Williams has told the churches pushing for change that it is not unreasonable to look for a much "wider and deeper consensus" before making such radical changes as blessing homosexual practice. It is tempting for all parties involved to want to go their own ways, but as a voice of unity, Williams pleads to all Anglican churches to continue to seek a way forward together based on the conviction that unity is the primary means for coming nearer the fullest possible truth. When you lose this conviction, to what can you appeal when division threatens the local context?[201] Endless free church fragmentation illustrates the force of this question.

Williams operates from a profound conviction that the church must work towards visible unity, but he operates from "no less a profound conviction that our identity as Anglicans is not something without boundaries."[202] It is not unity at all costs. And what the current tension has caused him to affirm is the need for more authoritative global structures of communion. He states that what the Anglican Communion now lacks is a "set of adequately developed structures" to cope with the diversity emerging from greater degrees of global communication. He expresses the need for "decision-making

---

200. Williams quoted in Wilkins, "Anglican Schism?" Theo Hobson sees the issue of homosexuality as the "loose end that threatens to unravel his [Williams] entire ecclesiology," because Williams believes a homosexual union can have sacramental significance, yet the church officially condemns homosexual practice. For Hobson, this means Williams has not dealt adequately enough with the potential for his highly sacramental ecclesiology to become an ideological justification for the power to police sacraments, even erroneously, "Policing of Signs," 389. Williams would likely admit a certain force to Hobson's critique, but Hobson fails to adequately acknowledge the pervasive theme of self-critique in Williams's thought.

201. R. Williams, "Challenge and Hope."

202. R. Williams, "Archbishop of Canterbury's Advent Letter." Setting these boundaries should not provide false confidence. Williams says that the church can articulate limits while also being relentlessly self-critical of the kinds of limits that might unjustly keep Christians from each other, *Ray of Darkness*, 227.

structures" that translate "this underlying sacramental communion into a more effective institutional reality."[203] We noticed in an earlier essay that he did not think of global structures, such as the Lambeth Conference, as decision-making bodies, but now he speaks in terms of the need for such global decision-making structures. He is still a long way from arguing for a highly centralized authority, but we do seem to observe a shift in his thinking toward the need for global structures that carry greater authority if meaningful communion is to result and not merely a loose federation of churches. He says that Anglicans have attempted to be a "family of churches willing to learn from each other across cultural divides," but the Communion is now in need of "a body which commands real confidence and whose authority is recognized."[204]

The structure that has won widest approval among Anglicans, and the one that Williams himself endorses, is the proposal for a covenant arrangement.[205] The idea of a covenant is that local churches would voluntarily "opt in" as an expression of their conviction that they are responsible to each other. It would involve "more visible formal commitments" in which local churches would "limit their local freedoms for the sake of a wider witness."[206] He still wants to steer clear of language that moves toward "jurisdiction and canonical supremacy." A more authoritative global structure is not about ruling from on high but a trustworthy and truthful method of coordinating discernment among churches, a structure that might involve a voice of "primacy," a person who expresses the discernment of the whole body of Christ rather than speaking from executive and canonical jurisdiction. The latter may be tidier, but it is not in Williams's view a wholly trustworthy method of discernment that takes seriously enough the importance of attending to the diverse gifts of the body of Christ in mutual exchange.[207]

He admits that such a covenant will not resemble anything Anglicans have known thus far, but he contends that given the current situation, something like the covenant is needed to embody visible unity in such a way that keeps member churches from becoming enslaved to the priorities of any surrounding culture or some momentary consensus. Institutionally, it would still be an association of local churches rather than a structure with

203. R. Williams, "Challenge and Hope."

204. R. Williams, "Second Presidential Address to the Lambeth Conference."

205. For the most recent draft of the covenant proposal, see "The Anglican Communion Covenant: The Ridley Cambridge Draft."

206. R. Williams, "Challenge and Hope."

207. R. Williams, "Debate on the Gift of Authority."

a controlling bureaucracy; it would only make the ties of association more binding.[208] He believes such a binding is needed if further disintegration is to be avoided.[209] While it would provide for a more authoritative global structure, the discernment would still derive from local churches being represented through their bishops rather than local churches deriving their integrity *as churches* from their association with the global structure. For Williams, it is still fundamentally about a mutual exchange of gifts among local churches; it is still about listening, and such processes of truthful listening are not easy. Not having a central executive authority makes matters more complicated, and the cost is patience.[210] A process of long and sustained listening and discernment is painful, but it is only in the painful way of the cross that the church will appear in the world as Christ's body.[211] This is an important point for understanding Williams. He is interested not only in conclusions but processes. It is this kind of process rooted in mutual exchange and debate that demonstrates a particular *kind* of unity and not just the bare *fact* of unity. It is a unity that emerges through giving attention and place to the other. A central executive office may provide an official measure for unity, but as a structure, it does not indicate the *kind* of body the church fundamentally is. A covenant type structure also indicates that Anglicans are realizing that voluntary association among churches that does not make ultimate commitments and does not give up a certain measure of local freedoms has nothing to preclude endless splintering. Free churches can learn from observing the Anglican debates at this point even if they only apply these insights within the local congregation for the time being.

Conclusion

The fundamental challenge of Williams's work for the free church tradition, the challenge that generates other challenges, is his systematic critique of the kind of individualism that has marked much of the free church tradition. For Williams, knowledge and the formation of human identity are always located in processes of historically contingent exchanges. Williams not only

208. R. Williams, "Challenge and Hope."

209. R. Williams, "Second Presidential Address to the Lambeth Conference."

210. R. Williams, "Archbishop of Canterbury, Rowan Williams, Speaks to the Press."

211. R. Williams, "Archbishop of Canterbury's Pentecost Letter to the Bishops of the Anglican Communion." In this letter, Williams announced that the central mode of listening among bishops for the 2008 Lambeth Conference was to be indaba groups, a Zulu term that indicates purposeful discussion among equals.

develops this point philosophically, he also develops it theologically by arguing that the body of Christ is fundamentally a network of mutual exchange of gifts for the building up of a discernible common way of life formed around Jesus and sustained within the worshipping life of the church. Such a view challenges all notions of the church as a voluntary association that plays a supporting role for the individual believer. It also undermines any account of ecclesial unity that leans primarily on the notion of the "invisible church."

Once visible unity becomes a pressing agenda, discerning the authorities that are necessary to govern the common life becomes increasingly important. We have seen that Williams argues for the authoritative function of Scripture, tradition, and a teaching office with global structure. These authorities never function simplistically as guardians or articulators of fixed truth. Scripture provides the most basic authoritative touch point for recognizing continuity with Christ's life, but its witness is complex. It witnesses to a unity "never visible without ambiguity in history."[212] The Bible's unity is discovered primarily by reference to the patterns of life that emerge from engagement with its testimony. It is the foundational witness but does not exhaust the vision of transformed life which is its goal. In this way, the tradition of its reading becomes crucial. If the one body of Christ is one network of mutual exchange, contemporary Christians are obligated to be open to receiving the gifts of those removed in space and time but who are nonetheless responding to the same summons of Christ.

Not only are Christians obligated to receive the gifts of those within the tradition who are removed historically, they are called to receive the gifts from contemporary Christians around the world so that the one body of Christ becomes visible. Historically, churches have been represented to each other through the bishop. Williams affirms this arrangement since the authority of bishops arises primarily out of their presiding role with respect to the Eucharist. The Eucharist is where the heart of Christian identity is most visibly demonstrated, and the teaching authority of the bishop arises primarily out his connection with this central authoritative symbol by which churches are recognizable to each other and accountable to each other in fellowship and discernment.

There is much in Williams' theology that resonates with that of Jenson. When it comes to the form of episcopal polity, however, Williams cannot subscribe to the necessity of a universal pastor as the head of the church.

---

212. R. Williams, "Unity of the Church," 19. We also recall Williams's statement in this same context that the Bible "warns us against a simplistic account of what unity we may reasonably hope for in the Church."

Jenson finds significance in the papal role as a symbol of ecclesial unity. Williams admits the attraction of such a view, but finally decides that knowledge and identity come only through a process involving painstaking webs of mutual exchange. This is true both for individuals and churches. Locating ultimate authority in one person does not, in the end, appear truthful in his view. Such a view leads to a much greater degree of ambiguity in many ways, but Williams eventually wants to convince us that the pursuit of truth is a difficult process that emerges only through slow and patient engagement with the strange other around the central Christian symbols. Being truthful about those processes of debate and exchange is crucial if the church is to further approach visible unity.

5

James Wm. McClendon Jr.:
Assessment and Critique

Introduction

WE WILL NOW RETURN our attention to the free church tradition and place it in conversation with what we have developed from both Robert Jenson and Rowan Williams, reminding ourselves that the question before us has to do with whether free churches concerned with visible unity can a) continue coherently without an explicit retrieval of the church's teaching tradition, and b) if not, whether it is coherent to retrieve the authority of the tradition without also retrieving a nonlocal teaching office. I have chosen to examine the Baptist theologian James McClendon as a representative free church theologian, and in the conclusion I will make some general observations about other contemporary theologians within the free church tradition who are now moving beyond McClendon in certain ways. Though any number of worthy free church theologians could be selected for special focus, I have chosen James McClendon for the following reasons:

a. McClendon is committed to the church first and foremost as a visible gathering and is, therefore, concerned about visible unity among followers of Jesus.

b. He believes that the proper *telos* for humans is essentially corporate, one new humanity in Christ.

c. In comparison with much of the free church tradition, he is generally more open to sacramental theology.

d. He believes catholicity is an essential quality of the church.

e. While profoundly biblical, he seeks to avoid the difficulties associated with attempts to provide foundationalist footing for the Bible's authority commonly found within the free church tradition.

f. His proposed strategy for reading Scripture moves toward important connections with the church's interpretive tradition.

g. He theoretically recognizes, unlike much of the free church tradition, the inherently conditioned nature of language and knowledge, and thus the importance of tradition.

While McClendon is not unique among free church theologians in any of these commitments, he has been an especially influential free church theologian in recent years.[1] I view all of these points as strengths of McClendon's theology in comparison with where free churches have historically been. Taking Robert Jenson and Rowan Williams as my guides, however, I will argue that in each of these areas, McClendon has not moved far enough. More specifically, I will contend that these several resulting weaknesses in McClendon's theology (with respect to the concerns of this volume) are rooted in two primary weaknesses that have important implications for his understanding of ecclesial union and authority: a) For all his emphasis on history and narrative, McClendon's theology turns out to be surprisingly ahistorical in some important respects, and b) despite some surface-level language to the contrary, McClendon does not exhibit a strong theology of participation/union (*theosis*) such as we have seen in Jenson and Williams. These particular shortcomings, if indeed I have located them accurately, have a direct bearing on what we can expect (or not expect as the case may be) from McClendon with regard to visible church unity.

McClendon's Basic Affirmation of Ecclesial Unity

We must first acknowledge the heart of McClendon's commitment to the goal of visible ecclesial unity. As noted in the first chapter, McClendon adamantly rejects appeals to the invisible church to account for its unity. McClendon's ecclesiology begins (though does not end) with the gathered flesh-and-blood church. This commitment has largely to do with what McClendon perceives

---

1. As noted in the first chapter, Veli-Matti Kärkkäinen considers McClendon the premier theologian of the free church tradition, *Introduction to Ecclesiology*, 142.

to be the proper *telos* of humanity, that is, "one embodied self, one new Adam . . . humanity on a new model, a corporate humanity in Jesus Christ."[2] He is so committed to the centrality of the visible church that he forthrightly admits that "the Christian reality today is, in fact, a divided reality." He states that this divided reality may be denied by two groups especially, either those who focus on the ideal (i.e., invisible) church or those who believe themselves to be the only authentic ecclesial form (i.e., sectarians).[3] Both of these groups have great representation in the free church tradition and McClendon admirably distances himself from both groups, which places a burden upon him to acknowledge and address ecclesial division. We may now assess whether his theology effectively deals with this problem.

Ahistorical Tendencies in McClendon's Theology

As we have seen, it is partly because of the historical contingency of Christian faith that Robert Jenson and Rowan Williams see the church's tradition and a nonlocal teaching office as important loci of authority. Conversely, I propose that it is partly because McClendon does not sufficiently highlight the historical contingency of the Christian faith that the church's tradition and a globally structured teaching office do not figure as centrally in his theology as authoritative loci. I will demonstrate briefly how McClendon's theology turns out to be surprisingly ahistorical given his unrelenting emphasis on history and narrative.

Scripture

There are several ways to uncover the ahistorical tendencies in McClendon's theology. Since he seeks above all to be a biblical theologian, we may begin with some observations concerning both his understanding of Scripture and his use of Scripture. To his credit, McClendon distances himself from attempts to ground the authority of Scripture in theories of inerrancy.[4] Similar to both Jenson and Williams, in accounting for the authority of Scripture, McClendon gives primary attention not to some inherent quality of "the book" per se, but to what occurs in the public reading of Scripture in

2. McClendon, *Doctrine,* 33.
3. McClendon and Yoder, "Christian Identity in Ecumenical Perspective," 565.
4. McClendon, *Doctrine,* 473ff.

the gathered church, in its liturgical usage.[5] Still, McClendon's account of Scripture tends in other ways to lean toward the kind of foundationalism he wishes to avoid. McClendon puts much confidence in Scripture for the practice of doctrine, because it is less subject to corruption than anything else; it is "objectively *there*, a given." McClendon, of course, knows that it still requires interpretation, which will inevitably be subjective to some degree. Nonetheless, he takes comfort in labeling the Bible "the objective norm."[6]

While both Jenson and Williams see Scripture as objectively *there* as well, they do so in a way that considers Scripture inextricable from the historical contingencies from which these writings arose and were collected. Jenson contends that Scripture arose alongside dogmatic tradition and a more formalized teaching office, and thus its authority cannot ultimately be extricated from the authority of these other two loci. If, as a matter of historical fact, these loci did emerge in a reciprocal relation, the burden is on those who wish to mute or ignore tradition or an extra-congregational teaching office. McClendon fails to adequately address this issue, as have many others in the free church tradition.

For someone who is so interested in Scripture as the objective norm for doctrinal practice, McClendon gives surprisingly little attention to the process of canon formation and how that is related to questions of its authority. Where he does address it, he resists the idea that the church created Scripture, a move that would commit him to assign more authority to the church's tradition than is comfortable for him. Rather, he prefers to say that the making of the canon was only a faithful act because churches recognized "scriptural attributes" already possessed by these books, and in so choosing, these churches showed themselves to be true churches.[7] He acknowledges that the canon testifies to historic decisions made by churches and councils but mutes this admission with the assertion that because of the reciprocity of these books in one coherent collection (i.e., they quote and presume one another), we could expect any Spirit-led church, if given time, to arrive at about the same collection of books if these were placed on a shelf alongside many others.[8]

5. Ibid., 41.

6. Ibid. See also 34–35.

7. It turns out that these "scriptural attributes" are the central convictions that guide McClendon's entire volume on doctrine; namely, that these writings are the story of both God and humans, are Chrstocentric, and elicit the "baptist vision" in their readers. We will soon return to the reading strategy that McClendon labels the "baptist vision."

8. McClendon, *Doctrine*, 476–77.

While there is probably some good caution to heed in resisting the bald assertion that the church "made" Scripture, McClendon's account of the existence and nature of Scripture runs the risk of downplaying the significance of real history in the process of canon formation. In his view, it does not seem important that contemporary Christians intentionally receive Scripture from the hands of specific churches in specific times and places being guided by specific theological concerns. Rather, whatever role ancient Christians played in shaping the canon, it is simply one occurrence that should, in principle, be repeatable by every generation. In fact, McClendon says, ". . . if the list thus produced is correct, it foreshadows an act that must be repeated whenever a church, Spirit-guided, uses any part of the Scripture *as* Scripture."[9] It is not altogether clear what this might mean precisely, but it does further suggest that for McClendon, while Scripture does in fact have a history, in principle, that history is more accidental to Scripture's existence than bound up with it. Contrast that with Jenson's view that the canon emerged through historical contingencies, and that if the canon were being formed today, a different canon might result. Jenson claims the Holy Spirit works precisely *through* these contingencies. What matters for McClendon more than the history is the Spirit's active presence in any church gathered around the reading of Scripture. In his view, this "correct list" of books is what any faithful church would repeatedly arrive at, more or less. Aside from this being a circular argument, notice that while McClendon wishes to avoid grounding the authority of Scripture in any theory of inerrancy, his account of Scripture eventually tends toward a kind of timeless fixation that motivates many inerrancy theories. Once formed, Scripture is objectively *there*, bounded, fixed. How it was formed is of relatively little concern, only *that* it was formed by the Holy Spirit's guidance, the same Spirit present in churches today. Such a view can only serve to relativize the importance of tradition and the historic teaching office in the reception and interpretation of Scripture, as modes of the Spirit's activity.

Not only does McClendon tend to downplay the history of canon formation, he also tends to downplay Scripture's own inner history. He adopts a perspective on Scripture similar to George Lindbeck, a perspective we noticed Rowan Williams critique in the previous chapter. McClendon talks about "discovering the world of the Bible to be our own real world."[10] Williams's problem with similar language in Lindbeck is that it tends to treat Scripture as a self-contained, monolithic world without any inner terrain to

9. Ibid., 476.
10. Ibid., 462.

be navigated. It is simply an undifferentiated world into which readers insert themselves. Certainly there is a place for speaking of Scripture's unity and coherence, but we will recall that Williams and Jenson are both alert to the distances within Scripture as well as its unity. That is, there is a real history to be navigated between and among these diverse texts. Both Williams and Jenson are supporters of contemporary retrievals of theological readings of Scripture like McClendon wants to pursue, but each is careful not to undertake these reading strategies in a way that mutes the historical distances within Scripture. And each proposes that this is one of the most valuable contributions historical-critical reading strategies still have to make in biblical study. McClendon does not regularly display Scripture's inner history, usually only the unified history it narrates, its grand narrative.[11] Perhaps this is why he is less eager to defend the need for historical-critical exegesis. He does acknowledge his debt to its gains, yet he does not offer his reader, as do Jenson and Williams, a careful treatment of the importance of addressing the real historical gap between ancient texts and modern readers and how historical-critical exegesis is crucial to minding these gaps. Attending to such distances within Scripture positions it less as a fixed and bounded reservoir for truth and more as a privileged instance of the ongoing debate that is tradition. Such a perspective then possibly suggests the need for voices to serve as recognized guardians and facilitators of the debate.

McClendon's ahistorical tendencies with regard to Scripture can be most clearly observed with regard to his basic hermeneutical approach to Scripture. His reading strategy has two major components. First, Scripture must be read with Christ at its center. Second, for Scripture to function authoritatively, it must be read according to what McClendon calls the "baptist vision." The baptist vision is McClendon's term for a figural or typological reading of Scripture. Figural reading is the way in which the story of Scripture is bound to the story of contemporary readers in an authoritative way. It is what allows us to speak of a unified story linking past, present, and future. McClendon's characteristic way of expressing the baptist vision is that past, present, and future are linked through a "this is that" and "then is now" relation.[12] In other words, it is a "shared awareness of *the present Christian community as the primitive community and the eschatological community.*"[13]

Comparatively, we have noticed how important a christological reading of Scripture is for both Jenson and Williams. Also, we have noticed how for

---

11. Ibid., 40, 464ff.

12. See McClendon, *Ethics*, 32–33; *Doctrine*, 45–46, 465–67.

13. McClendon, *Ethics*, 31.

both of these theologians, after the historical distances among scriptural texts and between these texts and later readers have been sufficiently acknowledged, some kind of figural reading strategy is key to realizing the unity of the Bible and its ongoing authority in the one church extended through time and space. We even noticed that Williams uses language almost identical to McClendon's "this is that" expression. McClendon offers a reading strategy that is certainly headed in the right direction, and he should be highlighted among free church theologians for helping free churches think about how to read the Bible as a unified authority without succumbing to the regular traps of rigid fundamentalism often rooted in difficult theories of inspiration.

While there are important connections to acknowledge between the reading strategies offered by Williams and Jenson, on the one hand, and McClendon, on the other, there are also crucial differences that have wide-ranging implications for issues of authority and ecclesial unity. First, while we should affirm these two prongs of McClendon's reading strategy, *how* we affirm them is important. McClendon states that they are "so nearly formal that it may not be possible flatly to reject them both without rejecting Christian faith itself," and that any suggestion for improvement or reformulation must be prepared to say why it is an improvement. My suggestion for improvement has more to do with how we affirm McClendon's proposal than in its actual formulation. First, while McClendon acknowledges the two prongs of his reading strategy are traditional, he mutes the importance of tradition in the emergence of both. He grounds the first prong (Christocentric reading) in the authority of Jesus, who makes the Bible authoritative for his followers. He grounds the second prong (figural reading) in the fact that this is Scripture's own way of reading itself.[14] While both of these arguments are valid, they are only valid in tandem with a teaching tradition that acknowledged these texts as authoritative and not others. For early Christian apologists, such as Irenaeus and Tertullian, both prongs of this reading strategy had to be argued from the church's tradition as enshrined primarily in the liturgy and the rule of faith. Many of their opponents were happy to read Scripture; what was at stake was how Scripture was to be read properly. Apart from traditional elements of the church's confession and teaching, this reading strategy would not have been obvious. Jenson is especially helpful in showing how early tradition was crucial in setting the course not only for

14. See, e.g., McClendon, *Doctrine*, 471–72. Peter's appropriation of the prophet Joel in his Pentecost sermon ("this is that which has been spoken through the prophet Joel," Acts 2:16 ASV) serves as one of McClendon's primary examples of Scripture's own use of this figural reading strategy, *Ethics*, 33.

how to read Scripture but for canon formation itself. McClendon's recognition that figural reading is the Bible's way of reading itself can only be part of what is needed. It is also the case that the Bible is the way it is because the church's tradition was the way it was. Such a recognition can only serve to raise the importance of the authority of tradition in the church. And if McClendon is right, as I think he is, that these two prongs of his reading strategy are so formal as to be inseparable from Christian faith, they are only so in conjunction with a lively ecclesial tradition through which they came to light. In advancing his figural reading strategy, McClendon has unwittingly made a stronger case than he realizes for the authority of the church's tradition.

A second difference between McClendon and our two interlocutors concerns how they understand a figural reading strategy. McClendon's "baptist vision" further reveals his ahistoric tendencies. The problem resides in how he understands the "is" in his "this is that" and "then is now" formula. He describes the force of this "is" as a "mystical and immediate" relation in contrast to a Catholic sense of development or succession. He writes, "The church now *is* the primitive church; *we* are Jesus' followers; the commands are addressed directly to *us*."[15] The problem with such a view is that it does not take seriously enough historical mediation. Christ's words are *not* spoken directly to us. The primitive proclamation only comes to us through processes of historical contingency.[16] Jenson and Williams rightly contend that if the words of Scripture are to be authoritative for us, we must first recognize their distance and strangeness. McClendon's strategy effectively removes the difficult distance between "this" and "that." The pattern for such a move is explicitly stated in his account of "then is now." That is, to live eschatologically as the people of God, followers of Christ must live with a "foreshortened sense of future time." They must live the life of the end *now*.[17] While there is value in such teaching, McClendon appears to apply

15. McClendon, *Ethics*, 33. To be fair, McClendon does nuance this claim elsewhere. For example, "By the baptist vision, our task is not mere replication of primitive Christian behavior, but acting in our own context with an understanding of what we do informed by our identity with Jesus' first disciples," *Doctrine*, 395. Yet even a statement such as this does not extricate him from the difficulties posed by his articulation of the baptist vision we will now address.

16. Barry Harvey has arrived at the same critique of McClendon on this point. Harvey challenges McClendon's comparison of the force of his "is" to that of the Roman Catholic understanding of "This *is* my body." Harvey rightly argues that even in the sacrament, the real presence of Christ is not immediate but is mediated sacramentally, *Can These Bones Live?*, 52.

17. McClendon, *Doctrine*, 92.

that foreshortening of time toward the past as well, collapsing the distance between contemporary followers of Christ and the primitive church.

McClendon is aware of the potential criticism that his baptist vision is a denial of the importance of history. Immediately on the heels of articulating the baptist vision, he states, "This is not meant as a denial of the facts of history, nor a rejection of their significance; it *is* a claim for the historic significance of this present time in the life of the church and therefore by implication of every other present time in her life."[18] Several years later, after having received the critique that his vision denies the importance of history,[19] McClendon again defends the baptist vision as being historically concerned when he writes, "History is real, *history matters*, exactly because in God's mysterious way the past is present. . . . [T]ime, though not abolished, is in this manner transcended, and the church that reclaims its past stands today before the great final Judge as well."[20] The problem with both of these statements is that McClendon is not affirming history *qua* history but only individual historical moments as they are immediately related to a primitive moment.

As we have seen, Jenson and Williams eschew such historical naïveté. Both are committed to affirming the unity of the body of Christ across time and space in one story, but neither will allow for an account that bypasses the necessary contingencies of historical mediation. Recall that for Williams, the "that" in "this is that" includes not only primitive history but the successive receptions and working out of primitive history in different times and places. "This is that" names not merely an analogy but an analogy of duration. In Williams's view, if the story is indeed unified, it is unified by a God who acts consistently throughout time so that it is possible to discern patterns of holiness across time, discernment that requires what he calls "skills of recognition." In practice, McClendon is sometimes very close to this. In his book *Biography as Theology*, he argues that holy lives are central to the working out of theological doctrine. Any doctrine is "validated, so far as it can be validated by the evidence of these lives."[21] Williams would likely be very sympathetic to this statement. To use the example we observed in the last chapter, Williams explains the Arian crisis largely as an attempt to

18. McClendon, *Ethics*, 31.

19. See Layman, "Inner Ground of Christian Theology," 480–503.

20. McClendon, *Doctrine*, 466. See also McClendon's direct refutation of Layman's attack on this point in McClendon and Yoder, "Christian Identity in Ecumenical Perspective," 569.

21. McClendon, *Biography as Theology*, 80.

answer the question of what must be said of God and of Jesus to account for the present experience of holiness. For Williams, then, it is crucial that we attend to the ways in which the Christian faith has been mediated and relived through history if we are to get a clearer understanding of its content. Skipping immediately from "this" to "that" (understood as a singular primitive moment) in one's reading of Scripture reduces the weight one must ascribe to the interpreting tradition

Tradition

If McClendon's account of Scripture reveals some ahistoric tendencies in his thought, his account of tradition also reveals some historically reductionistic tendencies as well. In the first chapter of this study, I highlighted McClendon as a free church theologian who has influenced other free church scholars to engage the Christian tradition more seriously. At this point in our study, however, it is important to highlight some inadequacies in his treatment of tradition, inadequacies that impinge ultimately upon his understanding of visible church unity.

First, while we can celebrate McClendon's willingness to engage the breadth of the Christian tradition, he does not always demonstrate careful engagement with historical resources. In chapter 1, we noticed an example of McClendon settling for an overgeneralization concerning early Christian understandings of the atonement. He also is capable of very basic historical inaccuracies. For instance, he states that the Council of Nicea generated a creed that supported Athanasius's *homoousios* while condemning Arius,[22] when, in fact, Athanasius only became a significant contributor to the debates after Nicea and did not champion *homoousios* until the middle of the fourth century, some twenty-five years after Nicea. By comparison, Jenson and Williams are far more careful as historians. The quality of historical work eventually affects the quality of constructive theology seeking its footing in conversation with the tradition.

Second, and more importantly, McClendon often seems to misunderstand what is at stake in certain instances of the church's tradition, even its most dogmatic statements such as Nicea and Chalcedon. He offers this assessment of Nicea:

> Is it not worth considering, finally, how different might have been the history of Christianity if after the accession of the Emperor

22. McClendon, *Doctrine*, 253.

Constantine the church's leaders had met at Nicea, not to anath-
ematize others' inadequate Christological metaphysics, but to
devise a strategy by which the church might remain the church in
light of the fateful political shift—to secure Christian social ethics
before refining Christian dogma?[23]

Among other things one could say about this kind of assessment, it fails to
take seriously the complexity and pressing nature of the issues surrounding
Nicea and seems to trivialize doctrinal precision, especially that which has
been central to the church's most fundamental dogma.[24] McClendon regularly speaks somewhat pejoratively of the classical dogmatic statements as
being, in many ways, distractions from the Gospel story. He suggests that
a focus on *substantia, hypostasis, ousia,* and *persona* were all "alien puzzles"
that were read into the Gospel narratives and that they represent a "long
contextual byway of the Christian intellectual journey."[25] Ancient Trinitarian
thought pressed the raw data of Scripture into an ahistorical form, and the
ultimate result was a remote philosophical deity rather than the dynamic
and personal God represented in Scripture.[26]

We can discern at least two significant missteps in McClendon's assessment of this classical tradition. First, he accuses the patristic tradition
of moving away from the Gospel story and pressing the content of Christian faith into an ahistorical mold. This is somewhat ironic since it is my
contention that McClendon himself displays ahistoric tendencies. We must
concede that what has followed from these classical dogmatic statements
has sometimes eclipsed the centrality of the Gospel narrative in Christian
practice and proclamation. But careful historical work reveals that the classical statements were born out of an attempt to speak the Gospel narrative
with coherence. It was precisely the preservation of the Gospel narrative,
as it was encapsulated in the ancient rule of faith, that was motivating the
drive toward greater theological precision. Second, for McClendon to suggest that the Nicene Fathers should have been more concerned with social
ethics than metaphysical wrangling reveals that he does not fully understand

23. McClendon, *Ethics*, 42; cf. *Doctrine*, 253.

24. Although an admirer of McClendon's work, Barry Harvey also makes the observation that McClendon sometimes slights certain classical themes (e.g., divine immuta-
bility and impassibility, original sin), "Beginning in the Middle of Things," 260.

25. McClendon, *Doctrine*, 278.

26. Ibid., 298. This characterization, of course, is not original with McClendon. It
has been especially influential since Adolph von Harnack advanced his version of this
basic thesis.

the connection between ethics and doctrine that was at stake in the ancient debates. As Rowan Williams demonstrates, these debates were about the possibility of *theosis*. Since *theosis* does not figure large in McClendon's theology, he is able to relativize (though not deny) the importance of this dogmatic tradition, as evidenced in the quote above. We will return to the theme of *theosis* momentarily form a different angle.

Part of the difficulty of treating McClendon's view of tradition is that it is hard to find consistency. On the one hand, he sometimes speaks affirmatively of tradition. As we highlighted in the first chapter, he can speak approvingly of traditional creeds and confessions of faith, and he can agree that they provide hermeneutical lenses for reading Scripture and were intended to represent the purport of Scripture. In answering the question about their authority, he refers to them as markers to show us where others have been in their reading of Scripture, and they "invite us to read it that way if we can." They are "simply hermeneutical aids."[27] Again, it is not clear what kind of authority attaches to "read it that way if we can." With this last phrase he is concerned to maintain that even the most classical dogmatic statements not become rivals to Scripture but only interpretive aids.

On the other hand, he can be quite dismissive of even the most time-honored tradition if it does not square with his theological preferences. For example, he briefly assesses what he refers to as different christological models throughout the Christian tradition.[28] His unswerving interest in the Gospel narratives and ethics leads him to read the Chalcedonian two-natures Christology as well-intended attempts at rational coherence, but ultimately failing on this point as well as failing to portray Jesus as a model of conduct for his disciples. In fact, he suggests that Chalcedon's metaphysically strained emphasis on natures unfairly marginalized groups such as the Monophysites and Nestorians who were centrally concerned with Christian conduct. He then concludes that in this way churches and monastic groups were "sometimes more Christian than the theology represented by the creeds."[29] After

---

27. Ibid., 471.

28. See ibid., 250ff. He refers to the "two-natures model" alongside other models such as the "logos model" and the more contemporary "historical model." To refer to the two-natures teaching as a model alongside other models from which to choose eclipses its historical and contemporary significance. It is not one model among several viable models, as might be the case with atonement theories. Historically, it was a dogmatic definition of the church in council.

29. Ibid., 256. This is yet another example of McClendon failing to see what was at stake for teaching about Christian conduct in the carefully balanced Chalcedonian definition.

providing his own alternative christological model,[30] he pointedly says, "Two-natures Christology has had its day, and we need not return to it save as to a monument of what has gone before. All honor to Athanasius and Basil and Leontius, but they did not write Scripture, and it is to Scripture that we must return in fashioning our convictions."[31]

Nonetheless, McClendon suggests we should not scorn these historic models. When taken together, what they teach us is that "if we would answer for our day such questions as they answered for theirs, we must be open to revising the *models* (not the biblical data, but the current scaffolds from which we work) that have served Christian thought." We must ask of each of these models "how it serves the task of Christian thought *in its own generation*."[32] McClendon is insistent that contemporary theology is not simply about preserving historic orthodoxies; rather, every generation must face the creative theological task.[33]

There are some elements in these thoughts that are similar to elements we found in both Jenson and Williams. First, the tradition teaches us that Christian reflection must be open to revision. As Williams argues, Nicea was precisely about the need for revising theological language in order to remain faithful to apostolic proclamation. Second, like McClendon, Jenson and Williams argue that the meaning of dogma cannot be separated from the historical conditions in which dogma arose. Third, orthodoxy cannot simply be about repetition of achieved dogmatic formulas. Every generation has to struggle with how it will speak the gospel. Both Williams and Jenson are very sensitive to this point.

Yet there is also significant dissonance between McClendon, on the one hand, and our interlocutors, on the other, with regard to the authority of tradition. McClendon's perspective does not appear to allow for genuine doctrinal development in any meaningful sense. As we noticed above, he articulates his baptist vision (i.e., "this is that") in explicit contrast to a Catholic understanding of development or succession. In this way, pieces of tradition stand as markers of where others have been. Tradition may be helpful for contemporary teaching (i.e., read by its light if you can), and it should be respected, but as historical monuments, even the most time-honored

30. McClendon suggests substituting an outdated two-natures Christology with a "two-narrative" Christology. While his proposal is rooted in sustained exegetical attention to Scripture, ultimately it does not avoid the strains he ascribes to the Chalcedonian definition. See *Doctrine*, 263ff.

31. McClendon, *Doctrine*, 276.

32. Ibid., 263.

33. Ibid., 265.

dogmatic statements cannot make authoritative claims on subsequent churches. We recall, by contrast, Jenson's argument that dogma is authoritative in such a way that if the church in council erred, there is no present church to reverse the decision.[34] For McClendon, each generation goes back to the "biblical data" and makes immediate contact with it. If he acknowledges teachers or theological contributions within the Christian tradition in the process, it often appears he is attempting to peer over their heads to catch an unadulterated view of the apostolic witness.[35] Jenson and Williams are equally concerned with apostolic witness, but they believe you approach it only *through* tradition and not around it. They also believe that while the apostolic witness is a privileged occurrence of speaking the gospel, it is not the only such occurrence. Therefore, we must be attentive to how the gospel has been expressed through time if, indeed, the church spread over time is the one body of Christ united in a common faith (a teaching McClendon's theology makes difficult to admit as we will see shortly). In this way, for Jenson and Williams, Scripture and tradition are not essentially different in nature even if they are different in priority.

For Jenson, one of the reasons for attending to the tradition so closely is that the Gospel is a linguistic reality, and a linguistic reality is what it is only through reception and handing on. Similarly, Williams presents knowledge as a process of receiving and extending connections that are always

34. Jenson and McClendon share some similar theological inclinations. Each finds himself resisting what he perceives to be the Hellenistic encroachment on the Bible's God of narrative, or better "narrative God." A major difference, however, is that Jenson feels bound to the most traditional dogma as an authority in such a way that he feels obligated to make his theology square with it. Some have judged that he has not done so successfully. McClendon, on the other hand, does not feel as tied to traditional dogma, formulae, or even the theological rationale behind them. Sometimes he simply dismisses the tradition politely. At other times, he seems to want to place himself under the umbrella of orthodoxy by accepting some labels and rejecting others. He conceives of his *Doctrine* volume as a "Trinitarian" work (317), even though much of what he says could have been said by an ancient modalist Monarchian (e.g., 320–22). Because of this, he cannot develop a compelling Trinitarian ecclesiology of communion. Further, he tries to deny that his is an adoptionist Christology, but does not do so satisfactorily in my view, largely because he does not feel accountable to Nicene or Chalcedonian theology (see 247ff.). Likewise, he sympathizes with the Monophysites and Nestorians, not because he has found a way to sort out the complexities of the theological issues involved, but because they were serious about discipleship. Conversely, the Chalcedonians were supposedly more concerned about Christ's two natures (256–57).

35. D. Stephen Long recognizes the same problem in the Mennonite theologian John Howard Yoder. Yoder claimed to look over the heads of all particular traditions in appealing to Scripture, but Long suggests that in practice, Yoder was unwittingly privileging the Anabaptist tradition over all others, *Goodness of God*, 94.

linguistically and historically embedded. In some ways, McClendon operates within this same general perspective, drawing on some of the same philosophical influences as both Jenson and Williams. For example, McClendon acknowledges the influence of both Ludwig Wittgenstein and Alasdair MacIntyre on his own work. He follows MacIntyre's understanding of tradition as a "community over time" shaped by shared practices and skills developed over generations, and which community is the very condition for further inquiry. McClendon extends this idea to suggest that the knowledge (in all senses of the term) of God depends on a community of shared practices,[36] doctrine being one of the Christian community's central practices.[37]

Yet McClendon does not emphasize the "over time" aspects of such a learning community as much as do MacIntyre, Jenson, and Williams. His focus is more squarely on the practices that have *traditionally* marked the Christian community. In his view, it is almost as if every church gets to learn afresh what it should teach as it engages in its community-constituting practices. Traditional theology may give us some insight, but we should ask how any church answered its pressing questions "in its own generation." Jenson and Williams might respond that just because the church in a historically conditioned time and place constructed theology to deal with questions in its own generation does not mean its theological responses were only *for* its own generation. The theological accomplishments in history shape, to varying degrees, how the practice of theology proceeds from that time forward. What parts of that tradition become most authoritative (and to what degree) in the ongoing task of doctrine is part of the debate and exchange that constitutes the Christian tradition. Williams emphasizes that knowledge occurs through chains of association, and he positions the church over time as a learning community. Thus, the church's tradition becomes an indispensable locus of authority as the church seeks to know itself and go forward.

McClendon's account of history, contingency, and continuity is more persuasive in his discussions of individual lives than in his discussions of the church. One can see, for example, in his *Ethics* volume that he understands very well the complexities of both contingency and continuity in individual lives.[38] When it comes to the church, however, McClendon appears to shift a bit. He still understands very well contingency in history; what he struggles to display with regard to the church in his *Doctrine* volume (as we have seen)

36. McClendon, *Doctrine*, 314–17.

37. See ibid., ch. 1

38. One can also observe these emphases played out at the social level in McClendon and Smith, *Understanding Religious Convictions*.

is a substantial account of continuity in history. In other words, he does not apply his account of how humans know things and develop over time to how the church knows things across time. By contrast, one of the things we observed in Williams was his willingness to apply his general epistemological commitments to the church across time. Part of the problem for McClendon is that his theology does not readily allow him to conceive of "the church" as a single learning community over time. In fact, his theology makes such a conception almost impossible in some ways. It is to that point we now turn.

Participation/Union (or Not) in the Theology of James McClendon

Along with McClendon's ahistoric tendencies, a second major difference between his theology and that of our interlocutors has to do with an issue of ontology. Specifically, McClendon makes little use of the notion of participation in the divine life—that is, *theosis*—as the proper *telos* of humans. By contrast a soteriology focused around *theosis* is central for both Jenson and Williams, a soteriological focus that ultimately bears fruit in their accounts of ecclesial unity. I suggest that McClendon's lack of emphasis on this soteriological theme is another primary reason for his different understanding of ecclesial unity and the authoritative loci by which that unity is partly nourished. Specifically, I will demonstrate that a lack of attention to *theosis* contributes to McClendon's free church ecclesial model that comfortably rejects the need for an extra-congregational teaching office.

One of the first places to notice McClendon's lack of emphasis on ontological union with the divine life is in his understanding of the body of Christ. McClendon makes surprisingly little use of Paul's body of Christ imagery in his discussions of the church. This is somewhat striking in a theologian who is so ecclesiologically concerned, especially since the body of Christ has been a center of focus in recent ecumenical discussions. By contrast, one of the explicit reasons Jenson gives for dealing so thoroughly with this notion is its ecumenical currency. The absence of this central Pauline image in McClendon is even more striking in a theologian who is so thoroughly biblical. The index of McClendon's *Doctrine* volume lists only one reference to the body of Christ. In fairness, the book contains more occurrences of this phrase than the one provided in the index, but these few references are very brief and never sustained treatments. One of McClendon's most interesting references to this phrase occurs in a discussion of sacraments in which he affirms Jesus' presence in the gathered assembly. He states, "The congregation, to be sure, is called 'Christ's body' (1 Cor. 12:27; Rom. 12:5), and in Christian thought, that powerful utterance has serious work to do. But his presence cannot be limited either to the fellowship of believers or to the signs of salvation. . . ."[39] Although this utterance "has serious work to do," McClendon does not give it a prominent position in his theology.[40]

The relative absence of the body of Christ in McClendon's theology may simply be a matter of placing his emphasis elsewhere. I suggest, however, that it is a subtle indicator of a deficiency in his soteriology that has important implications for his ecclesiology. The body of Christ was central to the ecclesiologies of both Jenson and Williams. Both develop this notion in ways that reveal a deep ontological connection between Christ and his church. To be sure, Jenson develops this in ways that may be theologically uncomfortable for many (including Roman Catholics!), but the primary point here is that neither Jenson nor Williams shrinks from the implications of this biblical notion, that the church participates in the very life of Christ and is his very own tangible presence in the world. McClendon, however, seems especially keen to emphasize the distinction between Christ and the church, and in doing so fails to demonstrate any strong participatory connection between them.

In his discussion of soteriology, McClendon briefly addresses the question of Christian mysticism, particularly in reference to the New Testament "in Christ" formula. While he is very careful to guard against the implication of mystical absorption, he does allow that this phrase is making "ontological" claims of union, but then he quickly describes this as Christ's presence "with" both the individual and the community. Although he uses the word *union*, his real emphasis here, as in the rest of the volume, is on Christ's presence *to* and *with* believers and the gathered church. Ontological union with Christ does not do any heavy lifting in McClendon's theology.[41] Nor is there any connection on his part of the idea of union with that of the mystical body of Christ, especially with regard to the real presence of Christ in eucharistic observance. He does briefly notice this connection as a "characteristic Catholic plan of salvation" that developed over the centuries, and

39. McClendon, *Doctrine*, 379.

40. He does, however, give significant attention to the biblical notion of the "people of God," which eventually serves his free church interest in "gathering" more than does the "body of Christ." See ibid., 363ff.

41. If he were making a strong claim for mystical union, one might expect to see the typical reference to 2 Peter 1:14 ("that . . . [you] might become participants of the divine nature"), a text that, as far as I can tell, makes no appearance in *Doctrine*, an otherwise biblically saturated volume.

he regards the notion of union with God as a strength of this "plan" but does not develop it within his own theology. After this brief treatment of the "in Christ" formula, he moves immediately to describe sanctification as a "state" of holiness granted to the believer, which is followed by a very brief account of the New Testament use of *teleios*, which McClendon exegetes primarily as a matter of conformity to the image of Christ.[42]

McClendon does not develop conformity to the image of Christ in relation to anything like *theosis*. His soteriological scope regularly narrows on discipleship in a way that does not emphasize union with Christ. For example, McClendon's Christology is developed to accentuate Christ's right to absolute lordship which demands "nothing less than perfect discipleship on our part." Christ opens a trail of obedience for others to follow.[43] McClendon's telescoped soteriological focus on obedience and discipleship shapes his understanding of baptism. He develops baptism primarily as conversion (*metanoia*) and commissioning for a new way of life in the eschatological community of God, a life marked by forgiveness and service.[44] To his great credit, McClendon challenges an individualistic conception of baptism common in free churches. Further, he rejects the common free church view that baptism is merely symbolic. He speaks of baptism as a sign that actually effects what it proclaims.[45] But of what is it a sign? For McClendon, baptism is a sign of inclusion into God's community, a sign of forgiveness made actual, a sign of conversion. But he does not develop baptism as a sign of entry into and ontological union with Christ. Interestingly, in his discussion of baptism, he cites Galatians 3:27 from the New English Bible, which reads, "Baptized into union with him, you have all put on Christ like a garment."[46] This citation is interesting for two reasons. First, few English translations use the word *union* here, because the Greek text simply speaks of being baptized *eis Christon* (into Christ). As we have already suggested, however, there is good reason to take this important Pauline phrase as an indication of mystical union, so McClendon's chosen translation is actually helpful. Yet, what is even more interesting about his use of this verse is that

---

42. For this entire discussion, see McClendon, *Doctrine*, 113–17.

43. Ibid., 278–79.

44. Ibid., 386ff. There are other features to McClendon's account of baptism, but conversion and commissioning occupy center stage for him.

45. Ibid., 388. McClendon explicitly appeals to J. L. Austen's speech-act theory in his articulation of the church's "sign language."

46. Ibid., 389.

he completely ignores the explicit reference to union, and uses the verse instead to highlight the double agency of baptism (i.e., human and divine).

In speaking of how one's life comes together with Christ's through baptism, McClendon says that earlier periods in Christian history spoke in terms of mystery or sacrament. He prefers, consistent with his overall methodology, to speak in terms more germane to a postmodern context; namely, narrative. Baptism is about two narratives coming together.[47] This is similar to, and even grows out of, his Christology. He believes that Chalcedonian two-natures Christology became encumbered in a nonbiblical obsession with natures and essences. He proposes a "two-narrative" Christology in which the story of God and the human story come together. Similarly, in baptism, he wants to bypass questions of ontology in favor of portraying baptism as one life consciously adopting the form of another life. It is not an account emphasizing ontological union with the living Christ and with those who together constitute his body, the church.

The result of this ontologically deficient theology reflected in a truncated account of baptism has a subsequent effect on his understanding of Eucharist. This is important because of the implications it has for his understanding of a teaching office. For both Jenson and Williams, the authority that adheres to the teaching office is tied closely to its association with the church's eucharistic observance, and for both theologians, the Eucharist is at the heart of their vision of ecclesial unity. As with baptism, there are aspects of McClendon's account of the Lord's Supper that are welcome contributions to free church eucharistic theology. The Lord's Supper is a sign rather than a mere symbol. McClendon rejects memorialist views of the Eucharist common within the free church tradition. He also sees it as one of the church's central and self-constituting practices, giving it a more central relevance than it has received in much of the free church tradition. The church becomes what it is through this practice especially. Further, for McClendon, the Lord's Supper is oriented toward the identity of the community rather than the individual as it often is in the free church tradition. As a communally oriented practice, it is the central sign of unity. Intentional engagement with this sign within the community of faith facilitates fellowship with the present Jesus and is an act of "re-membering," the means by which the gathered community is reconstituted as the body of Christ. Such "re-membering" has an eschatological character as it anticipates the coming fullness of God's kingdom.[48]

47. Ibid., 390.
48. For the full discussion, see McClendon, *Doctrine*, 400ff.

McClendon's account of the Eucharist, however, suffers from the same ontological deficiencies in his overall theology that we have been tracing. McClendon unswervingly emphasizes the "real presence" of Jesus in worship that occurs "in his name." Yet, he is hesitant to attach this presence too focally to the Eucharist (even less to its material objects of food and drink). He rather likes to emphasize that Jesus' presence is not limited to the fellowship of believers or to their central signs, including the Eucharist. In fact, he likes to speak of the "hidden" or "secret" presence of Jesus in worship. But Jesus is present "*in a way that matters*." And consistent with McClendon's narrative approach to Christology, he suggests that for Jesus to be present in a way that matters means that he is present "in such a way that *the story continues*."[49] There is no indication here of any kind of bodily presence. Again, we see a shift away from ontology in favor of the language of narrative.

McClendon suggests four themes of the eucharistic meal: it is about solidarity; it is about forgiveness; it is a thanksgiving meal; and it is an eschatological meal.[50] For the purposes of this study, the theme of solidarity is of the most significance. One of the strengths of McClendon's presentation is that he believes that the sharing of the Lord's Supper is aimed at reunification and that this unity is actualized *through* the sharing of the meal, as opposed to the meal merely being symbolic of a unity already established "spiritually." By taking such a view, McClendon moves closer to a more sacramental understanding of the Lord's Supper than many within the free church tradition would espouse.

Yet, has he moved far enough to justify his claims about the unity of the church being rooted in its eucharistic observance? Central to his brief discussion about solidarity is McClendon's treatment of what Jesus means by the statement "This is my body" (1 Cor 11:24). He distances himself from medieval interpretations which relied on a metaphysic of substance, then very briefly recognizes more recent (and "less foreign") theories of "transsignification" in Catholic thought. Finally, he develops an interpretation dependent on the thought of Austin Farrer.[51] In McClendon's view, when Jesus said, "This is my body," he spoke a truism that anyone in Jesus' day would not have found surprising; food, when ingested, becomes a part of the human body. The bread Jesus offered his disciples was "his body to be." When the church offers its bread to Jesus, it becomes his, and he offers it back to the church. Rather than Christ slaughtered on the table to be eaten by the

49. See ibid., 377–79.
50. Ibid., 401.
51. Specifically, see Farrer, *Faith of Our Own*, 146ff.

congregants, McClendon says, "Christ risen is present in our Eucharist to commune with us, to give us bread that is his, and so (by rights) his own body." It is through this "union" with Jesus that the members of the church are re-membered, re-united to one another as Christ's members.[52]

It is not clear to me what McClendon means by receiving bread from Jesus that "by rights" is his own body. It does seem one step removed from receiving Christ's body itself. In spite of his use of "union" and "communion," it seems that what matters to McClendon is Jesus' presence, in terms of proximity, or perhaps moral unity. His opening statement about the Lord's Supper locates its power in its "nearness to the person of Christ."[53] Elsewhere, he states that the *telos* of God's mission is "the bringing of the divine self and human selves into an unspeakable, ecstatic intimacy." McClendon refers to this intimacy as "union" and "participation" and "fellowship" drawing on Paul's term *koinonia*. Yet when he defines *koinonia*, it is "participation *with* someone *in* some common engagement." The fellowship of the Spirit, then, is "participation *in* nearness to God *with* others in whom the same Spirit works."[54] Thus, McClendon's use of "union" and "participation" language does not seem aimed at making strong ontological claims along the lines of *theosis* and the common union made possible by such a theological focus. Perhaps that is because for McClendon, it is stories that converge, not natures; and stories have no ontological status.

The logic of Paul's argument in 1 Corinthians seems to require a closer connection than McClendon develops among the physicality of Jesus, the eucharistic elements, and the church as the body of Christ. By participating in the one loaf that sacramentally and materially focuses the presence of Christ to the gathered worshipers, these worshipers become what they eat—a unified body by virtue of their participation *in* (not simply proximity to) the very life of Christ. McClendon rightly affirms the social implications of the Eucharist, including peacemaking and unity, but he does not provide a sacramental ontology that adequately identifies this new social reality with its Lord such that we may speak of the body of Christ as more than mere metaphor. And Jenson rightly argues that to treat the body of Christ simply as a metaphor makes mush of Paul's argument in 1 Corinthians.

52. McClendon, *Doctrine*, 401–2.

53. Ibid., 400. It is not clear what McClendon might mean by "nearness" here. One would not think he conceives of God as being otherwise spatially separated from humans.

54. Ibid., 443, emphases added.

Catholicity

To the degree that McClendon's theology allows any real force to the church being the body of Christ, he appears to limit that designation to the local, gathered congregation,[55] a limitation he expressly applies to the word *church* (*ekklesia*) as well.[56] Robert Jenson represents the widely held ecumenical agreement that *church*, as it occurs in the New Testament, can be applied at different levels. At the very least it includes two levels—local gatherings and the one great fellowship in Christ (e.g., 1 Cor 1:2; 12:28; Acts 9:31). By limiting the body of Christ to the local congregation, it is not clear how McClendon could speak meaningfully of "the" body of Christ that is "one," a central Pauline teaching (e.g., Eph 4:4, 12). It seems as though McClendon is letting his free church commitments govern his exegesis of Scripture at this point.

McClendon's surprising delimitation of "church" to the local congregation has implications for his vision of ecclesial unity. McClendon argues that the New Testament (especially Pauline) emphasis is not upon one "church" extended through many "branch outlets." Rather, its emphasis is upon local gatherings around the risen Jesus. Each assembly is original and dependent upon the Holy Spirit in its midst. For McClendon, this "primitive pattern" has "typical and lasting value" in contrast to those who would argue that such an early pattern represents an embryonic stage in ecclesiastical development.[57] He does not argue this point as much as he asserts the point. Part of McClendon's rationale for such a claim is rooted in his acceptance and extension of an ecclesiological typology he borrows from Lesslie Newbigin. Newbigin locates three ecclesiological "types," which he labels Catholic, Protestant, and Pentecostal. McClendon approves of much of how Newbigin describes the third group, but prefers to call it the "baptist type." McClendon summarizes Newbigin's description of this type as "local, Spirit-filled, mission-oriented, its discipleship always shaped by a practice of discernment."[58]

---

55. Ibid., 409. Here he says in its re-membering, the church reconstitutes "Christ's body in the gathering." See also *Ethics*, 215–16, where he addresses Paul's discussion in 1 Corinthians of the "powerful metaphor of the gathered church constituting the body of Christ."

56. McClendon, *Doctrine*, 364–65.

57. Ibid., 364.

58. Ibid., 343. McClendon adds to this description the "baptist vision" reading strategy. Elsewhere, he refers to this third type also by the terms *free church* and *believers church*, 362.

Much of what McClendon has to say about ecclesiology is calculated to defend and recommend this ecclesial type.[59] He does not claim it is the only legitimate ecclesial type. In fact, he argues that from an eschatological viewpoint, each type is only provisional. This ecclesiological provisionality is crucial to his own ecumenical strategy. According to McClendon, it is appropriate to talk about "the universal dimension Christian community" beyond the local gathering,[60] but as we have seen, such community is not properly labeled "church." It is a church (i.e., local gathering) that is marked by visibility, shared practices of identity formation (most centrally baptism and Eucharist), discernment, etc. To speak of Christian community beyond the local church, McClendon prefers the categories of "people" and "peoples." He derives this terminology from Scripture, where God calls "a people" together (ethnic Israel) that then opens to include another people (Gentiles), whom Paul calls "the Israel of God" (Gal 6:16). Thus, in the New Testament, we see the people of God including two peoples still being formed (but not yet fully formed) into one people.[61] McClendon connects the categories of "people" and "peoples" to Newbigin's ecclesial types to suggest that the one people of God includes all these types ("peoples") and their subtypes. While McClendon acknowledges that such diversity threatens unity, he also emphasizes that they make up "the rich plurality of the people of God."[62] His ecumenical strategy, then, seems to be a recognition that each type of Christian community is provisional, with none able to simply absorb the others. Fulfillment of the unity God desires remains an eschatological reality. In the meantime, "peoples" within "the people" of God can and should open themselves to each other.[63] We will return shortly to how McClendon conceives of such openness.

A strength of McClendon's ecclesiology over many free church accounts is his emphasis on the visible church as the focal point of Christian unity (contra those accounts, many of which are free church, that locate unity in the notion of an invisible church). Further, like Jenson and Williams,

59. In an aside, McClendon at one point states that ecclesiologies that are organized around ecclesial models or images "too easily conform to existing presuppositions about the church," *Doctrine*, 328. I suggest that McClendon himself is prone to move in the same direction. It seems exegetically unnatural, for example, to argue that *church* in the New Testament refers *only* to a local gathering.

60. Ibid., 328.

61. Ibid., 363–64. McClendon also appeals to Romans 9–11 to support the notion of the people of God encompassing two peoples.

62. Ibid., 365.

63. McClendon, *Doctrine*, 344, 370–71.

he rightly emphasizes that the Eucharist is the central practice by which the visible community is formed and reformed in unity as it gathers around Christ. It seems, however, that McClendon unnecessarily limits visible unity to the local congregation. Perhaps this is because he unnecessarily limits the context of central ecclesial practices, by which visible unity is most realized, to the local congregation. If you disallow any ecclesial contexts beyond the local congregation from being properly church, those contexts are not the proper place for the ecclesial practices by which the church's identity is formed and reformed. It is difficult to ascertain, then, what McClendon would mean by pursuing *Christian* unity at the level of "peoples" beyond local churches if Christian unity emerges specifically through Spirit-guided ecclesial practices.

Yet McClendon does in fact promote the issue of Christian unity beyond the local congregation. He asserts that all Christians have a duty to realize the unity for which Jesus prayed (that *all* his disciples would be one [John 17:20–23]) and which Paul commanded when he exhorted the Ephesian Christians to find unity in one Lord, one faith, and one baptism (Eph 4:5).[64] In fact, McClendon embraces the nonbiblical term *catholic* as a way of highlighting his concern for such unity. His use of the term, however, appears incomplete when viewed alongside Jenson's and Williams' understanding of catholicity. McClendon and Yoder together argue that the term *catholic* needs greater specification than it often receives and that the "baptist" ecclesial style can confidently lay claim to it when properly defined. They argue that the term *catholic* usually operates at three levels. The earliest instances of "catholic church" (which they designate catholic1) in the post-apostolic writings referred to a *quality* of churches, specifically a quality of wholeness that encompassed belief, worship, and ethics. A second sense of the term emerged in the second century according to which "catholic church" became roughly synonymous with a new understanding of the term

64. McClendon and Yoder, "Christian Identity in Ecumenical Perspective," 561. It is interesting that in this discussion of Ephesians 4:3–6 and broad Christian unity, McClendon does not at all mention the Pauline phrase "one body" that occurs in 4:4. Its absence is especially noteworthy in that this article is primarily about catholicity, albeit a "baptist" style of catholicity. That McClendon and Yoder can articulate a "baptist" catholicity and casually ignore the "body of Christ" readily at hand in one of their flagship biblical texts is revealing. The image of "one body" beyond the local congregation would suggest an ontological reality that McClendon likely finds uncomfortable given his theological commitments we have been tracing. What meaning could it have for him, except for something strictly metaphorical? A strictly metaphorical usage would be problematic since nothing else in the list found in Ephesians 4:4–5 is metaphorical (one lord, one faith, one baptism, one God, etc.).

church (*ekklesia*) in which *church* was used metaphorically to refer to "all the churches summed up as one" (even though this referent never gathered). This second sense (catholic2) is roughly equivalent to *ecumenical* in McClendon's and Yoder's usage—ecumenical in the modern sense of referring to the "universal Christian community" (both geographically and denominationally). The third sense of *catholic* (catholic3, or "the Catholic Church") came to be associated in the West with the Roman Catholic Church that (along with other groups in the East) claimed to be *the* catholic church on the basis of its unique organic structure which bound the prior two senses of *catholic* together.[65]

McClendon and Yoder forthrightly embrace the term *catholic2* as a way of expressing "the concept of *substantial* Christian unity."[66] They then declare their intention to argue that a believers church ecclesial style demonstrates catholicity1 (i.e., wholeness) in such as way as to make for catholicity2 (i.e., ecumenical unity).[67] First, we notice here that the unity they seek is "substantial" unity. We recall that for McClendon, substantial unity is visible and demonstrable unity rooted mainly in shared practices around the lordship of Christ. Second, when McClendon and Yoder attempt to describe catholicity1 in their own terms, the "wholeness" they describe includes several things: a typological reading of Scripture (i.e., the baptist vision); a particular conception of and practice of mission, liberty, discipleship, and community; a strongly sacramental emphasis (i.e., an objective view of the sacraments); and its own "concept of tradition."[68]

One problem with this description is that they have not shown why this particular list of descriptors represents "wholeness," except to say that the catholicity described here does not differ from ecclesial life in the first, second, or third centuries.[69] They assume that the church of the first three centuries is, in principle, the full measure of catholicity.[70] A second prob-

65. Ibid., 562–63, with special attention to n. 7.

66. Ibid., 564, emphasis added.

67. Ibid., 565. McClendon also refers to the ecumenical orientation of the baptist type as the "catholicity of intent." He points to the baptist emphasis on worldwide mission as evidence, *Doctrine*, 450–51.

68. McClendon and Yoder, "Christian Identity in Ecumenical Perspective," 570–72.

69. Ibid., 571.

70. I suggest that part of what motivates such a view is their ubiquitous concern, present in this essay as well, about the Constantinian settlement that emerged in the fourth century and gave rise to what is now called Christendom. While neither McClendon nor Yoder sets forth a clear theory of "the fall" of the church in this essay, as some in the Anabaptist tradition have done, each is very sensitive (and rightly so) to the

lem is that there may be important things missing here for a full account of catholicity. As McClendon and Yoder admit, whether their free church account of catholicity is valid is debatable and is an account best judged by historians.[71]

It seems to me that both Jenson and Williams provide more rigorous historical rationales for their respective accounts of catholicity. For example, like McClendon, Jenson describes catholicity in terms of wholeness, but he includes within that wholeness, for justifiable historical reasons we have already observed in chapter 2, things like apostolic tradition (including the rule of faith), ecumenical creedal statements, and episcopal ministry. In the context of this essay, the only specification McClendon and Yoder give to "tradition" is that the "baptist vision" is itself a biblical and ancient catholic tradition. As a description, this sits light with respect to tradition as mediating any determinative content by which Christians have historically been able to recognize each other (e.g., Nicene theology). Williams also describes catholicity in terms of wholeness, but he emphasizes the nature of that wholeness as having not only to do with a quality of apostolic origin but universal significance, relatable to the entire range of human condition and experience. This is all eventually rooted in the church's central proclamation of one new humanity in Christ, the proclamation central to McClendon's theology as well, as we have seen. As a result, Williams describes any local church's catholicity primarily in terms of its "mutual critical openness" to the entire range of believers, both past and present. In these terms, catholicity serves to free the local congregation from the prison of the local

---

serious risks involved with the collusion of church and state. It seems, however, that in their attempts to define the different markers of catholicity, they are led more by their free church aversions to historical Christendom than is necessary for trying to discern the heart of historic catholicity. In each of their markers of catholicity1, there seem to be veiled (in some cases, not so veiled) criticisms of the Roman Catholic Church as well as mainstream Protestant groups. Yet these criticisms sometimes seem to be responses to free church caricatures of such groups that, if they ever were accurate, no longer represent the complexity of the situation. For example, they want "mission" to be understood not as a Christian attempt to control history, but as the responsibility to witness to Christ, accepting the resulting suffering. This seems to be a stab at the Christendom model, yet thoughtful contemporary Roman Catholics are more sensitive than were their forebears to the problems with such a model. In fact, one could argue that many free church groups (especially those of a mainstream evangelical bent) have become too enamored in recent years with some form of a Christendom vision just when Roman Catholics are learning historical lessons about its dangers. Thus, the description here of a "baptist" style of mission appears less a description than a goal—or at the very least, it is a vision not unique to a baptist-style ecclesiology.

71. McClendon and Yoder, "Christian Identity in Ecumenical Perspective" 573.

perspective. This is not only a strictly theological argument for Williams; he demonstrates historically that early "catholic" churches were noteworthy for their high level of epistolary correspondence as they sought to recognize and sharpen among each other a common faith and practice. They perceived they were accountable to one another. What is missing in McClendon is the "mutual critical" portion of "mutual critical openness." Openness alone will not free individuals or local churches from the sometimes crippling effects of localism.

Visible Ecclesial Unity

McClendon is aware of this threat of isolation implicit within a free church perspective. He admits that placing ecclesial focus on the local congregation does not mean that churches can be churches in isolation. Each church exists in a "shared subordination to God's rule" as a church among churches.[72] What does McClendon mean by "shared subordination"? As a phrase, "shared subordination" does not necessarily express a vision of *substantial* and visible unity. In what sense does McClendon believe that subordination is "shared" among churches? Is it shared only in the sense that it describes a common feature of genuine churches (i.e., submission to God's rule)? It seems that McClendon is implying something more than that since he rejects the idea that a church can be a church in isolation from other churches. The implication is that genuine churches should (must?) actively demonstrate somehow that they are not living in isolation. Yet it is still unclear exactly what McClendon believes is shared.

Contrary to many in the free church tradition, McClendon actually provides somewhat of a justification for institutional structures beyond the local congregation that may help facilitate the kind of church relationships he has in mind. But is his vision for these structures sufficient for nurturing and displaying broad Christian unity? McClendon argues that churches need not only the shared Spirit-led practices around which they gather "in a place" but also the narrative tradition of their sharing along with a "modest institutional home in which these practices and this narrative inhere." At this level, we are talking not about churches but peoplehoods alongside other peoplehoods in the Israel of God. Examples of such institutional homes are the Roman Curia or the Southern Baptist Convention. Whether functioning on a very small scale or a worldwide scale, they are "agents of peoplehood

72. McClendon, *Doctrine*, 365–66.

and servants of each church" but are not themselves "churches." Their two main agendas are to serve churches and to function as "an ecumenical open window" through which churches can "reach out to one another in shared peoplehood" and to other peoplehoods in the Israel of God. After providing his justification for these institutional general bodies, McClendon says denominational agencies such as these cannot adequately facilitate a baptist style ecumenism, because "the true genius of Christian community lies not in them, but in the church."[73]

It is hard to imagine exactly what McClendon actually has in mind with all of this, and several problems surface upon reflection. What does it mean for churches to "reach out to one another"? What is the goal? Since this discussion happens under the heading "Toward the Israel of God," one would think the purpose is to realize more fully Christian unity, the very concern McClendon lays out at the beginning of this chapter on ecclesiology. Yet how do such nonlocal bodies function ecumenically to facilitate the kind of visible unity that McClendon believes is important and that will be fully realized only in the eschaton? What is the nature of that unity? How is it visibly expressed as specifically *Christian* unity? He does not say. He only says that through these agencies, churches "reach out" to other churches. We should not be surprised to see no mention here of the practices (or institutions such as a teaching office) by which McClendon believes Christians are known to and bound to each other within local churches (e.g., Eucharist or discernment), because for McClendon these practices (and institutions) mark the gathered church "in a place." Yet without sharing among themselves these and other fundamental identifying practices of Christian community, how can churches recognize each other in *Christian* unity?

In McClendon's description, nonlocal structures have no authority. Their role is simply one of service to churches and a means by which conversation is facilitated among churches. McClendon advocates churches reaching out to each other, but what is noticeably absent is any notion of churches being *accountable* to each other and in *need* of each other for wholeness. McClendon's account of catholicity that we sketched above reveals one of its weaknesses at this point. I have argued that while it is encouraging to see a free church theologian embracing the language of catholicity, his explication of catholicity comes up short. He rightly focuses on catholicity as "wholeness," but he fails to address crucial features of what the church has traditionally included in that wholeness. Jenson and Williams taken together point us to an understanding of catholicity that is theologically and

73. Ibid., 370–71.

historically more fulsome, one in which churches not only reach out toward but are accountable to their common tradition and to each other for matters of faith and practice. One of the primary ways in which this accountability is practically negotiated and embodied is through episcopal structures of authority. To quote again Williams's succinct summation of the matter, "If catholicity matters, then structures of authority matter."[74] The fact that McClendon does not see these structures as authoritative structures reveals more fully that he is working from a different understanding of catholicity than are Williams and Jenson. Catholicity, for Jenson and Williams, is borne by the conviction that all Christians are actually (ontologically) bound up together in the one body of Christ that transcends but is reflected in each ecclesial gathering. The body of Christ is not merely a metaphor. While "the peoples of God" or "the Israel of God" provide for meaningful theological reflection, such phrases do not make the ontological claims that the body of Christ makes. The risen Christ attaches to and within himself all those who come to him in faith, and by being included in him, they are thereby brought into communion with all others across time and space who find their place in the one Christ. When such a view of the body of Christ is in view, unity beyond the local congregation involves more than simply "reaching out to each other" in a perhaps friendly but essentially noncommitted or nonaccountable gesture of goodwill. It is a single ontological reality/possibility, variously embodied, that Christians are called to make perceptible in the world, the one body of Christ.

Ecclesial Authority

It is not that McClendon is without an appreciation for ecclesial authority; it is only that he limits ecclesial authority within the scope of the local congregation, and the result is obviously something quite distinct from what we have seen in both Jenson and Williams. The final chapter of McClendon's *Doctrine* deals specifically with the problem of authority. He rightly states that only God *is* authority; the debated questions are about the modes through which God's authority is manifested in the world. These authorities are what McClendon calls "proximate" authorities. He locates three primary modes of such authorities which he (somewhat awkwardly) relates to the Trinitarian persons: experience, Scripture (with its tradition), and the

74. R. Williams, "Authority and the Bishop in the Church," 93.

church.[75] We have already seen how he articulates the authority of Scripture. Again, that he would include tradition in his treatment of Scripture is a move beyond where much of the free church has been, yet we have also seen that his account of the authority that might attach to tradition is not as fully orbed as it might be, and in the context of this discussion of authority, tradition gets subsumed under his discussion of the authority of Scripture until it almost quietly dissolves into Scripture. One gets the impression that McClendon sees (theoretically) the inescapability of tradition, and yet for all that, he cannot finally escape the biblicist inclinations he inherited from within his own tradition. With regard to experience as a locus of authority, McClendon rightly critiques any conception that would treat experience as an independent or foundational authority.[76] He directs his critique specifically against Schleiermacher's *Gefühl*, but it also applies to more contemporary expressions of the personal and internal experience of the Spirit (e.g., "soul competency" among Baptists). McClendon acknowledges the reality of evangelical experience but insists that it be located and framed by the other two loci of Scripture and the church. In doing so, he rightly locates Christian experience in such a way as to resist the damaging individualism that has bedeviled so much of the free church tradition.

It is with the third locus of authority, the church, that we are most concerned at the moment. Whatever McClendon has to say about the authority of the church is premised on the understanding of the church as the fellowship of the Spirit. Further, the authority exercised by the church is a result of "the inevitability that in a living community, someone, somehow, shall indeed judge." Rather than beginning with any specific office of ecclesial authority within the congregation as being responsible for such discernment, McClendon's starting point is the affirmation that the entire community of faith serves as a proximate authority. The authority of the community is the authority to discern God's sole authority; communal discernment is a mode of God's presence as the Holy Spirit. For McClendon, Spirit-led discernment is one of the central and distinctive practices of the church (Matt 18; 1 Cor 5, 12–14). It takes place when disciples gather "in a certain

---

75. McClendon, *Doctrine*, 456–59.

76. For McClendon's discussion of experience as a locus of authority, see ibid., 459–62. I realize the role and weight of personal experience needs much attention within many free churches, but I have chosen to place my emphasis elsewhere for the purposes of this study.

place" and prayerfully deliberate the direction to take in their common life in light of Scripture and experience, "shaping the common judgment of all concerned."[77]

McClendon claims that the strength of a congregational polity of discernment does not lie in a democratic tallying of votes. Rather, it lies in the mutual trust of those who gather, the diversity of the Spirit's gifts represented in those present in the gathering, openness to the voice of outsiders, and obedience to the Spirit. He then claims that the strength of what he calls a "connectional polity" lies in the extension of these same qualities to the exchange between congregations at the level of peoplehood.[78] After acknowledging (even if, perhaps, only out of politeness) the strength of connectional polities, he returns immediately to providing a rationale for a local form of ecclesial polity. He primarily roots his case in the fact that all three kinds of authority he ascertains to be part of personal authority (i.e., "authorities on," "authorities in," and criterial authority) can be found within any local congregation. In any congregation, there will be "authorities on" things such as the Bible, doctrine, missions, etc. These experts (e.g., theologians and historians) in certain areas exercise a proximate authority over the common life whether in person or through their writings.[79] Secondly, there are "authorities in" the congregation. McClendon is not clear about what precisely constitutes such authority. He only lists examples such as pastors, deacons, church callers, and church secretaries. He calls them "servant offices" and says they are only authoritative to the degree that they reflect the servanthood of Jesus. He also distinguishes the "solitary expert" (i.e., "authority on") from "the designated leader," so it seems that "authorities in" have a distinct function of leadership. It is not clear what conception of leadership McClendon is working with by collecting pastors and church secretaries under this "kind" of authority. Lastly, there is criterial authority, which is the authority members of the congregation have simply by being members. This authority comes to expression only in the members' gathering that is empowered by the Holy Spirit. The proximate authority of the "authorities on" and "authorities in" is dependent upon this criterial authority.[80]

77. McClendon, *Doctrine*, 478–79.

78. Ibid., 479.

79. If McClendon's concern is to show how each of these authorities is found within the congregation, it is a bit strange that he would suggest that these "authorities on" may exercise authority either in person or through their writings. How would the latter case support his argument for congregationalism?

80. For this discussion of the three kinds of authority, see McClendon, *Doctrine*, 479–80.

All of this leads McClendon to a view of ecclesial authority modeled on a Ferris wheel. Since all human authority is proximate and only God's authority is final, each expression of human authority and each "kind" of authority in the Ferris wheel of authority finds its place in a moving circle of discernment that "has no top chair, no priestly summit—not 'the clergy,' not the solitary 'believer-priest' with his or her Bible, not 'the whole church in council,' since each of these is secured to and depends on others in the wheel, and since each in turn must swing beneath the discerning judgment of God."[81] McClendon's free church sensitivities lead him to react against anything resembling hierarchy. He argues that God's consistent desire for his people is to overcome distinctions rooted in authoritative power. For example, unlike the nations around them, Israel was to be a nation of priests not a nation with priests.[82] Further, McClendon calls for the "radical abolition" of the distinction between clergy and laity. He roots this in the Pauline idea of gifts within the church, expressed in the image of Christ's body in which all members are distinct yet equal, equally gifted for the building up of the community "whose accomplishment is the fullness of Christ" (Eph 4:13).[83] McClendon is most concerned about avoiding a special class of people for ministry within the church. All members are called to ministry. He interprets baptism as a commissioning for ministry, and so baptism functions as

---

81. Ibid., 478.

82. Ibid., 368.

83. Ibid., 369. I include the final phrase verbatim because McClendon states it without qualification. We have already seen that McClendon is not ignorant about the possible force of the word *is* (e.g., "this is that"). Yet what can *he* intend by it here? Paradoxically, it occurs in this discussion of the body of Christ, which we have seen he does not develop with much ontological heft. On the surface, however, he seems to read this Ephesian phrase ("the fullness of Christ") in a way that would resonate with Jenson's emphasis on the patristic notion of the *totus Christus*. The fact that he does not at all develop the body of Christ in this direction within the same paragraph makes it hard to believe that he really intends the ontological identification between Christ and the church that the closing quote above suggests on a surface reading. For his discussion of "the fullness of Christ," McClendon expressly draws upon John Yoder's book *The Fullness of Christ*. In a condensation of that book's theme, Yoder develops this Pauline phrase in connection with Paul's use of the body of Christ. It is very much in tune with the things we have observed here in McClendon. And it is clearer in Yoder's exposition than in McClendon's that he does not intend by this phrase to suggest an ontological connection between Christ and his church. In fact, not only does he treat the body of Christ as simply metaphorical, but he also seems to treat "the fullness of Christ" as a metaphor for a new mode of relationships in which each individual has a divinely given and specific role in relation to the whole. See *Body Politics*, 47–60, esp. 47. That McClendon so closely follows Yoder at this point suggests that McClendon does not intend to indicate ontological union between Christ and the church.

ordination in free churches rather than ordination referring to a process by which some members are separated off from others for special ministry.[84] He states plainly, "If *leadership* in the church is a gift among gifts granted in the fullness of Christ, then ordination (not provided in the New Testament) and hierarchy (opposed there) are not essentials of leadership, and may concretely resist the realization of that fullness."[85]

There are certain things to appreciate about McClendon's account of ecclesial authority. His emphasis on discernment involving the entire worshipping community is a strong affirmation of the church as the fellowship of the Spirit. He rightly roots this in the notion that the unity of the ecclesial body of Christ arises from the mutuality of the wide range of various gifts the Spirit provides. Historically, this has not been appreciated enough by hierarchically oriented churches (or free churches for that matter). While McClendon may sometimes argue against a caricature of the Roman Catholic hierarchy as an authoritarian disseminator of doctrine that the faithful are simply to accept and repeat, there is some truth within the caricature. A strong emphasis upon local discernment of the entire congregation is thoroughly biblical and theologically sound; yet, it need not be the sole property of a free church style. Both Jenson and Williams demonstrate a profound regard for the necessity of local discernment, but they do not believe the importance of local discernment implies a strictly congregational polity.

While McClendon admirably articulates the importance of local discernment, he does not adequately deal with the subsequent ecumenical question. He acknowledges that one of the strengths of "connectional polities" is that they extend the strengths of the local congregation to larger levels of conversation. This begs the question: if this is possible, why would it not be preferable, or even required? On what basis would one continue to argue for the superiority of a congregational polity if connectional polities extend the unity made possible by congregational practices, and thus effect greater visible unity? McClendon consistently makes his case based on what he finds in Scripture. In his view, the New Testament reveals that discernment is a central Christian practice that occurs "in a certain place" (i.e., locally) via the differentiated gifts of the congregation and in such a way that a common judgment is shaped. First, why could not a meeting for discernment among representatives from different churches constitute "a certain place"? Jenson and Williams argue that just such representatives, in the form of bishops, carry the crucial local discernment to be weighed by the wider mind of the

84. McClendon, *Doctrine*, 369.
85. Ibid., 371.

church. But as we have seen, McClendon has not provided much theological basis for any ontological union beyond the local congregation that could emerge in anything like "the mind of the church." Jenson and Williams have provided an ontology of union that can sustain a more robust commitment to visible ecclesial unity.

Second, if McClendon finds value in the differentiation of gifts for the process of discernment, why would not global processes of discernment be even more desirable? Congregationalism still risks entrapment within a local perspective, even with an array of spiritual gifts.[86] Just as in a local congregation, the members submit themselves to the discernment of the whole so that a common judgment emerges. Why would local churches not be eager to submit to the authority of a global process of discernment that weighed seriously the local processes of discernment, trusting that the unity of the body of Christ emerges through attending to the wide array of God's gifts in the church, across both time and space? Jenson and Williams demonstrate, each in his own way, how extra-congregational forms of teaching authority properly emerge from the gifts of local churches rather than beginning at the global level and filtering into local churches.

Third, McClendon's assertion that the New Testament model of discernment is only local is questionable at best. It is interesting that for all his interest in discernment as a central churchly act, he refers to the so-called Jerusalem Council of Acts 15 only twice in *Doctrine*.[87] In each of these instances, it is only a passing reference. The Jerusalem Council is perhaps the quintessential instance of Spirit-led discernment in the New Testament. McClendon quickly passes by it as just one illustration of a congregation (i.e., "the Jerusalem church") practicing discernment, but it seems to indicate more than this.[88] It was a council of discernment involving representatives from both Antioch (Paul and Barnabas) and Jerusalem (the apostles and elders). The goal was to seek a common mind and then to urge that shared discernment upon churches within their missionary scope. After

---

86. McClendon provides two essential Christian convictions. First, "my own story is inadequate" (the doctrine of the church). Second, "*our* story is inadequate" (the doctrine of salvation), *Ethics*, 356. By the second, he means each church's story is dependent upon God's overarching story, but it could become more theologically rounded if by this he also intended to say that each church's story is incomplete without converse with the others in the one body of Christ.

87. See 142 and 253.

88. Given the prominence of the Jerusalem Council in Roman Catholic and Orthodox churches, it would seem the burden of proof would lie with those who deny that it justifies in some sense extra-congregational patterns of authority.

all had been heard, James stood and declared what "I have decided" (even with the apostles present). After receiving consent from "the whole church" (i.e., the Jerusalem church), the leaders constructed a letter to be read to the Gentile churches that laid out what the council had decided "unanimously" (ὁμοθυμαδὸν). The letter declared what "seemed good to the Holy Spirit and to us," which included the primary message of Gentile freedom from Mosaic law (primarily freedom from circumcision) along with the few impositions they did decide to place on the Gentile churches. Whatever the historical outcome of this council and its letter, it clearly indicates a process of discernment involving representatives from more than one congregation, the common mind of which was expected to have authoritative influence in other churches.[89] In matters that greatly affect visible unity, Jenson and Williams likewise believe in processes of global discernment that begin by hearing the full range of local discernment and aim toward a common mind. Williams has historically been more tentative than Jenson about the authority of such discernment as it bears on local churches but has increasingly advocated the need for greater accountability among churches mediated by episcopal structures that facilitate global discernment. Still, for both theologians, the process includes a genuine reciprocity between the global and local modeled for each upon his Trinitarian theology.

McClendon is largely concerned to resist hierarchy, and as we have seen, this instinct finds expression not only in disallowing structures of authority beyond the local congregation (such structures exist to serve local churches), it also finds expression within the congregation as exemplified in his use of the image of the Ferris wheel with no top chair. He sees resistance to hierarchy as the ideal of God's people represented in Scripture, but once again, it seems his free church instincts govern his reading of Scripture. To say Israel was to be distinguished from other nations by being a nation *of* priests not a nation *with* priests is only half true; clearly Israel had a special class of priests internal to herself even as she served her sacerdotal function as a whole. Further, McClendon uses Paul's image of the body to press the point that the distribution of the Spirit's various gifts creates a polity in which each member is distinct yet equal. His emphasis falls on the "equal" portion of this formula, where equality means primarily eliminating all distinctions between clergy and laity. There is no ecclesial function that any member cannot perform. Williams, however, argues that a radically egalitarian approach

89. How this actually played out, especially in Paul's missionary travels, is difficult to assess. For our purposes, it is sufficient to show that Acts presents a situation that does not appear to reflect congregationalism as it is defended by many free churches today.

fails to appreciate enough the distinction of gifts in the body of Christ. While in agreement with McClendon that the pastoral function is one gift among others, for Williams it comes with a distinct authority to govern the teaching of the church, not in isolation from the church's discernment, but also not simply as a voice to articulate a general consensus.

For both Jenson and Williams, the authority of the teaching office arises out of its eucharistic connection. This is because for both of them the teaching office functions primarily as a sign of unity, not simply a voice of discernment. Since the Eucharist is the church's central practice by which unity is realized and nourished, the manner of openness to other churches is primarily oriented toward eucharistic recognition among churches. The extra-congregational teaching office is the personal representation and sign of any local church's unity to itself and to the rest of the body of Christ. For this reason, it is theologically significant that the person occupying the teaching office regularly preside at the Eucharist. Whatever teaching authority inheres in the office emerges from this primary function of the office as a sign of unity. It is most centrally through eucharistic recognition among churches represented to each other through their personal signs of unity that the one body of Christ becomes visible. Herein lies the problem for McClendon. Without an ontology that can account for a unified body of Christ beyond the local congregation, and without a sacramental account of the Eucharist that really emphasizes union through participation, an account of the teaching office will lack substance in comparison with what we find in Jenson and Williams.

Conclusion

McClendon rightly points to a singular and unified human race as the eschatological goal of God. And he rightly emphasizes that this new human reality is to be made visible by the church, which is continually renewed through its Spirit-led central practices. Eventually, McClendon does not see it as a great burden to realize full visible unity among churches because it will only be fully realized in the eschaton. He does affirm that churches should work toward whatever unity may be possible, but he seems fairly satisfied to affirm the legitimacy of the different ecclesial types, even as he argues that the free church type is preferable. Jenson and Williams also affirm that full visible unity is an eschatological reality, but both feel more compelled than McClendon to work toward that unity in the present. They are not as satisfied as McClendon to see the different ecclesial types as a beautiful display of the rich variety of God primarily because the goal of the church is to embody one new humanity. I have tried to show that McClendon's justification of the free church tradition is made possible in part by a) suppressing the possibility and reality of actual theological development and historical contingency, a suppression made possible partly through his brand of biblicism, and b) developing a soteriology that is ontologically anemic such that the notion of the one body of Christ and its sacramental sinews cannot be supported, and thus, the demonstration of Christian unity beyond the local congregation is rendered almost unintelligible. Jenson and Williams find some important points of contact with McClendon, but it is primarily because of a fundamentally different orientation regarding these two points that they cannot eventually argue for the adequacy of the free church tradition. The first point is not truthful, and the second grows out of the first by not recognizing what is at stake in the church's most fundamental dogma.

6

Conclusion

As we observed in the first chapter, there is an increasing resistance among free church scholars to depend on the notion of an invisible church to account for ecclesial unity. Scholars such as James McClendon and John Yoder have been influential among free church theologians in their insistence that the church's witness is rooted primarily in its visible communal life and that its visible unity is paramount to that witness. We also observed there is a new generation of free church theologians who are wrestling more closely and seriously with the church's tradition than did pioneers such as McClendon and Yoder who contributed so much in moving free church scholars toward friendly engagement with the church's larger tradition and contemporary ecumenical discussions. Not only are these recent scholars attending more carefully to engaging the tradition, they are increasingly calling for tradition to be approached as a locus of authority. We observed some of their primary rationales for doing so, rationales that are compelling both historically and theologically.

The primary aim of this study has been to question, via engagement with Robert Jenson and Rowan Williams, whether these contemporary free church scholars have gone far enough in assessing the implications of such retrievals, implications especially with regard to ecclesial unity. Namely, is it possible to both promote an ecumenical agenda for visible unity and embrace the authority of the church's tradition without also discovering the need (or at least the usefulness) for some sort of authoritative extra-congregational teaching office? Once the historical nature of tradition and catholicity come into view, is it possible, or even desirable, to retrieve the catholic tradition congregationally "as Baptists" or "for free churches" as suggested by some of these leading free church theologians? While the main purpose of this study is primarily to press the question from within the free church tradition, my own tentative response to the question is that such goals are too short-sighted. Just as McClendon helped move free church theologians forward in some important ways, these more recent theologians have made invaluable contributions in an ecumenical direction and toward leading free churches closer to resources for nurturing catholicity. But upon careful historical and theological reflection, it becomes increasingly difficult to see how it is coherent to advocate a deepening engagement with the church's tradition with the expressed goal of sustaining free churches *as* free churches, especially when the episcopal office has been so important in the development of that very tradition.

The question of a teaching office presents itself more forcefully the more one engages the Christian tradition as a locus of authority and not simply as a resource. Without a teaching office, who (i.e., what authority) says what parts of the tradition are to be retrieved, to what extent, and how? How are such decisions made either by individuals or single congregations to avoid the trap of provincialism or mere preferences in what they choose to engage, which would be yet another expression of the kind of individualism (personally or congregationally) these theologians are seeking to combat in the first place by leading free churches toward tradition? The historic role of the bishops in the church's developing tradition is worthy of far more consideration than it has yet been given by the free church theologians advocating a free church retrieval of the tradition.

Only recently has this lacuna been clearly acknowledged and addressed by one of the most active voices in this newer generation of free church scholars. Steven Harmon essentially sidestepped the question in his book *Toward Baptist Catholicity*. More recently, however, Harmon has acknowledged that he avoided the issue both because of his target audience and because he was not satisfied with his own provisional solution at the time he wrote his book. In this more recent piece, he attempts to provide a modest response. He argues that even free churches operate with a magisterium. In contrast to both Roman Catholic and magisterial Protestant accounts, the free church magisterial authority resides in the gathered congregation. It is what Harmon calls the "magisterium-hood of all believers," which basically amounts to the process of local discernment emphasized so heavily by McClendon and Yoder. Ideally, says Harmon, local congregations are not absolutely independent but through different levels of association seek the mind of Christ together, interdependently. In this way, free churches avoid the negative implications of descriptors such as "independent" or "autonomous." Harmon concludes by listing eight kinds of resources (aside from Scripture) that should be weighed in free church processes of discernment, ranging from ancient creeds to contextual theologies. Almost all these resources come from outside the free church tradition and should be weighed carefully, "even if such weighing results in heavily qualified reception."[1]

While there is much to commend in this lecture, the notion of a free church magisterium does not, in my view, provide a satisfactory response to the questions that occasioned the lecture. The fact remains that, on this account, free churches have the option of "heavily qualified reception" of some or any of these resources, or perhaps in some cases no reception at all beyond initially weighing them. Harmon's "magisterium-hood of all believers" is a process that begins with local discernment (using resources mostly from outside the free church tradition) and ideally emerges in wider discernment among congregations as they seek a "fuller grasp of the truth, as one ecclesial communion," and perhaps the process might even eventually move outside one's own tradition. At some point, this begins to look like something other than free church polity. If it still reflects a free church polity, then it is only because each congregation sees the others as partners in discernment, but eventually they are not accountable to each other for the decisions they make as local churches.[2] We have seen that a similar polity, although preferable to radical congregational autonomy, has not been sufficient to maintain visible unity among Anglicans in recent years and who are now considering how they might increase their levels of mutual accountability and have this reflected in their global structures.

We have engaged the thought of Robert Jenson and Rowan Williams, two theologians from outside the free church tradition, to see how each construes the relationship between visible ecclesial unity and the requisite authorities by which such unity is nourished and maintained. Each of these theologians argues that authority is exercised through a complex of

1. Harmon, "Nicene Faith and the Catholicity of the Church." The final quotation comes from 90.

2. While this lack of accountability remains an implication in Harmon's presentation, it is stated more clearly in the work of free church theologian Miroslav Volf. Like Harmon, Volf emphasizes the importance of local congregations being open to each other, freely networked through structures that facilitate such openness. This is one mark of catholicity. But he argues that an ordained office is not necessary for ecclesiality, even if good and useful. Each congregation is a church and is connected to other churches because of a common confession of Christ (strikingly, Volf does not even mention classic creeds in this discussion). Extra-congregational councils have no authority over local congregations because Christ is fully present to each congregation, and each congregation is "self-complete," *After Our Likeness*, 275, 154–55.

Scripture, tradition, and an extra-congregational teaching office. They end up with somewhat different visions of ecclesial unity, differences most noticeable in their approaches to the teaching office. Jenson argues for an episcopally oriented polity with a universal pastor representing the unity of the church, and pragmatically he argues that that pastor should be the bishop of Rome. Williams argues for a non-centralized episcopal polity (a conciliarist model) and, increasingly in his role as archbishop, has acknowledged the potential need for a voice of unity from among the bishops that would represent the mind of the global church to the particular churches in such a way that the global discernment would carry a greater degree of authority in the local churches than perhaps it has in the past among Anglicans. In terms of visible unity, these are different models. Taken together, however, Jenson and Williams provide many common and compelling points of challenge to the free church tradition while being able to support some of the main concerns of those within the free church tradition.

Both Jenson and Williams have a concern for visible unity that arises partly out of a soteriological ontology of divine participation. Not only is *theosis* the goal of individual believers, participation in the Trinitarian life of God is the communal goal of all humanity made possible by participation in the resurrected life of Jesus. The church is the body of Christ, not simply in a metaphorical sense, but in that believers truly participate in Christ's very life, and are thereby held in a common fellowship of union with each other. This communion is locally and visibly manifested in gathered churches as well as in their demonstrated relationships of unity. Christ has included within his own life this fellowship of the Spirit and has chosen its visible manifestation as his very own embodiment in the world. That is not to say that Christ's presence in the world is limited to the church, but it is to affirm the visible church as Christ's chosen means of embodiment, or tangible availability to use Jenson's terminology. It is this ontology of participation that largely undergirds the sacramental theology of each of these theologians. The sacraments, primarily baptism and the Eucharist, are the means by which this union is effected and regularly nourished. So for Jenson and Williams, the sacraments become crucially important in any discussion of ecclesial unity, not only within local congregations but among them as well, because the body of Christ is one.

As long as free churches were willing to emphasize the invisible church as the true church, there was no great pressure toward realizing visible unity among churches. Now that more free church theologians are emphasizing the visible church, they have to work harder to make the case for a congregational polity, since the church's unity is one of its primary means of witness to a united humanity in Christ. One way to do this is to reject or downplay an ontological connection between Christ and the church as his body.[3] But as more free church theologians give ontological weight to the one ecclesial body of Christ and its relation to the sacraments (especially the Eucharist),[4] the pressure toward extra-congregational visible unity mounts, and it becomes even harder to argue that the free church polity is a preferred ecclesial model. The episcopal office has historically been the means for embodying the unity of the one body of Christ among churches. Such an understanding of the importance of this office arises primarily from the eucharistic practice of local churches seeking to recognize each other as participants in the life of the same God.

We have also noticed how recent free church scholars have begun to deal more carefully with the complex historical and theological issues surrounding early Christianity in ways that have led them to challenge simplistic notions of *sola scriptura* along with their inevitable tendency toward individualism. These scholars are calling for a closer connection to the church's tradition, especially the church's early tradition as enshrined in its liturgical practices, interpretive practices, catechetical instructions, and most of all in its ecumenical dogmatic teaching. They are encouraging their free church brothers and sisters to consciously read Scripture and formulate their teaching by the light of these ancient interpretive guides, treasures that belong equally to all Christians. These same free church scholars affirm the inevitability of genuine doctrinal development and so will urge, for example, faithfulness to Nicene theology as a marker of orthodoxy and that orthodoxy

3. We saw this already with McClendon, who is ambiguous on the issue and largely ignores it. Miroslav Volf accepts only a metaphorical and non-organic usage of the term, *After Our Likeness*, 142–45. The illustrious Church of Christ historian Everett Ferguson argues that the body of Christ functions beyond the merely metaphorical, but he thinks it likely expresses the idea of "corporate personality" rather than an ontological or organic union with Christ. His concern is to acknowledge an intimate connection between Christ and the church while maintaining the proper distinction between them, *Church of Christ*, 94.

4. E.g., Harvey, *Can These Bones Live?*, ch. 6. It is worth noting in this connection that Harvey operates throughout this book with the patristic doctrine of *theosis* as the proper *telos* of humans. Elizabeth Newman makes sacramental union the theological underpinning of her exposition on Christian hospitality, *Untamed Hospitality*, ch. 6. For a brief summary of other Baptist scholars moving in the direction of sacramental union, see Harmon, *Towards Baptist Catholicity*, 13–14. A recent ecclesiology written by evangelical theologians from the free church tradition sounds a surprisingly clear note regarding the church's sacramental participation in Christ. See Harper and Metzger, *Exploring Ecclesiology*, ch. 7.

is not static but develops through processes of historical contingency. They believe that without recourse to this tradition, free churches will have nothing to keep them from coming untethered from the church's one faith. These arguments are compelling.

Through engagement with Jenson and Williams, however, we have reason to question whether turning to the authority of tradition as independent congregations is sufficient. First, congregationalism could not have produced the very tradition these free church theologians want their churches to retrieve. The historic episcopate was crucial to the complex development of both the canon of Scripture and the church's theological tradition. Jenson rightly asks on what basis the authority of tradition could be meaningfully recognized without also recognizing the episcopal authority that was crucial to its formation. Second, to argue for the legitimacy of doctrinal development and the authority attending to such development, and then to argue that a free church polity is capable of retrieving this tradition and bearing it forward, is to imply that doctrinal development is no longer possible or needed. For who would speak for "the church" in such a divided state of affairs? The implication in the work of some of these newer free church voices is that orthodoxy was genuinely accomplished through historical contingency, but it then became locked within a particular time period (e.g., the patristic period). To "fix" orthodoxy in this way is to do to the tradition what these scholars say free churches have tended to do with Scripture; it is the same impulse of biblicism just applied to a larger pool of data. If the issues leading up to Nicea were truly historically contingent and could not have been known ahead of time, there is no reason to assume that the church/churches will not have to face equally threatening crises in the future; and we cannot know ahead of time what they might be. To advocate a free church polity oriented toward the tradition fixes the tradition in such a way that these free churches are crippled to be able to respond in the face of new crises. The church must have a living voice by which she can retrieve and promulgate the tradition if tradition is to maintain its lively quality that Jenson and Williams most ably demonstrate it must have (and that some of these free church theologians advocate as well). If, as with Jenson and Williams, the meaning(s) of Scripture and tradition turn out to be less static than sometimes thought, then a living voice of discernment is needed for those who seek to embrace the one apostolic faith reflected in both Scripture and tradition.

Further, if the church is to bear witness to its proper *telos* primarily by its unified life, then the living teaching voice of the church that oversees that unified life must itself reflect the one true humanity in Christ. As Jenson and Williams argue, however else it might have happened, the episcopal polity has been the mode of this voice historically, and it was largely by means of this mode of speaking that classical orthodoxy took shape. Whether or not one argues for the essentiality of the episcopal office to the church, it is understandable why one would affirm along with both Jenson and Williams that, in the absence of any obvious reasons to the contrary, the church should embrace the means by which the tradition has in fact been handed on and by which Christians for centuries have been able to recognize in each other a common faith.

Neither Jenson nor Williams makes exaggerated claims about what a teaching office can guarantee. Nor are they bashful about acknowledging the problems and failures of episcopal polities as they have been practiced. Perhaps this modest position opens the door to a more sympathetic hearing from free churches. There may be problems in practice with episcopal forms of polity, but to cavil about these problems and not fully own up to the critical problems of a free church polity is dishonest. Congregational forms of polity can be just as hierarchically authoritarian as any episcopal polity, only on a smaller scale. Congregations can be as enslaved to local prejudices, preferences, and individualistic notions of rights as any free church caricature of episcopal churches being enslaved to the theology of remote ecclesial office holders.

Since the one body of Christ is *about* overcoming that which divides humans, churches cannot afford to emphasize only the local perspective. In a world of increasing globalization, the church cannot afford to be provincial, even while emphasizing the importance of the gathered community. The church must show forth what genuine globalization looks like. Rowan Williams's emphasis on *gift* is crucial at this point. In their global connections and accountability to each other, churches should be bodying forth the one true humanity in Christ that rejects all barriers of racial and nationalistic self-interest in favor of acting in the interest of the other, knowing that we cannot know ourselves rightly apart from the strange other. The perspective from the strange other is one of the central means by which we are challenged to truthfulness in our means of knowing. A church that is not willing to be truthful in its processes of knowing is a church that cannot hold out much hope for increased visible unity. A teaching office that represents local eucharistic congregations to each other is one of the primary ways in which such truthfulness is pursued. And it is one of the primary ways the one new humanity in Christ is visibly demonstrated and the one body of Christ discerned.[5]

While Williams argues that a global perspective is crucial to the church's truthfulness, free church theologians may be tempted to respond that conciliatory processes and decisions facilitated by episcopal structures may not themselves be the measure of truthfulness. They may argue that dissenting voices are crucially important in any truthful process of discernment. Some free church theologians continue to see their own traditions as primarily dissenting traditions within the larger Christian tradition. That is, in the wide spectrum of the variety of gifts in the body of Christ, the primary role they play in the larger body is that of the dissenting voice.[6] It may be true that there are legitimate occasions for dissent, but to root one's primary identity in dissent within an overall program that is essentially about unity is unintelligible. Dissent, when called for, must be a principled and occasional action, not an identity.[7]

To argue against a global teaching office by asserting that it is not found in Scripture or in the apostolic period is simply not an effective argument if we hold to a view of developing tradition and the church's developing self-understanding such as we find in Jenson or Williams. First, the degree of autonomy among early churches is sometimes overplayed, especially by free church theologians. As we have seen, Williams shows how the epistolary evidence among early Christians demonstrates a degree of accountability among churches often overlooked by historians.[8] Second, Jenson effectively argues that something can emerge through historically contingent circumstances that then becomes an integral part of the fabric of the reality in which

5. After rehearsing the strengths of a congregational polity, free church theologians Metzger and Harper acknowledge that it is the least suitable to express the universality and oneness of the church, *Exploring Ecclesiology*, 198–99. If the proper *telos* of humanity is communal participation in the divine life such that one unified humanity is made a reality, it seems strange that anyone would advocate the polity least suitable to embodying its eschatological end. Rowan Williams rightly argues that any expression of authority must be consonant with the *telos* toward which it is heading.

6. E.g., see Freeman, "Confession for Catholic Baptists," 85–86.

7. For a very good discussion of the important role of "loyal dissent" within the church, see Schlabach, *Unlearning Protestantism*, ch. 5.

8. Wendell Willis, a New Testament scholar from the Church of Christ tradition, argues that the Pauline corpus demonstrates churches that expected to be compared with and corrected by believers in other congregations. He argues (rather provocatively for a Church of Christ scholar), "The widespread Pauline congregations were not independent franchises adapting their gospel to a local market, but the nascent form of an ecumenical church," "Networking of the Pauline Churches," 78.

it functions. In this case, the episcopate was not original to the church's organization or self-understanding. Once it emerged, however, it became integral to how the church knew itself and proclaimed its common faith in increasingly complex situations. Free church theologians have increasingly been willing to admit such a process with regard to Trinitarian theology, but generally do not allow it at the level of ecclesial organization.

Free churches cannot truthfully claim the theological treasures of the tradition while easily rejecting one of the central means by which the tradition was formed. That is not to say the churches within the free church tradition are not genuine churches.[9] In fact, it is the fact that Jenson and Williams would consider them churches that might allow free churches to hear them more easily than perhaps they could hear others from outside the free church tradition. Jenson and Williams operate with an understanding of degrees of catholicity. Many or most free churches are within this spectrum of catholicity, but because of a lack of formal connection to the wider body of Christ, their catholicity exists in a diminished form. Whatever catholicity they embody and whatever theological orthodoxy they reflect may be a matter of closeness in historical proximity to their theological roots (and the grace of God) rather than anything inherent in the free church polity. There is nothing to suggest they will not eventually float away from traditional teaching if there is no accountability to remain close to it.

Both Jenson and Williams are agreed with a number of free church scholars that the unity of the church is eventually an eschatological reality. What they may disagree about is the urgency with which churches should pursue a eucharistically centered visible unity. Robert Jenson acknowledges the church exists in a state of waiting, but its time of waiting must be an active waiting, working diligently toward visible unity. If, as Jesus prays in the Gospel of John, the unity of the Christian community is the means by which the world comes to know Christ, then demonstrable unity does not appear to be a luxury the church can leisurely pursue.

Both Jenson and Williams operate with a vision that takes Scripture seriously, that does not underestimate the importance of the local eucharistic gathering, that has no illusions about the flaws and potential hazards within an episcopal ecclesial arrangement, and that is always cautious about the abuse of authoritarian exercises of power sometimes found

---

9. Though one could legitimately question whether they were churches on their own, apart from the Catholic and Orthodox bodies. It is possible to interpret the Catholic use of "ecclesial communities" along these lines. For this discussion, see Turner, *When Other Christians Become Catholic*, 116–21.

within hierarchical churches. For these reasons, among others, free churches should be able to enter into patient conversation with these two theologians without too much initial defensiveness. What they will find are two generous theologians who, nonetheless, will put some difficult questions to the long-term viability of the free church tradition. They will find two theologians committed to the visible manifestation of the one body of Christ and to the idea that a truthful embodiment of this unity now requires a church willing to submit to God's authority as it is mediated principally through a complex interconnection of Scripture, tradition, and a living teaching office, the latter of which takes its rise first and foremost from the church's most visible unifying practice, the Eucharist. They will find in these two theologians an account of unity in which the very exchanges between the local and global come to reflect the eternal Trinitarian exchange into which the church herself is always being drawn.

This study has placed a question mark over the long-term theological viability of the free church tradition. That is not to say that free church members must leave free churches to be located in the catholic church. If this study has arrived at any trustworthy conclusions, however, those within free churches cannot afford to willfully operate apart from churches that preserve their catholicity through deep engagement with the tradition and a global teaching office. Further, they cannot see their own continuance, *qua* free churches, as an admirable goal. By virtue of the Bible they use and their general affirmation of the central tenants of orthodoxy (e.g., Trinitarian doctrine), free churches *do* participate in the church's tradition. The question is, will they, like a growing number of free church theologians, truthfully acknowledge this fact? For those who will acknowledge that fact, how will they pursue a more intentional engagement with the church's tradition?

Those who are convinced of the force of the questions raised by this study and who choose to remain in free churches should remain not only to honor the heritage that brought them to faith (however deficient in its content), they should also remain as a gift to that same heritage with the commitment to bring their churches toward the one body of Christ. This may occur in any number of unofficial ways, many of which are suggested by free church theologians such as Harmon and Volf. But these ways of keeping our churches "close to home" through unofficial conversation with those beyond our borders are no substitute for full, visible eucharistic fellowship in which each part is accountable to all other parts and in which the body of Christ becomes most fully transparent to a watching world.

Bibliography

Allen, Leonard. "The Future of the Restoration Movement." *Leaven* 14:4 (2006) 150–65.

Allert, Craig D. *A High View of Scripture? The Authority of the Bible and the Formation of the New Testament Canon.* Evangelical *Ressourcement*. Grand Rapids: Baker Academic, 2007.

Armstrong, Chris. "The Future Lies in the Past: Why Evangelicals Are Connecting with the Early Church As They Move into the 21st Century." *Christianity Today*, February 8, 2008, 22–29.

"The Anglican Communion Covenant: The Ridley Cambridge Draft." Online: http://www.anglicancommunion.org/commission/covenant/ridley_cambridge/draft_text.cfm.

Davis, Ellen F., and Richard B. Hays, editors. *The Art of Reading Scripture.* Grand Rapids: Eerdmans, 2003.

Avis, Paul. "Church." In *The Encyclopedia of Protestantism*, edited by Hans Hillerbrand, 1:416–19. New York: Routledge, 2004.

———. Foreword to *Towards Baptist Catholicity: Essays on Tradition and the Baptist Vision*, by Steven R. Harmon. Studies in Baptist History and Thought 27. Milton Keyes: Paternoster, 2006.

Bauer, Walter. *Orthodoxy and Heresy in Earliest Christianity.* Philadelphia: Fortress, 1971.

Baptism, Eucharist and Ministry. Faith and Order Paper No. 111. Geneva: WCC, 1982.

Barton, Stephen C. "New Testament Interpretation as Performance." *Scottish Journal of Theology* 52:2 (1992) 179–208.

Bezzant, Rhys. "The Ecclesiology of Rowan Williams." In *On Rowan Williams: Critical Essays*, edited by Matheson Russell, 1–24. Eugene, OR: Cascade Books, 2009.

Bonhoeffer, Dietrich. *Conspiracy and Imprisonment.* Edited by Mark S. Brocker. Translated by Lisa E. Dahill. Dietrich Bonhoeffer Works 16. Minneapolis: Fortress, 2006.

———. *Discipleship.* Edited by Geffrey Kelly and John Godsey. Translated by Barbara Green and Reinhard Krauss. Dietrich Bonhoeffer Works 4. Minneapolis: Fortress, 2001.

Boring, M. Eugene. *Disciples and the Bible: A History of Disciples Biblical Interpretation in North America.* St. Louis: Chalice, 1997.

Braaten, Carl. "Robert William Jenson—A Personal Memoir." In *Trinity, Time, and the Church: A Response to the Theology of Robert W. Jenson*, edited by Colin Gunton, 1–9. Grand Rapids: Eerdmans, 2000.

Braaten, Carl, and Robert Jenson, editors. *The Catholicity of the Reformation.* Grand Rapids: Eerdmans, 1996.

———. *Church Unity and the Papal Office: An Ecumenical Dialogue on John Paul II's Encyclical* Ut Unum Sint. Grand Rapids: Eerdmans, 2001.

———. *The Ecumenical Future: Background Papers for* In One Body Through the Cross: The Princeton Proposal for Christian Unity. Grand Rapids: Eerdmans, 2004.

———. *In One Body Through the Cross: The Princeton Proposal for Christian Unity.* Grand Rapids: Eerdmans, 2003.

Broadway, M., et al. "Re-Envisioning Baptist Identity: A Manifesto for Baptist Communities in North America." *Perspectives in Religious Studies* 24:3 (1997) 303–10.

Buckley, James J. "Intimacy: The Character of Robert Jenson's Theology." In *Trinity, Time, and the Church: A Response to the Theology of Robert W. Jenson,* edited by Colin Gunton, 10–22. Grand Rapids: Eerdmans, 2000.

Burgess, Andrew. *The Ascension in Karl Barth.* Barth Studies. Burlington, VT: Ashgate, 2004.

"The Chicago Call: An Appeal to Evangelicals." In *The Orthodox Evangelicals: Who Are They and What They Are Saying?,* edited by Robert E. Webber and Donald Bloesch. Nashville: Thomas Nelson, 1978.

Childers, Jeff, Douglas Foster, and Jack Reese. *The Crux of the Matter: Crisis, Tradition, and the Future of Churches of Christ.* Heart of the Restoration Series 1. Abilene, TX: Abilene Christian University Press, 2001.

Congar, Yves M. J. *Tradition and Traditions: An Historical and Theological Essay.* New York: Macmillan, 1966.

Congregation for the Doctrine of the Faith. "Declaration '*Dominus Iesus*': On the Unicity and Salvific Universality of Jesus Christ and the Church." Online: http://www.vatican.va/roman_curia/congregations/cfaith/documents/rc_con_cfaith_doc_20000806_dominus-iesus_en.html.

Crisp, Olilver. "Robert Jenson on the Pre-Existence of Christ." *Modern Theology* 23:1 (2007) 27–45.

Cumin, Paul. "Robert Jenson and the Spirit of It All: Or, You (Sometimes) Wonder Where Everything Else Went." *Scottish Journal of Theology* 60:2 (2007) 161–79.

Cunningham, David. "Living the Questions: The Converging Worlds of Rowan Williams." *Christian Century,* April-May, 2002, 18–29.

Dawson, John David. "Figural Reading and the Fashioning of Christian Identity in Boyarin, Auerbach and Frei." *Modern Theology* 14:2 (1998) 181–96.

Durnbaugh, Donald F. *The Believer's Church: The History and Character of Radical Protestantism.* 2nd ed. Scottdale, PA: Herald, 1985.

Erickson, Millard. *Christian Theology.* Grand Rapids: Baker, 1985.

Fackre, Gabriel. "The Lutheran *Capax* Lives." In *Trinity, Time, and the Church: A Response to the Theology of Robert W. Jenson,* edited by Colin Gunton, 94–102. Grand Rapids: Eerdmans, 2000.

Farrer, Austin M. *A Faith of Our Own.* Cleveland: World Press, 1960.

Farrow, Douglas, David Demson, and J. Augustine Di Noia. "Robert Jenson's 'Systematic Theology': Three Responses." *International Journal of Systematic Theology* 1 (1999) 89–104.

Ferguson, Everett. *The Church of Christ: A Biblical Ecclesiology for Today.* Grand Rapids: Eerdmans, 1996.

Fiddes, Paul S. *Tracks and Traces.* Studies in Baptist History and Thought 13. Carlisle: Paternoster, 2003.

Florovsky, Georges. "The Work of the Holy Spirit in Revelation." *The Christian East* 13:2 (1932) 49–64.

Forde, Gerhard O. "Robert Jenson's Soteriology." In *Trinity, Time, and the Church: A Response to the Theology of Robert W. Jenson*, edited by Colin Gunton, 126–38. Grand Rapids: Eerdmans, 2000.

Fowl, Stephen, editor. *The Theological Interpretation of Scripture: Classic and Contemporary Readings*. Blackwell Readings in Modern Theology. Oxford: Wiley-Blackwell, 1997.

Freeman, Curtis. "A Confession for Catholic Baptists." In *Ties That Bind: Life Together in the Baptist Vision*, edited by G. Furr and C. W. Freeman, 83–97. Macon, GA: Smyth & Helwys, 1994.

———. "Where Two or Three Are Gathered: Communion Ecclesiology in the Free Church." *Perspectives in Religious Studies* 31:3 (2004) 259–272.

Freeman, Curtis, et al. "Confessing the Faith." In *Towards Baptist Catholicity: Essays on Tradition and the Baptist Vision*. Studies in Baptist History and Thought 27. Milton Keyes: Paternoster, 2006.

Frei, Hans. *The Eclipse of Biblical Narrative: A Study in Eighteenth and Nineteenth Century Hermeneutics*. New Haven: Yale University Press, 1974.

———. "The 'Literal Reading' of Biblical Narrative in the Christian Tradition: Does It Stretch or Will It Break?" Abridged and edited by Kathryn Tanner. In *The Return of Scripture in Judaism and Christianity*, edited by Peter Ochs, 55–82. New York: Paulist, 1993.

George, Timothy. "The Sacramentality of the Church." In *Baptist Sacramentalism*, edited by A. Cross and P. Thompson, 5:21–35. Studies in Baptist History and Thought. Carlisle: Paternoster, 2003.

Grenz, Stanley. *Renewing the Center: Evangelical Theology in a Post-Theological Era*. Grand Rapids: Baker Academic, 2000.

———. *Theology for the Community of God*. Grand Rapids: Eerdmans, 1994.

Grenz, Stanley, and John R. Franke. *Beyond Foundationalism: Shaping Theology in a Postmodern Context*. Louisville: Westminster John Knox, 2001.

Grudem, Wayne. *Systematic Theology: An Introduction to Biblical Doctrine*. Grand Rapids: Zondervan, 1994.

Gunton, Colin. "Creation and Mediation in the Theology of Robert W. Jenson." In *Trinity, Time, and the Church: A Response to the Theology of Robert W. Jenson*, edited by Colin Gunton, 80–93. Grand Rapids: Eerdmans, 2000.

Hanson, R. C. P. *The Search for the Christian Doctrine of God: The Arian Controversy, 318–381*. Grand Rapids: Baker Academic, 2006.

Harmon, Steven R. "The Nicene Faith and the Catholicity of the Church: Evangelical Retrieval and the Problem of Magisterium." In *Evangelicals and Nicene Faith: Reclaiming the Apostolic Witness*, edited by Timothy George, 74–92. Grand Rapids: Baker Academic, 2011.

———. *Towards Baptist Catholicity: Essays on Tradition and the Baptist Vision*. Studies in Baptist History and Thought 27. Milton Keyes: Paternoster, 2006.

Harnack, Adolph von. *History of Dogma*. Translated by Neil Buchanan. 5 vols. New York: Dover, 1961.

Harper, Brad, and Paul Metzger. *Exploring Ecclesiology: An Evangelical and Ecumenical Introduction*. Grand Rapids: Brazos Press, 2009.

Hart, David Bentley. "The Lively God of Robert Jenson." *First Things* 156 (2005) 28–35.

Harvey, Barry. "Beginning in the Middle of Things: James McClendon's Systematic Theology." *Modern Theology* 18:2 (2002) 251–65.

————. *Can These Bones Live? A Catholic Baptist Engagement with Ecclesiology, Hermeneutics, and Social Theory*. Grand Rapids: Brazos, 2008.

————. "Doctrinally Speaking: James McClendon on the Nature of Doctrine." *Perspectives in Religious Studies* 27:1 (2000) 39–61.

————."Where, Then, Do We Stand? Baptists, History, and Authority." *Perspectives in Religious Studies* 29:4 (2002) 359–80.

Heine, Ronald E. *Reading the Old Testament with the Church: Exploring the Formation of Early Christian Thought*. Evangelical *Ressourcement*. Grand Rapids: Baker Academic, 2007.

Highfield, Ron. *Great Is the Lord: Theology for the Praise of God*. Grand Rapids: Eerdmans, 2008.

Higton, Mike. *Difficult Gospel: The Theology of Rowan Williams*. New York: Church Publishing, 2004.

Hobson, Theo. *Anarchy, Church and Utopia: Rowan Williams on Church*. London: Darton, Longman & Todd, 2005.

————. "The Policing of Signs: Sacramentalism and Authority in Rowan Williams' Theology." *Scottish Journal of Theology* 61:4 (2008) 381–95.

Hollerich, Michael J. "Retrieving a Neglected Critique of Church, Theology and Secularization in Weimar, Germany." *Pro Ecclesia* 2:3 (1993) 305–32.

Holmes, Stephen. *Listening to the Past: The Place of Tradition in Theology*. Grand Rapids: Baker Academic, 2002.

Hunsinger, George. "Robert Jenson's *Systematic Theology*: A Review Essay." *Scottish Journal of Theology* 55 (2002) 176–79.

Ive, Jeremy. "Robert Jenson's Theology of History." In *Trinity, Time, and the Church: A Response to the Theology of Robert W. Jenson*, edited by Colin Gunton, 146–57. Grand Rapids: Eerdmans, 2000.

Jenson, Robert W. *Alpha and Omega: A Study in the Theology of Karl Barth*. New York: Thomas Nelson, 1963. Reprint, Eugene, OR: Wipf & Stock, 2002.

————. "Can a Text Defend Itself? An Essay *de Inspiratione Scripturae*." *Dialog* 28 (1989) 251–56.

————. *Canon and Creed*. Interpretation: Resources for the Use of Scripture in the Church. Louisville: Westminster John Knox, 2010.

————. "Catachesis for Our Time." In *Marks of the Body of Christ*, edited by Carl Braaten and Robert Jenson, 137–49. Grand Rapids: Eerdmans, 1999.

————. *Christian Dogmatics*. Edited by Carl Braaten and Robert Jenson. 2 vols. Philadelphia: Fortress, 1984.

————. "The Church and the Sacraments." In *The Cambridge Companion to Christian Doctrine*, edited by Colin Gunton, 207–25. New York: Cambridge University Press, 1997.

————. "The Church as *Communio*." In *The Catholicity of the Reformation*, edited by Carl Braaten and Robert Jenson, 1–12. Grand Rapids: Eerdmans, 1996.

————. "The Church as Communion: A Catholic-Lutheran Dialogue-Consensus-Statement Dreamed in the Night." *Pro Ecclesia* 4:1 (1995) 68–78.

————. *Essays in Theology of Culture*. Grand Rapids: Eerdmans, 1995.

————. "The Future of the Papacy: A Symposium." *First Things* 111 (2001) 28–36.

————. "Hermeneutics and the Life of the Church." In *Reclaiming the Bible for the Church*, edited by Carl Braaten and Robert Jenson, 89–106. Grand Rapids: Eerdmans, 1995.

————. "How the World Lost Its Story." *First Things* 36 (1993) 19–24.

———. *The Knowledge of Things Hoped For.* Oxford: Oxford University Press, 1969.

———. "Male and Female He Created Them." In *I Am the Lord Your God: Christian Reflections on the Ten Commandments,* edited by Carl Braaten and Christopher Seitz, 175–88. Grand Rapids: Eerdmans, 2005.

———. "On the Authorities of Scripture." In *Engaging Biblical Authority: Perspectives on the Bible as Scripture,* edited by William P. Brown, 53–61. Louisville: Westminster John Knox, 2007.

———. "On the 'Joint Declaration' of the LWF and the RC Church on the Doctrine of Justification." *Pro Ecclesia* 5 (1966) 137–41.

———. "On the Problem(s) of Scriptural Authority." *Interpretation* 31 (1977) 237–50.

———. *A Religion Against Itself.* Richmond: John Knox, 1967.

———. "Response to Watson and Hunsinger." *Scottish Journal of Theology* 55:2 (2002) 225–28.

———. Review of *On Christian Theology,* by Rowan Williams. *Pro Ecclesia* 9:3 (2002) 367–69.

———. "Scripture's Authority in the Church." In *The Art of Reading Scripture,* edited by Ellen F. Davis and Richard B. Hays, 27–37. Grand Rapids: Eerdmans, 2003.

———. "A Second Thought about Inspiration." *Pro Ecclesia* 13:4 (2004) 393–98.

———. *Song of Songs.* Interpretation. Louisville: John Knox, 2005.

———. *Story and Promise: A Brief Theology of the Gospel about Jesus.* Philadelphia: Fortress, 1973.

———. *Systematic Theology.* 2 vols. New York: Oxford University Press, 1997–99.

———. "A Theological Autobiography, to Date." *Dialog* 46:1 (2007) 46–54.

———. *The Triune Identity: God According to the Gospel.* Philadelphia: Fortress, 1982.

———. *Unbaptized God: The Basic Flaw in Ecumenical Theology.* Minneapolis: Fortress, 1992.

———. *Visible Words: The Interpretation and Practice of the Christian Sacraments.* Philadelphia: Fortress, 1978.

Jorgenson, Cameron H. "Bapto-Catholicism: Recovering Tradition and Reconsidering the Baptist Identity." PhD diss., Baylor University, 2008.

Kärkkäinen, Veli-Matti. *An Introduction to Ecclesiology: Ecumenical, Historical and Global Perspectives.* Downers Grove, IL: InterVarsity, 2002.

Köster, Helmut. "GNOMAI DIAPHOROI." *Zeitschrift für Theologie und Kirche* 65 (1968) 160–203.

Lash, Nicholas. *Theology on the Way to Emmaus.* London: SCM, 1986.

Layman, David Wayne. "The Inner Ground of Christian Theology: Church, Faith, and Sectarianism." *Journal of Ecumenical Studies* 27 (1990) 480–503.

Lindbeck, George. *The Nature of Doctrine: Religion and Theology in a Postliberal Age.* Philadelphia: Westminster John Knox, 1984.

———. "Papacy and the Ius Divinum: A Lutheran View." In *Papal Primacy and the Universal Church,* edited by Paul Empie and T. Austin Murphey, 5:193–207. Lutherans and Catholics in Dialogue. Minneapolis: Augsburg, 1974.

Long, D. Stephen. *The Goodness of God.* Grand Rapids: Brazos, 2001.

Lossky, Vladimir. *The Mystical Theology of the Eastern Church.* London: J. Clarke, 1957.

Lubac, Henri de. *Catholicism: Christ and the Common Destiny of Man.* Translated by Lancelot Sheppard and Elizabeth Englund. San Francisco: Ignatius, 1988.

———. *The Church: Paradox and Mystery.* Translated by James Dunne. New York: Ecclesia, 1969.

―――. *Medieval Exegesis: The Four Senses of Scripture.* Translated by Marc Sebanc. 3 vols. *Ressourcement:* Retrieval and Renewal in Catholic Thought. Grand Rapids: Eerdmans, 1998–2009.

―――. *The Splendour of the Church.* Translated by Michael Mason. New York: Sheed & Ward, 1956.

MacIntyre, Alasdair. *After Virtue.* 2nd ed. Notre Dame: Notre Dame University Press, 1984.

―――. *Whose Justice? Which Rationality?* Notre Dame: Notre Dame University Press, 1988.

Martin, Dennis. "*Evangelicals and Tradition: The Formative Influence of the Early Church,* a review." *Pro Ecclesia* 18:2 (2009) 216–19.

Mattes, Mark C. "An Analysis and Assessment of Robert Jenson's *Systematic Theology.*" *Lutheran Quarterly* 14:4 (2000) 463–94.

―――. *The Role of Justification in Contemporary Theology.* Grand Rapids: Eerdmans, 2004.

McClendon, James W., Jr. *Biography as Theology: How Life Stories Can Remake Today's Theology.* Nashville: Abingdon, 1974. Reprint, Eugene, OR: Wipf & Stock, 2002.

―――. *Doctrine.* Vol. 2 of *Systematic Theology.* Nashville: Abingdon, 1994.

―――. *Ethics.* Vol. 1 of *Systematic Theology.* Nashville: Abingdon, 1986.

―――. *Witness.* Vol. 3 of *Systematic Theology.* Nashville: Abingdon, 2000.

McClendon, James W., Jr., and James M. Smith. *Convictions: Defusing Religious Relativism.* Rev. ed. Valley Forge, PA: Trinity, 1994.

―――. *Understanding Religious Convictions.* Notre Dame: Notre Dame University Press, 1975.

McClendon, James W., Jr., and John Howard Yoder. "Christian Identity in Ecumenical Perspecitve." *Journal of Ecumenical Studies* 27:3 (1990) 561–80.

Medley, Mark. "Catholics, Baptists, and the Normativity of Tradition." *Perspectives in Religious Studies* 28:2 (2001) 119–29.

―――. "Stewards, Interrogators, and Inventors: Toward a Practice of Tradition." *Pro Ecclesia* 18:1 (2009) 69–92.

Milbank, John. "'Postmodern Critical Augustinianism': A Short *Summa* in Forty-Two Responses to Unasked Questions." *Modern Theology* 7:3 (1991) 225–37.

―――. *The Word Made Strange: Theology, Language and Culture.* Oxford: Blackwell, 1997.

Molnar, Paul. "Robert W. Jenson's *Systematic Theology, Volume 1: The Triune God.*" *Scottish Journal of Theology* 52:1 (1999) 117–31.

Moody, Andrew. "The Hidden Center: Trinity and Incarnation in the Negative (and Positive) Theology of Rowan Williams." In *On Rowan Williams: Critical Essays,* edited by Matheson Russell, 25–46. Eugene, OR: Cascade Books, 2009.

Murphy, Nancey. *Beyond Liberalism and Fundamentalism: How Modern and Postmodern Philosophy Set the Theological Agenda.* Valley Forge, PA: Trinity, 1996.

Myers, Benjamin. "Disruptive History: Rowan Williams on Heresy and Orthodoxy." In *On Rowan Williams: Critical Essays,* edited by Matheson Russell, 47–67. Eugene, OR: Cascade Books, 2009.

Neuhaus, Richard. "Jenson in the Public Square." In *Trinity, Time, and the Church: A Response to the Theology of Robert W. Jenson,* edited by Colin Gunton, 238–51. Grand Rapids: Eerdmans, 2000.

Newbigin, Lesslie. *The Household of God: Lectures on the Nature of the Church.* New York: Friendship, 1954.

Newman, Elizabeth. "The Priesthood of All Believers and the Necessity of the Church." In *Recycling the Past or Researching History? Studies in Baptist Historiography and Myths*, edited by P. E. Thompson and A. R. Cross, 11:50–66. Studies in Baptist History. Waynesboro, GA: Paternoster, 2005.

———. *Untamed Hospitality: Welcoming God and Other Strangers*. The Christian Practices of Everyday Life. Grand Rapids: Brazos, 2007.

Newman, John Henry. *An Essay on the Development of Christian Doctrine*. 6th ed. Notre Dame: Notre Dame University Press, 1989.

———. *On Consulting the Faithful in Matters of Doctrine*. Kansas City: Sheed & Ward, 1961.

———. *The Via Media of the Anglican Church*. Edited by H. D. Weidner. Oxford: Clarendon, 1990.

"Nine Theses on the Interpretation of Scripture." In *The Art of Reading Scripture*, edited by Ellen Davis and Richard Hays, 1–8. Eerdmans: Grand Rapids, 2003.

Norris, Frederick W. "The Canon of Scripture in the Church." In *The Free Church and the Early Church: Bridging the Historical and Theological Divide*, edited by D. H. Williams, 3–26. Grand Rapids: Eerdmans, 2002.

Nugent, John C., editor. *Radical Ecumenicity: Pursuing Unity and Continuity after John Howard Yoder*. Abilene, TX: Abilene Christian University Press, 2010.

Ochs, Peter. "A Jewish Reading of *Trinity, Time and the Church: A Response to the Theology of Robert Jenson*." *Modern Theology* 19:3 (2003) 419–27.

O'Donovan, Oliver. "Archbishop Rowan Williams." *Pro Ecclesia* 12:1 (2003) 5–8.

Pannenberg, Wolfhart. "Eternity, Time and the Trinitarian God." In *Trinity, Time, and the Church: A Response to the Theology of Robert W. Jenson*, edited by Colin Gunton, 62–70. Grand Rapids: Eerdmans, 2000.

Pelikan, Jaroslav. *The Christian Tradition: A History of the Development of Doctrine*. Vol. 1, *The Emergence of the Catholic Tradition (100–600)*. Chicago: University of Chicago Press, 1971.

Ratzinger, Joseph. "Fragen zur Sukzession." *KNA-Kritischer Ökumenischer Informationsdient*, 28/29:5.

———. *Theologische Prinzipienlehre*. Munich: Erich Wewel, 1982.

Ricoeur, Paul. *Essays on Biblical Interpretation*. Edited by L. S. Mudge. London: SPCK, 1980.

Ritschl, Dietrich. *Logic of Theology: A Brief Account of the Relationship between Basic Concepts in Theology*. London: SCM, 1986.

Schlabach, Gerald. *Unlearning Protestantism: Sustaining Christian Community in an Unstable Age*. Grand Rapids: Brazos, 2010.

Schreiner, Susan E. "Church." In *The Oxford Encyclopedia of the Reformation*, edited by Hans Hillerbrand, 1:323–27. New York: Oxford University Press, 1996.

Schwöbel, Christoph. "Once Again, Christ and Culture: Remarks on the Christological Bases of a Theology of Culture." In *Trinity, Time, and the Church: A Response to the Theology of Robert W. Jenson*, edited by Colin Gunton, 103–25. Grand Rapids: Eerdmans, 2000.

Seitz, Christopher. "Canterbury and Unity." *Pro Ecclesia* 12:1 (2003) 11–14.

Sholl, Brian. "On Robert Jenson's Trinitarian Thought." *Modern Theology* 18:1 (2002) 27–36.

Shortt, Rupert. *Rowan Williams: An Introduction*. Harrisburg, PA: Morehouse, 2003.

Steinmetz, David C. "The Superiority of Pre-Critical Exegesis." *Theology Today* 37 (1980) 27–38.

Stephanopoulos, Robert G. "The Lima Statement on Ministry." *St. Vladimir's Theological Quarterly* 27 (1983) 273–79.

Stiver, Dan. "Theological Method." In *The Cambridge Companion to Postmodern Theology*, edited by Kevin J. Vanhoozer, 170–85. Cambridge: Cambridge University Press, 2003.

Stringfellow, William. *A Keeper of the Word: Selected Writings of William Stringfellow*. Edited by Bill Kellerman. Grand Rapids: Eerdmans, 1994.

Tabernee, William. "Alexander Campbell and the Apostolic Tradition." In *The Free Church and the Early Church: Bridging the Historical and Theological Divide*, edited by D. H. Williams, 163–80. Grand Rapids: Eerdmans, 2002.

Thils, Gustav. *Primaut et infallibility du Pontife Romain a Vatican I et autres etudes d'ecclesiologie*. Louvain: Peeters, 1989.

Thompson, James W. "What Is Church of Christ Scholarship?" *Restoration Quarterly* 49:1 (2007) 33–38.

Thompson, Philip E. "Re-envisioning Baptist Identity: Historical, Theological, and Liturgical Analysis." *Perspectives in Religious Studies* 27:3 (2000): 287–302.

Thurian, Max, editor. *Churches Respond to BEM: Official Responses to the "Baptism, Eucharist and Ministry" Text*. Vol. 6. Faith and Order Paper No. 144. Geneva: WCC, 1986.

Tillard, J.-M.-R. *Church of Churches: The Ecclesiology of Communion*. Translated by R. C. de Peaux. Collegeville, MN: Liturgical, 1992.

Tillich, Paul. *Systematic Theology*. Vol. 3. Chicago: University of Chicago Press, 1963.

Tjørhom, Ola. *Visible Church—Visible Unity: Ecumenical Ecclesiology and "The Great Tradition of the Church"*. Collegeville, MN: Liturgical, 2004.

Treier, Daniel J. *Introducing Theological Interpretation of Scripture: Recovering a Christian Practice*. Grand Rapids: Baker Academic, 2008.

Turner, H. E. W. *The Patristic Doctrine of Redemption: A Study of the Development of Doctrine in the First Five Centuries*. London: A. R. Mowbray, 1952.

———. *The Pattern of Christian Truth: A Study in the Relations between Orthodoxy and Heresy in the Early Church*. London: A. R. Mowbray, 1954.

Turner, Paul. *When Other Christians Become Catholic*. Collegeville, MN: Pueblo, 2007.

Vanhoozer, Kevin J. *Dictionary for Theological Interpretation of the Bible*. Grand Rapids: Baker Academic, 2005.

Volf, Miroslav. *After Our Likeness: The Church as the Image of the Trinity*. Grand Rapids: Eerdmans, 1998.

Wainwright, Geoffrey. "Rowan Williams on Christian Doctrine." *Scottish Journal of Theology* 56:1 (2003) 73–81.

———. *"Vera Visibilia*: Robert Jenson on the Sacraments." In *Trinity, Time, and the Church: A Response to the Theology of Robert W. Jenson*, edited by Colin Gunton, 281–97. Grand Rapids: Eerdmans, 2000.

Watson, David. *I Believe in the Church*. Grand Rapids: Eerdmans, 1978.

Watson, Francis. "'America's Theologian': An Appreciation of Robert Jenson's *Systematic Theology*, with Some Remarks about the Bible." *Scottish Journal of Theology* 55:2 (2002) 201–23.

Webster, John. "Rowan Williams on Scripture." In *Scripture's Doctrine and Theology's Bible*, edited by Markus Bockmuehl and Alan J. Torrance, 105–24. Grand Rapids: Baker Academic, 2008.

Westcott, B. F. *Lessons from Labour*. London: Macmillan, 1901.

Wilken, Robert Louis. "Is Pentecost a Peer of Easter?" In *Trinity, Time, and the Church: A Response to the Theology of Robert W. Jenson*, edited by Colin Gunton, 158–77. Grand Rapids: Eerdmans, 2000.

Wilkins, John. "Anglican Schism? Archbishop Rowan Williams Strives to Preserve the Communion." *National Catholic Reporter*, September 14, 2007. Online: http://www.highbeam.com/doc/1G1-168748377.html.

Williams, A. N. "The Parlement of Foules and the Communion of Saints." In *Trinity, Time, and the Church: A Response to the Theology of Robert W. Jenson*, edited by Colin Gunton, 188–200. Grand Rapids: Eerdmans, 2000.

Williams, D. H. *Evangelicals and Tradition*. Evangelical *Ressourcement*. Grand Rapids: Baker, 2005.

———, editor. *The Free Church and the Early Church: Bridging the Historical and Theological Divide*. Grand Rapids: Eerdmans, 2002.

———. Preface to *The Free Church and the Early Church: Bridging the Historical and Theological Divide*, edited by D. H. Williams. Grand Rapids: Eerdmans, 2002.

———. *Retrieving the Tradition and Renewing Evangelicalism: A Primer for Suspicious Protestants*. Grand Rapids: Eerdmans, 1999.

———. "Scripture, Tradition, and the Church: Reformation and Post-Reformation." *The Free Church and the Early Church: Bridging the Historical and Theological Divide*, edited by D. H. Williams, 101–26. Grand Rapids: Eerdmans, 2002.

———. *Tradition, Scripture, and Interpretation: A Sourcebook of the Ancient Church*. Evangelical *Ressourcement*. Grand Rapids: Baker Academic, 2006.

Williams, Rowan. *Anglican Identities*. London: Darton, Longman & Todd, 2004.

———. "Archbishop of Canterbury's Advent Letter." December 14, 2007. Online: http://www.anglicancommunion.org/acns.news.cfm/2007/12/14/ACNS4354.

———. "Archbishop of Canterbury's Pentecost Letter to the Bishops of the Anglican Communion." May 13, 2008. Online: http://aco.org/acns/news/cfm/2008/5/13/ACNS4403.

———. "Archbishop's Contribution during the Presentation on 'Episcopacy in the Church of England.'" November 16, 2005. Online: www.archbishopofcanterbury.org/sermons speeches/2005/051115b.htm.

———. "Archbishop's Lecture Given at the Pontifical Academy of Social Sciences, Rome." November 23, 2006. Online: www.archbishopofcanterbury.org/sermons_speeches/061123a.htm.

———. "Archbishop's Presidential Address to the 14th Meeting of the ACC." Online: http://www.archbishopofcanterbury.org/2410.

———. *Arius: Heresy and Tradition*. Rev. ed. Grand Rapids: Eerdmans, 2001.

———. "Authority and the Bishop in the Church." In *Their Lord and Ours: Approaches to Authority, Community, and the Unity of the Church*, edited by Mark Santer, 90–112. London: SPCK, 1982.

———. "Being a People: Reflections on the Concept of the Laity." *Religion, State and Society* 27:1 (1991) 11–21.

———. "The Bible Today: Reading and Hearing." Speech delivered on April 1, 2007, in Toronto, Canada. Online: http://www.archbishopofcanterbury.org/sermons_speeches/070416.htm.

———. "The Body's Grace." In *Theology and Sexuality: Classic and Contemporary Readings*, edited by Eugene F. Rogers Jr., 309–21. Oxford: Blackwell, 2002.

———. "The Challenge and Hope of Being an Anglican Today: A Reflection for the Bishops, Clergy and Faithful of the Anglican Communion." Online: http://www.episcipalchurch.org/3577_76411_ENG_Print.html

———. *Christ on Trial: How the Gospel Unsettles Our Judgment.* London: HarperCollins*Religious*, 2000.

———. "The Christian Priest Today." Lecture on the occasion of the 150th anniversary of Ripon College, Cuddeson on May 28, 2004. Online: http://www.archbishopofcanterbury.org/sermons_speeches/2004/040528.html.

———. "The Creed and the Eucharist in the Fourth and Fifth Centuries." March 11, 2004. Online: http://archbishopofcanterbury.org/sermons_speeches/2004/040311.html.

———. "Debate on the Gift of Authority—Archbishop of Canterbury's Remarks." Online: http://www.archbishopofcanterbury.org/articles.php/1836/general-synod-debate-on-the-gift-of-authority-archbishop-of-canterburys-remarks.

———. "Defining Heresy." In *The Origins of Christendom in the West*, edited by A. Kreider, 313–35. Edinburgh: T. & T. Clark, 2001.

———. "The Deflections of Desire: Negative Theology in Trinitarian Discourse." In *Silence and the Word: Negative Theology and Incarnation*, edited by Oliver Davies and Denys Turner, 115–35. Cambridge: Cambridge University Press, 2002.

———. "Does It Make Sense to Speak of Pre-Nicene Orthodoxy?" In *The Making of Orthodoxy: Essays in Honour of Henry Chadwick*, edited by Rowan Williams, 1–23. Cambridge: Cambridge University Press, 2002.

———. *The Dwelling of the Light: Praying with the Icons of Christ.* Grand Rapids: Eerdmans, 2003.

———. "Eastern Orthodox Theology." In *The Modern Theologians: An Introduction to Christian Theology Since 1918*, edited by David Ford, 499–512. 3rd ed. Malden, MA: Blackwell, 2005.

———. "The Goal of Visible Unity and the Limits of Diversity." In *Returning Pilgrims: Insights from British and Irish Participants in the World Faith and Order Conference, Santiago de Compostela, August 3–14, 1993*, edited by Rowan Williams, Colin Davey, and Flora Winfield, 12–14. London: CCBI, 1994.

———. *Grace and Necessity: Towards a New Theology for the 21st Century.* Harrisburg, PA: Morehouse, 2005.

———. "Historical Criticism and Sacred Text." In *Reading Texts, Seeking Wisdom: Scripture and Theology*, edited by David Ford and Graham Stanton, 217–28. Grand Rapids: Eerdmans, 2004.

———. "Imagining the Kingdom: Some Questions for Anglican Worship Today." In *Identity of Anglican Worship*, edited by Kenneth Stevenson and Bryan Spinks, 1–13. Harrisburg, PA: Morehouse, 1991.

———. "'Is It the Same God?' Reflections on Continuity and Identity in Religious Language." In *The Possibilities of Sense*, edited by John H. Whittaker, 204–18. London: Palgrave, 2002.

———. "Less a Roman Holiday, More an Italian Job—An Interview with Paul Handley." *Church Times*, November 17, 2006.

———. *Lost Icons: Reflections on Cultural Bereavement*. Harrisburg, PA: Morehouse, 2000.

———. "The Lutheran Catholic." A lecture given in Durham Cathedral on November 23, 2004. Online: http://www.archbishopofcanterbury.org/sermons_speeches/2004/041123.html.

———. "Making Moral Decisions." In *Cambridge Companion to Christian Ethics*, edited by Robin Gill, 3–15. Cambridge: Cambridge University Press, 2001.

———, editor. *The Making of Orthodoxy: Essays in Honour of Henry Chadwick*. Cambridge: Cambridge University Press, 2002.

———. "Mission-Shaped Church Conference—Keynote Address." June 23, 2004. Online: www.archbishopofcanterbury.org/sermons_speeches/2004/040623.html

———. "The Nicene Heritage." In *The Christian Understanding of God: Theological Colloquium on the Occasion of the 400th Anniversary of the Foundation of Trinity College, Dublin*, edited by James Byrne, 45–48. Dublin: Columbia, 1993.

———. *On Christian Theology*. Challenges in Contemporary Theology. Oxford: Blackwell, 2000.

———. "On Doing Theology." In *Stepping Stones: Joint Essays on Anglican Catholic and Evangelical Unity*, edited by Christina Baxter, 1–19. London: Hodder & Stoughton, 1987.

———. "One Church, One Hope." Freiburg Lecture given on August 9, 2006. Online: http://www.archbishopofcanterbury.org/sermons_speeches/060809a.htm.

———. "One Holy Catholic and Apostolic Church." Address to the 3rd Global South to South Encounter, Ain al Sukhna, Egypt, October 28, 2005. Online: http://www.archbishopofcanterbury.org/articles.php/1675/one-holy-catholic-and-apostolic-church.

———. "Paper for Seminar 'Scriptures in Monotheistic Faith' at St. Egidio Conference." October 22, 2007. Online: www.archbishopofcanterbury.org/sermons_speeches/071022.htm.

———. *A Ray of Darkness: Sermons and Reflections*. Boston: Cowley, 1995.

———. *Resurrection: Interpreting the Easter Gospel*. 2nd rev. ed. London: Darton, Longman & Todd, 2002.

———. "Saving Time: Thoughts on Practice, Patience and Vision." *New Blackfriars* 73 (1992) 319–327.

———. "Second Presidential Address to the Lambeth Conference." July 29, 2008. Online: http://www.archbishopofcaterbury.org/1916.

———. "Sermon at the 350th Festival Service of the Sons of the Clergy Corporation." May 18, 2004. Online: www.archbishopofcanterbury.org/sermons speeches/2004/040518.html.

———. "Service to Celebrate the Bicentenary of the British and Foreign Bible Society." March 8, 2004. Online: www.archbishopofcanterbury.org/sermons_speeches/2004/040308.html.

———. *Teresa of Avila*. Outstanding Christian Thinkers. Harrisburg, PA: Morehouse, 1991. Reprint, New York: Continuum, 2004.

———. "Theology and the Churches." In *Michael Ramsey as Theologian*, edited by Robin Gill and Lorna Kendall, 9–28. London: Darton, Longman & Todd, 1995.

———. "To Stand Where Christ Stands." In *An Introduction to Christian Spirituality*, edited by Ralph Waller and Bendicta Ward, 1–13. London: SPCK, 1999.

———. *Tokens of Trust: An Introduction to Christian Belief*. Louisville: Westminster John Knox, 2007.

———. *The Truce of God*. London: Faith Press, 1983. Reprint, Grand Rapids: Eerdmans, 2005.

———. "The Unity of the Church and the Unity of the Bible: An Analogy." *Internationale Kirchliche Zeit Schrift* 91 (2001) 5–21.

———. "What Is Catholic Orthodoxy?" In *Essays Catholic and Radical: A Jubilee Group Symposium for the 150th Anniversary of the Beginning of the Oxford Movement 1833–1983*, edited by Kenneth Leech, 11–25. London: Bowerdean, 1983.

———. "Who Are You Looking At? Faith and Seeing." November 10. 2007. Online: www.archbishopofcanterbury.org/1512.

———. *Why Study the Past? The Quest for the Historical Church*. Grand Rapids: Eerdmans, 2005.

———. *The Wound of Knowledge: Christian Spirituality from the New Testament to St. John of the Cross*. 2nd ed. Cambridge: Cowley, 1991.

———. *Wrestling With Angels: Conversations in Modern Theology*. Edited by Mike Higton. Grand Rapids: Eerdmans, 2007.

Willis, Wendell. "The Networking of the Pauline Churches: An Exploratory Essay." *Restoration Quarterly* 50:2 (2008) 69–78.

Wood, Susan. "Robert Jenson's Ecclesiology from a Roman Catholic Perspective." *Trinity, Time, and the Church: A Response to the Theology of Robert W. Jenson*, edited by Colin Gunton, 178–87. Grand Rapids: Eerdmans, 2000.

———. *Spiritual Exegesis and the Church in the Theology of Henri de Lubac*. Grand Rapids: Eerdmans, 1998.

Yeago, David. "The Church as Polity? The Lutheran Context of Robert W. Jenson's Ecclesiology." In *Trinity, Time, and the Church: A Response to the Theology of Robert W. Jenson*, edited by Colin Gunton, 201–37. Grand Rapids: Eerdmans, 2000.

Yoder, John Howard. *Body Politics: Five Practices of the Christian Community before the Watching World*. Nashville: Discipleship Resources, 1992.

———. *The Fullness of Christ: Paul's Revolutionary Vision of Universal Ministry*. Elgin, IL: Brethren, 1987.

———. *The Priestly Kingdom: Social Ethics as Gospel*. Notre Dame: Notre Dame University Press, 1984.

———. *The Royal Priesthood: Essays Ecclesiastical and Ecumenical*. Edited by Michael Cartwright. Grand Rapids: Eerdmans, 1994.

Zizoulas, John D. *Being as Communion: Studies in Personhood and the Church*. Crestwood, NY: St. Vladimir's Seminary Press, 1985.